MBA
FUNDAMENTALS

ACCOUNTING AND FINANCE

Also in the MBA Fundamentals series:

MBA Fundamentals Statistics

MBA Fundamentals Business Law

MBA Fundamentals Business Writing

MBA Fundamentals Project Management

MBA Fundamentals International Business

MBA Fundamentals Strategy

From the #1 graduate test prep provider, Kaplan MBA Fundamentals helps you master core business basics in a few easy steps. Each book in the series is based on an actual MBA course, providing direct and measurable skills you can use today.

For the latest titles in the series, as well as downloadable resources, visit:

www.kaplanmbafundamentals.com

MBA
FUNDAMENTALS

ACCOUNTING AND FINANCE

Michael P. Griffin, MBA, CMA

PUBLISHING

New York

Published by Kaplan Publishing, a division of Kaplan, Inc.
1 Liberty Plaza, 24th Floor
New York, NY 10006

Printed in the United States of America

Library of Congress Cataloging-in-Publication Data

Griffin, Michael P.
   MBA fundamentals : accounting and finance / Michael P. Griffin.
      p. cm. — (MBA fundamentals series)
   ISBN 978-1-4277-9719-3
   1. Accounting. 2. Finance. I. Title. II. Title: Accounting and finance.
   HF5636.G75 2009
   657—dc22   2008039307

10 9 8 7 6 5

ISBN-13: 978-1-4277-9719-3

Kaplan Publishing books are available at special quantity discounts to use for sales promotions, employee premiums, or educational purposes. Please email our Special Sales Department to order or for more information at kaplanpublishing@kaplan.com, or write to Kaplan Publishing, 1 Liberty Plaza, 24th Floor, New York, NY 10006.

Contents

For two bonus chapters to this book, please visit
www.kaplanmbafundamentals.com.

To My father, Philip D. Griffin

Introduction

Accounting is the language of business, and certainly a strong background in accounting is a great value when working with the concepts of finance. In a business college, the first business courses our students take include the principles of accounting (both financial and managerial) followed by business finance. The same is true in our MBA program where the foundation courses contain accounting and finance principles and concepts. It makes good sense to get the core business concepts of accounting and finance under your belt before you move deeper into the study or practice of business.

A business plan makes no sense without some basic understanding of accounting and finance. How can one read a pro forma finance statement without knowing the essence of the accounting equation, the assumptions of the accounting process, and the ideas behind capital investment? How can a manager with responsibility for costs, profits, or even investment do a good job without a basic understanding of cost accounting? How can an employee be held accountable for various financial results without an understanding of the math of finance and accounting?

The connections between accounting and finance have existed for hundreds of years and those links are evidenced throughout this book. The text begins with the basics of accounting. It takes a journey through the balance sheet, weaving its way through assets, liabilities, and equity. The next stops include the discovery of other financial statements and the analytical procedures, such as ratio analysis, that can bring out the important messages conveyed by the financial statements.

Eventually this book transitions into the field of management accounting. Moving away from chapters on financial accounting and into content about managerial accounting is an apt way of showing how management utilizes both financial and nonfinancial information to make important decisions and to monitor the performance of the entity. Many of the key decisions that managers make and the critical variables that they manage are financial. Thus, the last section of this book covers topics such as time value of money (the math of finance), financial asset valuation (stocks and bonds), and the capital budgeting process, including the review and analysis of capital investments.

Mastering the foundations of accounting and finance is not only important for the business executive, it is critical for the manager who has an engineering background but must run a manufacturing division, a nurse leader who oversees a staff of health-care providers, or an academic administrator who manages a school.

It does not matter if you work for a profit-seeking corporation of a non-profit enterprise or if you plan, organize, direct, and control the operations of any subunit or organization; you need the fundamentals of accounting and finance. This book won't make you a Certified Public Accountant (CPA®) or a Chartered Financial Analyst (CFA®). It won't replace the curriculum of a BS in finance or an MS in accounting. What it will do is help you converse with financial executives, understand the budgets you manage, and understand how accounting and finance are integral functions in the value chain of all organizations—from the fledgling entrepreneurial enterprise to the billion-dollar multinational corporation.

This book can be used in a variety of ways. It can be the textbook for an MBA-level foundations course that will get you ready for bigger and better things (more advanced business study) in grad school. If you have been away from business school for a while and want a refresher, this is an excellent primer on the topic of accounting and finance. If you are an executive with a nonbusiness background, you may find this book to be an excellent desktop reference—a handbook you can use to get down the basics and move beyond the basics to perform the financial aspects of your job. However you use it, I hope you find it helpful.

I look forward to hearing from you as you use this book. Your suggestions and comments are always welcome. My email is *mgriffin@umassd.edu*. I also maintain a companion site for this book. Visit it at: *www.accountingfinancebook.com*.

Michael P. Griffin
January 2009

PART

1

FINANCIAL ACCOUNTING

Financial Accounting Basics

INTRODUCTION

Accounting is the systematic recording, reporting, and analysis of financial transactions of a business. But beyond the critical role accounting plays as a financial information system, it provides much of the vocabulary utilized in our financial markets. Accounting also supplies the data needed to perform a variety of finance-critical applications, including financial planning, financial statement analysis, and capital asset investment analysis, and therefore there is a very strong link between accounting and finance. Accounting allows us to keep track of what is happening in our businesses (and nonprofit organizations and government).

WHAT'S AHEAD

In this chapter, you will learn:

- The objectives of financial accounting
- Who the users of accounting information are
- What is meant by usefulness, a key quality of accounting information
- How accounting principles are developed
- The principles and concepts that underlie the balance sheet and income statement
- The limitations and risks of accounting information

IN THE REAL WORLD

Convergence doesn't sound like an accounting term; in fact it almost sounds scientific. But convergence has been on the tongues of many accounting professionals, both in the United States and abroad, as the profession wrestles with ways of making international accounting information more useful by bringing together the U.S standards with those of the rest of the world.

On June 6, 2007, board and staff members from the Financial Accounting Standards Board (FASB) and the Accounting Standards Board of Japan (ASBJ) met in Tokyo to discuss serious pursuit of convergence—the development of a common set of accounting standards for both domestic and international use.

Experts believe that common global reporting standards are necessary to produce credible, comparable, conceptually sound, and extremely useful financial information—information used by managers, investors, and creditors to make significant decisions.

The concept of convergence has been on the front burner since October 2002 when FASB and the International Accounting Standards Board (IASB) first announced the issuance of a memorandum of understanding called the "Norwalk Agreement" (FASB has its headquarters in Norwalk, Connecticut). Both the FASB and IASB pledged to use their best efforts to make their existing financial reporting standards fully compatible as soon as is practicable and to coordinate their future work programs to ensure that once achieved, compatibility is maintained.

The speed at which convergence of United States and international standards is achieved will depend on many compromises. It has been reported that one of the most positive developments as a result of collaboration between FASB and IASB has been the updating of the conceptual framework. The conceptual framework forms the basis for specific accounting standards. It defines the underlying terms, such as what an asset is, what a liability is, and what revenues and expenses are. The conceptual framework, developed on a joint basis by these two leading, standard-setting boards, sets in place the fundamental building blocks of accounting.

KEY CONCEPTS

Some years ago, the American Institute of Certified Public Accountants issued a definition of accounting that in part referred to it as the "art of recording, classifying, and summarizing business transactions and interpreting results." To some extent accounting is an art; however, it should be understood that it is practiced within a body of knowledge that includes concepts and principles that have evolved and have been tested over time and are in response to the needs of users of accounting information.

To get the fundamentals of accounting under your belt, you must gain a basic understanding of the objectives of the practice of accounting. Although there are a number of objectives, each one has one thing in common: it promotes useful information so as to serve the needs of the user of financial accounting information. Never lose sight of the fact that the user of accounting information is at the heart of all the concepts, standards, and principles that fill accounting, tax, and auditing textbooks.

OBJECTIVES OF FINANCIAL ACCOUNTING

In the United States, the Financial Accounting Standards Board serves as an overseer of financial accounting. The FASB's conceptual framework spells out the objectives of financial accounting. These objectives apply to information that is useful to anyone interested in an enterprise's ability to meet its obligations and to reward its investors.

The first two objectives of financial accounting are related to usefulness. Financial information is useful if it helps current and potential investors and creditors in making investment and credit decisions. According to the FASB, financial accounting information must be comprehensible to those who "have a reasonable understanding of business and economic activities and who are willing to study information with reasonable diligence."

Financial accounting information must also help users of financial statements "assess amounts, timing, and uncertainties of prospective cash flows from their investments." This means financial accounting helps us determine risk; the likelihood that future cash inflows will be enough to cover future cash outflows. Someone once said that cash flow is the lifeblood of the enterprise, and therefore financial accounting helps us determine the vitality of an entity.

Another important objective of financial accounting is that it helps to inform users about the economic resources of and claims against enterprises. Strengths and weaknesses of companies are disclosed through financial accounting. Concepts like liquidity and solvency come to light when financial information is prepared properly. Performance as measured by earnings can shed light on management's stewardship of resources: in effect, financial accounting can help us to see how efficient and profitable management can be when managing the resources of the firm.

USERS OF ACCOUNTING INFORMATION AND USEFULNESS

Who uses accounting information? Just about everyone. A simple way to understand the needs of accounting information users is to divide the users into two groups—external and internal.

External users are those groups or individuals who are not directly involved in the operations of the enterprise but have an interest in the results and the financial position of the entity. These groups include stockholders, creditors, constituents (in the case of government accounting), potential investors, prospective creditors, labor union representatives, and federal regulators. Understanding the goals of each of these groups can lead you to a basic understanding of what type of accounting information they might need. For example, creditors and prospective creditors want to monitor cash flow and the ability to make loan payments.

Internal users of accounting information include all the people within an enterprise who make decisions, including all executives and managers who are responsible for planning, organizing, directing, and controlling operations. Internal users need information for budgeting and data to judge performance. In some entities, bonuses and promotion decisions are based on accounting data (profit goals, achieving budgeted objectives, etc.). Managerial accounting serves the needs of internal users only.

Accounting information is used to help managers make important decisions every day. These systems are populated with data derived from accounting, and key metrics like ratios and earnings guide management decision making—from where to invest to the pricing of products and services. Tax returns contain financial accounting data. Government agencies—such as the Federal Reserve and the FDIC, which manage our economy and safeguard our financial institutions—have insatiable appetites for financial accounting information.

Two related but distinct branches of accounting have developed to meet the needs of accounting information users. Financial accounting systems produce the information found in financial statements used by investors and creditors. Management accounting systems are designed to supplement financial accounting information and to assist managers in making operating decisions.

Whether it is financial or managerial accounting information, it is essential that the information be reliable and reasonably understandable for it to be of value to users. That's the essence of usefulness, and although there are many accounting concepts and standards that need to be mastered to be a proficient accountant, the one guiding light is usefulness. It is the primary quality of accounting information—one which users of accounting reports count on.

Reliability is found in information that is dependable and free from error or bias. Reliability should not be confused with absolute accuracy. Contrary to popular belief, reliable accounting information is often based on estimates and forecasts and therefore cannot always be precise. Relevant information is a bit different but equally as important in achieving usefulness.

Relevant accounting information makes a difference in a decision maker's formation of expectations. If a user of accounting information can better predict future consequences based on information about past events and transaction then such information is relevant.

Timeliness is an element of relevance. Accounting information is usually promptly presented to users before it becomes stale and rendered useless.

It is as simple as this: Accounting exists because of users. Every member of the accounting profession should work to meet the needs of accounting information users.

DEVELOPING ACCOUNTING PRINCIPLES

In the early years of the 20th century, the formation of large corporations and the introduction of federal and state income tax laws made it necessary to develop accounting principles. Initially, the American Institute of Certified Public Accountants (AICPA), a professional organization of practicing Certified Public Accountants, issued most of the bulletins, statements, and opinions that formed the guidelines for reporting the financial activities of enterprises. In 1973, the Financial Accounting Standards Board was established to replace the AICPA's Accounting Principles Board. The FASB became the key organization responsible for establishing and improving financial accounting standards and reporting practices.

The FASB serves as an overseeing board whose mission is "to establish and improve financial accounting and reporting for the guidance and education of the public, including issuers, auditors, and users of financial information." The FASB issues written standards and interpretations that form the basis of generally accepted accounting principles (GAAP).

The FASB recognizes that its actions affect many organizations. Therefore, the FASB utilizes a rigorous and open due process that actively encourages constituent input. That process involves public meetings, roundtables, field visits, field tests, liaison meetings, and other means designed to solicit participation and comment. It also includes exposure of the FASB's proposed standards to external review and public comment. Members of the FASB and its staff also regularly meet with a wide range of interested parties to obtain their input and to better understand their views.

After the stock market crash of 1929, the federal government became very concerned about regulation of the capital markets, and in 1934 an act of Congress created the Securities and Exchange Commission (SEC). The SEC requires that publicly traded companies follow certain prescribed accounting standards. The SEC has largely relied on the accounting profession, and specifically the FASB in recent decades, to formulate accounting principles. However, the SEC keeps a diligent watch over the development of accounting concepts and principles. The SEC wants to make sure that companies that sell their stocks and other financial instruments to the public file audited financial statements with the SEC and for public consumption. From time to time, the SEC will identify accounting problems for the FASB to study and address.

A number of organizations and groups have an impact on the development of generally accepted accounting principles. The U.S. Congress can pass laws, such as the Sarbanes-Oxley (SOX) Act, that have an impact on the accounting systems of companies. The SEC administers SOX and further influences GAAP by introducing regulatory requirements. All the groups shown above issue comments, reports, various standards, bulletins, and positions that all come together to form GAAP.

Illustration 1.1. Organizations Involved with Development of GAAP

The FASB deals with standards and concepts that impact public corporations and private enterprises, while another organization, the Governmental Accounting Standards Board (GASB) oversees accounting standards for government entities. The mission of the GASB is to establish and improve standards of state and local governmental accounting and financial reporting that will result in useful information for users of financial reports. It will also guide and educate the public, including issuers, auditors, and users of those financial reports. The GASB is an independent, private sector, not-for-profit organization that—through an open and thorough due process—establishes and improves standards of financial accounting and reporting for U.S. state and local governments. Governments and the accounting industry recognize the GASB as the official source of generally accepted accounting principles for state and local governments.

The GASB's span of influence covers over 84,000 state, county, and other local governmental units. Also impacted by the GASB's financial reporting standards are organizations such as public utilities, municipal hospitals, and state universities. The GASB, which does not impact the federal government, establishes concepts and standards that guide the preparation of external financial reports. The GASB establishes generally accepted accounting principles that are utilized by auditors charged with evaluating state and local government financial statements.

In the case of government accounting, the user is often a constituent: citizens, citizen groups, a state, a county, legislators and creditors, and persons involved in the municipal bond industry. The GASB standards help constituents to determine the ability of their government to provide services and repay its debt. The GASB's standards also help government officials demonstrate accountability to constituents, including their stewardship over public resources. The GASB standards help to ensure that those who finance government or who participate in the financing process have access to relevant, reliable, and understandable information that assists them to make better, more informed decisions.

An example of a GASB standard that had a significant impact on the accounting reporting of governments was a standard called GASB 34, "Basic Financial Statements—and Management's Discussion and Analysis—for State and Local Governments."

In June 1999, the GASB established GASB 34 as a new financial reporting standard that required that major infrastructure assets acquired or having major additions or improvements in fiscal years beginning after June 15, 1980, be shown as capital assets in the entities' financial statements. Infrastructure assets for governments include roads, bridges, tunnels, drainage systems, water and sewer systems, dams, and lighting systems.

PRINCIPLES AND CONCEPTS

The financial statements are the output of an accounting system. Since financial statements are the principal communication means through which an enterprise reveals its financial position and the results of its activities, rules are in place to help assure that clear and complete messages are transmitted. Following are the four primary *financial statements*:

1. **Balance Sheet:** Also called the statement of financial position. Provides information about the entity's financial position at a particular point in time. Reveals the assets, liabilities, and equity of the enterprise.

2. **Income Statement:** Provides the net income (or net loss) of an enterprise over a stated period of time. Reveals the revenues earned and expenses incurred during a specific time period.

3. **Statement of Changes in Equity:** Summarizes the adjustments to equity over a specific period of time (same period as the income statement), including changes in capital and earnings retained.

4. **Statement of Cash Flows:** Shows the amount of cash collected and paid out by the enterprise over a specified period of time (same period as the income statement and statement of changes in equity) for operating activities, investing activities, and financial activities.

There are important accounting principles and concepts that underlie the financial statements and help assure that they communicate everything that users need to know. The concepts that underlie the *balance sheet* are the following:

- **Economic Entity:** The accounting for an entity (i.e., a business) should be kept separate from the accounting for the owners of that entity. This assumption establishes the idea that economic resources and obligations shown on the balance sheet should not be confused with the resources and obligations of the owners of the entity. Owner's assets should not be listed along with the assets of a business and the debts of the business should only include the obligations of the business and not the personal debts of the owner. The economic entity assumption also requires that if a business does own or control the assets or liabilities of another entity or has assumed significant risks associated with the assets or liabilities of another entity, then those assets and liabilities must be included on the balance sheet.

- **Going Concern:** The presumption that in the absence of any evidence to the contrary, an entity will operate indefinitely. This assumption triggers other accounting procedures, such as the depreciation of assets over their useful life, recognition of revenue in the period it is earned, and the valuation of some assets based on expected future cash flows (as opposed to liquidation value).

- **Historical Cost:** A principle that guides the valuation of assets and liabilities. This rule states that an asset or liability should be initially recorded (and reported) at its original (historical) cost. The theory is that historical costs are easier to verify than are current values (i.e., a market value can only be proven when a sale is consummated).

- **Monetary Unit:** A concept that assumes currency is the appropriate unit of measure for assessing value and that the currency is not adjusted for inflation. Therefore, if a company purchased land 20 years ago for $100,000 and still owns that land, it will still be listed at $100,000 on the balance sheet today. It will not be adjusted for inflation.

The concepts that underlie the *income statement* are the following:

- **Periodicity:** Also called the time period assumption, this rule states that it is meaningful to measure a firm's activities in terms of arbitrary time periods. This rule is necessary because users of financial statements (investors, creditors, etc.) periodically need to know how an enterprise is doing. Therefore, companies issue income statements based on a quarter or an entire year.

- **Accrual Accounting:** This is a practice of accounting but also an assumption that financial statement users make when reviewing the income statement. This rule says that the economic impacts of transactions are recorded in the period that they occur rather than in the period when cash is received. Accrual accounting is the most fundamental concept not only underlying financial statements but all generally accepted accounting principles. It is the first concept taught to college students of accounting (Principles of Accounting I).

- **Revenue Recognition:** This rule states that revenue (earnings from selling goods and services) should be recognized when the amount and timing are reasonably determined and when the earnings process is complete. In most cases, the recognition of revenue is clear cut—the goods or services are sold and something of value (cash or a promise) is received. In other cases, such as when something of value has been received but not all the goods and services have been delivered, an analysis must be done to determine how much can be claimed as revenue.

- **Matching:** This concept holds that expenses (costs incurred in the process of delivering, producing, and rendering goods and services) should be reported in the same period as the revenues to which they are related.

- **Conservatism:** According to the FASB, this is the principle that requires a "prudent reaction to uncertainty to try to ensure that the uncertainty and risks inherent in a business situation are adequately considered." When faced with a choice, values must be chosen that are least likely to overstate an entity's net income (the difference between revenues and expenses) and financial position. A financial statement user should be able to assume that values are conservatively estimated as opposed to overstated and misleading.

- **Full Disclosure:** A principle that requires financial statements and related notes to include any information that is significant enough to change the decisions of financial statement users. Financial statements often include footnotes that explain complicated transactions (leases, stock options, etc.), potential losses (e.g., lawsuits), or significant events that took place after the financial statement date.

LIMITATIONS

There are many limitations to accounting information. Since financial reports include mostly numbers, they emphasize those specifics about an enterprise that can be quantified. Many significant facts about an economic entity cannot be put into numbers and therefore such characteristics as reputation, product quality, customer service, innovative thinking, management experience, and technological advantages are not revealed via accounting reports.

The cost principle and monetary unit assumption also present some important limitations. Inflation has caused many currencies to lose a great deal of purchasing power, while on the other hand, some assets such as land and buildings purchased many years ago can be greatly undervalued on the balance sheet. In short, the historical cost principle can lead to serious value distortions on balance sheets.

Accounting is not a science but an art, and although much of accounting information is based on objective evidence, there are times when absolute objective evidence is not available. Often, judgments and estimates are necessary. Financial statements may not be of uniform quality and reliability because of differences in the character and quality of judgments exercised by accountants and management. Estimates and judgments are made for such things as depreciation, future warranty claims, cost of complete long-term contracts, loss reserves for receivables, and tax expenses. Many of these estimates have a dramatic influence on earnings and financial position, and the accuracy of such estimates can take years to be verified through subsequent events.

Users also must be aware of certain risks when working with financial statements. There is always the risk that something significant has not been disclosed. The accounting system must also provide internal controls to ensure that enterprise policies are followed, accounting records are accurate, assets are used effectively, and steps are taken to reduce chances of fraud.

An enterprise's system of internal controls usually includes an auditing function. There are a variety of audits that can be performed in an organization (see box below). Auditors use a variety of approaches, including observation of current activities, examination of past transactions, and simulation—often using sample or fictitious transactions—to test the accuracy and reliability of the system. However, there is audit risk including failure on the part of the auditor to detect fraud or to take a representative sampling of transactions.

TYPES OF AUDITS

Financial Audit: A historically oriented, independent evaluation performed for the purpose of attesting to the fairness, accuracy, and reliability of financial data. This audit is performed by a certified public accounting firm.

Operational Audit: A future-oriented, systematic, and in-dependent evaluation of organizational activities. Financial data may be used, but the primary sources of evidence are the operational policies and achievements related to organizational objectives. Internal controls and efficiencies may be evaluated during this type of review.

Department Review: A current period analysis of administrative functions, to evaluate the adequacy of controls, safeguarding of assets, efficient use of resources, and compliance with related laws, regulations, and enterprise policy.

Information Systems (IS) Audit: There are three basic kinds of IS audits that may be performed: general controls review, applications controls review, and a system development review. All are designed to ensure that internal controls are in place in the IS function so as to protect the operation and security of IS systems and to safeguard enterprise data.

Investigative Audit: This is an audit that takes place as the result of a report of unusual or suspicious activity on the part of an individual or a department. It is usually focused on specific aspects of the work of a department or individual.

TEST YOURSELF

1. List three objectives of financial accounting.

2. What makes accounting information reliable?

3. How is financial accounting different from managerial accounting?

4. What are the four primary financial statements?

5. Although accounting systems are subject to audits, why are there still limitations and risks associated with financial reporting?

KEY POINTS TO REMEMBER

- Accounting is a system of recording, reporting, and analyzing transactions. It is also a profession with roots in 14th century Italy.

- There is a direct link between accounting and finance. In fact, accounting is the language of finance and accounting systems provide the information and analysis consumed by the financial markets to value investments and to make financial decisions.

- Accounting data exists to meet the needs of users, including investors, management, creditors, and government regulators.

- Accounting principles or GAAP (generally accepted accounting principles) are always evolving and are influenced by many groups and organizations, including the Financial Accounting Standards Board (FASB), the American Institute of Certified Public Accountants (AICPA), professional accounting groups, and the U.S. Securities and Exchange Commission (SEC).

- A set of principles and concepts underlie financial statements. These assumptions are the rules that help create clear and effective messages received by users of financial statements.

- Limitations and risks are inherent in accounting information. Accounting is more of an art than a science, and many estimates and judgments must be made to produce financial reports.

The Accounting Process and Cycle

INTRODUCTION

Accounting is a process designed to capture the economic impact of everyday transactions. Each day, many events and activities occur in an entity which change the elements of the accounting equation—the basis for all accounting systems. Periodically, financial statements are prepared to reveal the financial position and the results of operations. These financial statements are the output of an accounting cycle; at the same time the financial statements become an input into the analysis and decision-making activities of business owners, investors, managers, creditors, and government regulators. Users of financial statements move ahead with their analysis and decision making with confidence because of the work performed and the opinion expressed by independent auditors.

In this chapter, you will learn:
- The accounting equation
- The steps in the accounting cycle
- How transactions impact the accounting equation

- The auditor's role in the accounting process
- The meaning behind the various audit reports
- The different types of auditors needed in a 21st century economy

IN THE REAL WORLD

For years, small businesses utilized paper-based, checking account–based accounting systems like the Dome system and the one-write system. There are still manual methods used by small businesses to maintain a basic bookkeeping system. Bookkeeping systems are the basis for tax return preparation and financial statements for small businesses. However, for most small businesses, computerized systems like QuickBooks (Intuit) and Peachtree (Sage) are most prevalent because they are relatively inexpensive, easy to use, and offer many features.

Small business accounting software allows you to prepare vendor purchase orders to purchase the goods to be sold, prepare payroll for employees, record payments to vendors, and keep track of inventory and shipments to the customer (including the packing slip). For example, you can use QuickBooks to invoice the customer and track the amounts due (accounts receivable) from the customer. Peachtree helps you to keep track of sales tax and receive and apply money to customer balances, and it prints bank deposit forms. Recent versions of small business accounting software help users reconcile bank and credit card balances, provide online banking capabilities, allow you to prepare loan amortization schedules, and conduct fixed asset tracking.

A database of sorts, software like QuickBooks and Peachtree help business owners analyze, classify, and record business transactions and ultimately help the business owner or accountant prepare a variety of useful reports, including the following:

- Balance sheets and income statements
- Accounts receivable reports
- Sales reports
- Purchasing reports
- Accounts payable reports
- Account registers
- Customer and vendor reports
- Time and mileage reports
- Inventory reports
- Sales tax reports
- Payroll reports

KEY CONCEPTS

The basis for transaction analysis, the mechanics of the accounting system, and the structure of the balance sheet are the accounting equation. It can be said that every transaction has an impact on the accounting equation and yet at the conclusion of recording of the transaction, the equation is always in balance. The transaction is the start of the accounting cycle. Once it is analyzed and understood by the accountant, the transaction makes its way into the accounting system—a collection of journals and ledgers (most likely computerized). Financial statements are the final output of an accounting cycle, on which users must base a great deal of faith, as they will use financial statements to make a multitude of important decisions. Adding credibility and reliability to the financial statements is the audit, performed by an independent, external accountant who must follow auditing standards to help assure that the statements have been prepared in accordance with generally accepted accounting principles (GAAP).

THE ACCOUNTING EQUATION

The financial position of a company is measured by the following items:

- Assets (what it owns)
- Liabilities (what it owes to others)
- Owner's equity (the difference between assets and liabilities)

The accounting equation offers us a simple way to understand how these three financial items relate to each other:

$$\text{Assets} = \text{Liabilities} + \text{Stockholders' Equity}$$

Assets are a company's resources—things the company owns. Examples of assets include cash, accounts receivable, inventory, prepaid insurance, investments, land, buildings, equipment, and goodwill. From the accounting equation, we see that the amount of assets must equal the combined amount of liabilities plus owner's (or stockholders') equity.

Liabilities are a company's obligations—amounts the company owes (including debts like amounts owed to vendors and bank loans). Examples of liabilities include notes payable, accounts payable, salaries and wages payable, interest payable, and income taxes payable.

Liabilities can be viewed in two ways:

1. Claims by creditors against the company's assets
2. Source of funds—along with owner or stockholder equity—of the company's assets

Stockholders' equity is the amount left over after liabilities are deducted from assets:

$$\text{Assets} - \text{Liabilities} = \text{Stockholders' Equity}$$

Owner's or stockholders' equity also reports the amounts invested into the company by the owners plus the cumulative net income of the company that has not been withdrawn or distributed to the owners.

If a company keeps accurate records, the accounting equation will always be "in balance," meaning the left side should always equal the right side. The balance is maintained because every business transaction affects at least two of a company's accounts. For example, when a company borrows money from a bank, the company's assets will increase and its liabilities will increase by the same amount. When a company purchases inventory for cash, one asset will increase and one asset will decrease. Because there are two or more accounts affected by every transaction, the accounting system is referred to as *double-entry accounting*.

A company keeps track of all of its transactions by recording them in accounts in the company's general ledger. Each account in the general ledger is designated as to its type: asset, liability, owner's equity, revenue, expense, gain, or loss account.

THE ACCOUNTING CYCLE

The sequence of activities that a business transaction triggers is known as the *accounting cycle*. The cycle begins with a transaction, involves getting the impact of transactions into the "books" of the company (through journal entries and posting to ledgers), entails the preparation of financial statements, and concludes with the "closing of the books." The sections that follow will walk you through the accounting cycle.

Identify and Gather Transaction Information

Accounting initially focuses on events called transactions. A *transaction* is an exchange between a business (or some other type of organization such as a nonprofit firm) and one or more external parties, or it is a measurable internal event such as certain adjustments for the use of assets in operations. Transactions have an economic impact on an organization; they have some impact on the accounting formula. Therefore, a transaction will result in a change in assets, liabilities, or equity.

Part of the accounting function is to identify all transactions and to translate those transactions to financial results, which are done by the use of accounts. An *account* is a standardized format that organizations use to accumulate the dollar effect of a transaction. Account balances are kept so that financial statements can eventually be prepared. When you examine the balance sheet of a corporation, many of the accounts are really a summation or aggregation of several accounts. For example, accounts receivable (money owed to the business by customers who have purchased on credit) shown on a balance sheet could be comprised of hundreds of subsidiary accounts of all the company's customers.

Companies maintain a chart of accounts—a list of all the account names, usually organized by financial statement elements. For example, the chart of accounts lists all the asset, liability, and equity accounts. Transaction analysis is the process of studying an event to determine its economic effect on the accounting equation. To perform transaction analysis, two important rules need to be followed:

1. Every transaction affects at least two accounts.
2. The accounting equation must remain in balance after each transaction. In other words, this equilibrium must always be in place (both before and after the transaction's effects have been recorded): Assets = Liabilities + Stockholders' Equity.

To understand the workings of the accounting equation, review a few examples. Keep in mind the rules. Also, to make this easy, assume there are only four assets: cash, inventory, equipment, and accounts receivable. Cash, inventory, and equipment are self-explanatory. Accounts receivable is amounts that are owed to the organization by customers who have purchased goods or services on credit. For liabilities, assume only two accounts: notes payable for dollars borrowed by the firm and accounts payable for amounts owed to suppliers. For simplicity's sake, assume just one equity account, where we will record sales and expenses:

Cash of $10,000 is invested in the business by the owner.

Effect on accounting equation:

Assets =	Liabilities +	Equity
Increase in Cash $10,000	No change in Liabilities	Increase in Equity $10,000
Assets $10,000 =	Liabilities $0 +	Equity $10,000

Purchased $3,000 of equipment paying cash.

Effect on accounting equation:

Assets =	Liabilities +	Equity
Increase in Equipment $3,000 Decrease in Cash $3,000	No Change in Liabilities	No Change in Equity
Assets: Cash $7,000 Equipment $3,000 Total Assets $10,000 =	Liabilities $0 +	Equity $10,000

Purchased inventory on credit for $1,200.

Effect on accounting equation:

Assets =	Liabilities +	Equity
Increase in Inventory $1,200	Increase in Accounts Payable $1,200	No Change in Equity
Assets: Cash $7,000 Inventory $1,200 Equipment $3,000 Total Assets $11,200 =	Liabilities + Accounts Payable $1,200	Equity $10,000

Sell $2,000 of goods to customer on credit. The goods cost $1,200.

Effect on accounting equation:

Assets =	Liabilities +	Equity
Increase in Accounts Receivable $2,000		Increase in Equity (Revenue) of $2,000
Decrease in Inventory $1,200		Decrease in Equity $1,200 (Cost of Goods Sold)
Assets: Cash $7,000 Accounts Receivable $2,000 Equipment $3,000 Total Assets $12,000 =	Liabilities + Accounts Payable $1,200	Equity $10,800

As you can see from each example transaction, the accounting equation was always in equilibrium (Assets = Liabilities + Equity) after each transaction.

Analyze and Journalize

In double-entry accounting systems, each transaction is recorded in at least two accounts. Each transaction results in at least one account being debited and at least one account being credited, with the total debits of the transaction equal to the total credits. A debit is an entry made to the left-hand side of an account, while a credit is made to the right-hand side. The rules of debit and credit are taught in bookkeeping classes and in college accounting principles courses; however, debit and credit rules are not critical to the understanding of the accounting process. What is more important is the understanding that transactions are analyzed and then recorded in a *journal* (journalized). A journal is used once the accountant or bookkeeper has examined a source document (such as an invoice, a contract, a loan agreement, a calculation, etc.). *Journalizing* is the recording of the details of all of these source documents into multicolumn journals (also known as books of first entry). Several journals may be used. For example, all credit sales are recorded in the sales journal, and all cash payments are recorded in the cash payments journal.

The act of recording transactions into a journal (usually a computer file) is like recording important events in a diary. It is a chronological record of the transactions of a business. However, the journal should not be confused with the *ledger*—the collection of accounts used by the firm and the real heart of the accounting system.

Every transaction has either a debit or a credit. The abbreviations for debit and credit are DR and CR, respectively. *Debits,* which are always entered on the left-hand side of an account, are a component of an accounting transaction that will increase assets and decrease liabilities and equity. *Credits,* which are always entered on the right-hand side of an account, are a component of an accounting transaction that will increase liabilities and equity and decrease assets.

Accountants memorize these rules:

- Credits increase liabilities and equity; credits decrease assets.
- Debits decrease liabilities and equity; debits increase assets.

Posting to Ledgers

Posting to ledgers is done after the transaction has been analyzed and journalized. Ledgers are simply a collection of accounts. The general ledger is the core of the organization's financial records and constitutes the central books of your system. Every transaction flows through the general ledger: a permanent history of all financial transactions since day one of the life of the organization.

Posting means simply that you have debited or credited an account in the general ledger (or subsidiary ledgers, such as those for accounts receivable and accounts payable).

By posting, the account balances are brought up to date. For example, if at the beginning of the day the firm has $10,000 cash and during the day a total of $2,000 is withdrawn or paid out for expenses, $2,000 would be posted (credited) to the cash account to bring the account balance to a day-end balance of $8,000.

Unadjusted Trial Balance

A *trial balance* is a list of all of the accounts of the organization with their balances. The trial balance is a check on the equality of the debits and credits in the ledger. Accountants will not move forward in the cycle until the trial balance is in equilibrium. The trial balance lists all the assets first, followed by the liabilities, stockholders' equity, revenues, and expenses. That is called financial statement order, as the balance sheet contains assets, liabilities, and equity, and the income statement contains revenues and expenses.

Adjustments

A series of adjustments called *accruals* and *deferrals* is usually needed to bring the financial records in line with reality. There are always some events and activities that have not been incorporated into the accounting records. For example, there may be interest owed on debt or salaries owed but not yet paid to employees. Calculations must be done to determine those expense accruals—both an expense and a liability that are building over time. Revenue accruals are also possible. For example, interest may be accruing on an entity's investments and therefore an interest income accrual would need to be recognized that would have the effect of increasing assets (interest receivable) and increasing revenue (interest income). There are many types of accruals that may need to be recognized through a series of adjustments at the end of a period.

Deferrals are also a possible source of adjusting entries. There can be both deferred revenues and deferred expenses. If cash or something of value has been received for future products or work to be performed, since the product hasn't been delivered or the service provided, the income must be deferred to a future date. Deferred income is recorded as an asset (most likely cash) and a liability (deferred revenue). Prepaid rent received by a landlord is an example of a deferral.

Expenses can also be deferred. For example, if your company pays its insurance bill in advance for a period covering the next three years, only the amount attributed to this period's insurance coverage would be an expense, while the remainder of the payment would be classified as a deferred expense. In this case, an asset called prepaid insurance would be established for the insurance paid representing future coverage.

Preparing Financial Statements

The financial statements are the reason the accounting cycle exists. At some point, users want to take a look at the financial position of the entity and the results of operations. The journals, ledgers, trial balances, and adjusting entries are done to put the accountants in the position to prepare the financial statements: a balance sheet, income statement, statement of retained earnings, and a cash flow statement. It is with these reports that important decisions are made, such as whether to invest in the entity or to extend credit. A set of financial statements may be required by regulators (i.e., the Securities and Exchange Commission), and management will certainly want to check on progress toward financial goals. They will make a performance evaluation that is fed by the metrics for which the financial statements serve as important inputs. The key financial statements will be explored in great detail in later chapters of this book.

Closing the Books

Closing of the books is a type of housekeeping function that book-keepers and accountants must perform to accomplish a couple of important tasks:

- Closing procedures are how profits or losses get reflected in the equity accounts of the business.

- Closing procedures set certain temporary accounts back to zero.

By closing the books, the profits or losses for the period are added or subtracted from the equity accounts. In a corporation, the retained earnings account is updated via the closing process. In a partnership, the closing procedure divides up the profits and losses into the partners' equity accounts. The closing of the ac-counts also resets the scoreboard. In other words, there are certain accounts called *temporary accounts* that are to only show the score for the current period. Revenues, expenses, and dividends are ex-amples of temporary accounts. For example, if the company sells $5,000,000 of goods for the year 2009, at the end of 2009 the sales account should be set back to zero so that the sales from 2010 can be accumulated.

THE ROLE OF AUDITING IN THE ACCOUNTING PROCESS

The accounting process helps us move from the transaction to the financial statement. Tools like journals and ledgers are utilized, along with debit and credit rules and generally accepted account-ing principles, to help us get to the point where financial state-ments can be prepared and analyzed so that a variety of financial decisions can be made.

To maximize the confidence that users have in the finan-cial statements of an organization, an independent audit is often

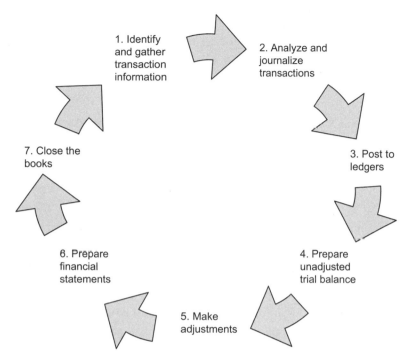

Illustration 2.1. The Accounting Cycle

required. An *audit* involves the examination of the financial reports and testing of the internal control systems of the organization to ensure that the financial statements represent what they claim and that they conform to GAAP.

Audits are performed by independent Certified Public Accountants. The idea is that an audit performed by an independent, external auditor provides assurances to external users of the financial statements as to the objectivity of the auditor's opinion. Three concepts are important in auditing: materiality, audit risk, and evidence.

According to the Financial Accounting Standards Board, materiality is an omission or misstatement of accounting information that, in light of surrounding circumstances, makes it probable that the judgment of a reasonable person relying on the information would have been changed or influenced by the omission or misstatements. Auditors establish thresholds of material dollar amounts. For example, in a very large organization with millions of dollars of inventory, a $500 error will be deemed insignificant.

The audit process is guided by the audit plan, a program developed by the auditor. An audit program lists in reasonable detail the procedures the auditors will follow. The objective is to express an opinion (attest to) whether the entity's financial statements present fairly its financial position (balance sheet), results of operation (income statement), and cash flows (statement of cash flows), in conformity with GAAP.

Underlying transactions are examined and tested along with the internal controls that help assure that accurate record keeping is achieved. Not all transactions are examined and not all internal controls are tested in an audit. However, professional approaches and techniques (including sampling) are used to ascertain beyond a reasonable doubt that transactions are measured and reported properly.

Most audit reports are standard in that they include the following:

- **Introductory Paragraph:** Identifies the financial statements and period(s) under audit and describes the responsibilities of management and the auditor.

- **Scope:** Describes the nature of the audit and discusses how the audit was conducted according to generally accepted auditing standards (GAAS), attempting to offer reasonable assurances that GAAP has been followed, that tests were performed, and that the accounting principles used and management estimates made were carefully examined by the auditors.

- **Opinion:** Presents the auditor's conclusion. This is the most important element of the auditor's report because it is from this sentence that users of financial statements will either gain great confidence and faith in the financial statements or will consider the statements within varying degrees (depending on the nature of the opinion) of skepticism and doubt.

There are basically four different opinions that can be expressed in an auditor's report: *unqualified, qualified, adverse,* and a *disclaimer of opinion.* The best type of audit report is an unqualified opinion. It states that the financial statements present fairly, in all material respects, the financial position, results of operations, and the cash flows of the entity, in conformity with GAAP. A qualified opinion states that *except for the effects of the matter or matters to which the qualification relates,* the financial statements present fairly the financial position, results of operations, and the cash flows of the entity, in conformity with GAAP.

An adverse opinion states that the financial statements do not present fairly the financial position, results of operations, and the cash flows of the entity, in conformity with GAAP. Certainly, users of financial statements that have an adverse opinion audit report would have great concerns about relying on those statements to make important financial decisions.

Finally, a disclaimer of opinion states that the auditor does not express an opinion on the financial statements, and it is appropriate when the auditor has not performed an audit sufficient in scope to enable forming an opinion. There are a few reasons why a disclaimer opinion can result, including audits that haven't complied with GAAS or any other major reservations the auditor might have that the financial statements may not present financial position in accordance with GAAP. An example of a disclaimer of opinion is as follows:

> The company did not make a count of its physical inventory. Further, documentary evidence supporting the cost of a significant amount of equipment is no longer available. Company records do not permit the application of auditing procedures to inventories or equipment; therefore, the scope of the audit was not sufficient to allow us to express an opinion on these financial statements.

TYPES OF AUDITS

Financial Statement Audit: Determines whether the financial statements conform to generally accepted accounting principles.

Compliance Audit: Determines the extent to which rules, policies, laws, or government regulations are followed by the entity being audited.

Operational Audit: Is a systematic review of an organization's activities to determine if they are efficient and effective.

Forensic Audit: Detects or uncovers fraudulent activities, including employee fraud.

TYPES OF AUDITORS

External Auditors: Independent auditors; often certified public accountants who maintain their objectivity and independence during an audit.

Internal Auditors: Auditors employed by the organizations being audited who conduct compliance and operational audits for the entity that employs them.

Government Auditors: Auditors employed by local, state, and federal agencies.

Forensic Auditors: Auditors employed by corporations, government agencies, public accounting firms, and consulting firms to conduct audits to detect or uncover fraud.

TEST YOURSELF

1. A company purchases $1,500 of equipment, paying cash. Update the accounting equation below based on this transaction.

Assets of $20,000 =	Liabilities of $12,000 +	Equity of $8,000
Assets of $_____ =	Liabilities of $_____ +	Equity of $_____

2. A company provides $5,000 of services to a customer and is paid cash.

Assets of $30,000 =	Liabilities of $18,000 +	Equity of $12,000
Assets of $_____ =	Liabilities of $_____ +	Equity of $_____

3. A company purchases $25,000 of inventory on credit and a $100,000 parcel of land for cash.

Assets of $300,000 =	Liabilities of $180,000 +	Equity of $120,000
Assets of $_____ =	Liabilities of $_____ +	Equity of $_____

4. List the steps in the accounting cycle.

5. When is an adverse opinion given in an audit report?

KEY POINTS TO REMEMBER

- The accounting equation Assets = Liabilities + Equity is the foundation of the accounting system.

- Assets are resources that an entity owns, liabilities are what is owed, and equity is the difference between assets and liabilities.

- The accounting cycle is a sequence of activities that begins with transactions and ends with the preparation of financial statements and the closing of the books.

- Every transaction affects at least two accounts and after the transaction has been recorded, the accounting equation remains in equilibrium.

- Financial audits, which are performed by external auditors, add a strong sense of reliability and confidence to the accounting process and the financial statements they produce.

- Other types of audits serve other purposes: for example, compliance audits check that employees are following policies and procedures, operation audits check on effectiveness and efficiency, and forensic audits detect fraud.

The Balance Sheet

INTRODUCTION

The *balance sheet* is one of the financial statements. Also called the *statement of financial position*, the balance sheet is a basic snapshot of a company's financial position at a particular point in time and is a logical starting point for assessing a company's financial position. The balance sheet shows the entity's resource structure, or major classes and amounts of assets, as well as its capital structure, or major classes and amounts of liabilities and equity.

Put another way, the balance sheet provides information about an entity's assets (what is owned), liabilities (what is owed), and equity (the difference between assets and liabilities). It is a key report for users of financial statements to review and analyze. From the balance sheet, we can learn a great deal about liquidity, solvency, financial flexibility, risk, and the sources of funds for the assets.

In this chapter, you will learn:

- The elements of a balance sheet
- The logic behind the order of presentation of assets, liabilities, and equity
- The two commonly used presentation formats of balance sheets: horizontal and vertical

- How current assets are classified and defined
- How current liabilities are classified and defined
- The uses of a personal balance sheet and how it is different from a business balance sheet

IN THE REAL WORLD

The federal securities laws require publicly traded companies to disclose information on an ongoing basis. U.S. corporations that sell their stock to the public must submit annual reports on Form 10-K. This is a document filed with the SEC which contains a detailed explanation of a business. It is reported annually and contains the same financial statements that the annual report to investors shows but in a more detailed form. The balance sheet (Assets = Liabilities + Equity) is one of the key financial statements included in a 10-K.

The benefit of the 10-K is that it allows you to find out additional information such as the amount of stock options awarded to executives at the company, as well as a more in-depth discussion of the nature of the business and marketplace.

The Securities and Exchange Commission uses EDGAR, the Electronic Data Gathering, Analysis, and Retrieval system, to perform automated collection, validation, indexing, acceptance, and forwarding of submissions by companies, including the 10-K.

Another key report, called the annual report, contains the balance sheet and other financial statements. The annual report to shareholders is the principal document used by most public companies to disclose corporate information to their shareholders. It is usually a state-of-the-company report, including an opening letter from the chief executive officer, financial data, and results of continuing operations, market segment information, new product plans, subsidiary activities, and research and development activities on future programs.

KEY CONCEPTS

You can't possibly understand the balance sheet without digging into it and learning its basic elements. Balance sheet accounts are listed in a logical manner that is dictated by generally accepted accounting principles (GAAP). The order of the listing, the classifications used (current versus noncurrent), and even the commonly utilized formats make the balance sheet more useful to users, including analysts such as credit managers and investors.

ELEMENTS OF THE BALANCE SHEET

The balance sheet is a detailed presentation of the accounting equation: Assets = Liabilities + Equity. Within those major classifications, subclassifications are used on balance sheets. Assets are broken out into current assets and noncurrent assets. Liabilities use the same current and noncurrent classification, while equity can be detailed out into a variety of accounts based on the type of company. For example, a corporation will have some variation of equity classifications of contributed capital and retained earnings.

Assets are presented in descending order of liquidity—the ability of an asset to be converted into cash quickly and without any price discount.

Here is a typical order:

> Assets
> Current assets
>   Cash
>   Accounts receivable
>   Inventory
> Noncurrent assets
> Investments
> Property, plant, and equipment
> Intangible assets

Current assets are all assets that are reasonably expected to be converted into cash or consumed by the entity (e.g., supplies) within one year in the normal course of business or within the normal operating cycle.

The operating cycle of an entity is the period of time in which a company purchases inventory or materials, sells the products for cash or credit, and collects the cash from credit sales.

Current assets include cash and other monetary assets, such as accounts receivable, inventory, marketable securities, prepaid expenses, and other liquid assets that can be readily converted to cash. Cash is always listed first because it is the most liquid of all assets. Noncurrent assets, also called long-term assets, are to be held by the entity for a period longer than one year.

Noncurrent assets are those assets whose benefits are expected to be realized or consumed over more than one year or a normal operating cycle. They are often separated into the following categories:

- Long-term investments
- Property, plant, and equipment
- Intangible assets

Long-term investments are funds set aside for long-term use and are assumed to be not available to settle current liabilities. Long-term note receivables, investments in equities (common stock and preferred stock) of other companies, and investment in the debts (bonds) of corporations and governments that won't mature until sometime after the current period are all examples of long-term investments.

Property, plant, and equipment are also called operating assets since they are used to create revenue from the operations. Operating assets are carried at their acquisition cost minus accumulated depreciation. *Depreciation* is the reduction in historical cost of an operating asset over its useful life (how long you believe it will provide benefits).

Intangible assets, such as patents and trademarks, are also listed at their cost but their book value is reduced over time through a concept called amortization. *Amortization* refers to the periodic write-off of the cost of intangible assets over their useful lives. Intangible assets have no physical substance but have value based on rights, privileges, or advantages belonging to the owner.

Liabilities are shown in a similar manner—in ascending order of time to maturity. They are broken down into current and noncurrent (or long-term) liabilities. Current liabilities are obligations that will be paid (liquidated) by utilizing current assets. Payables are a typical current assets, including amounts owed to vendors for purchases of inventory and supplies, wages and salaries owed, and rent and taxes to be paid. The portion of long-term debt that is due in the current period is also classified as a current liability.

Noncurrent liabilities do not qualify as current liabilities and include long-term notes and bonds, amounts owed as a result of long-term leases, and obligations as a result of pensions promised to employees.

Leases can be long-term liabilities. Leases are contractual agreements in which the owner (lessor) of the property allows another party (lessee) to use the property for a stated period of time. Entities lease all types of real estate, equipment, and machines and often enter into agreements that extend beyond the current period. When that happens, the lease could be capitalized and shown as a long-term liability. In a capital lease, the lessee assumes most of the risk and rewards of ownership; therefore, accounting rules require that the lease be shown as an asset (capitalized) and the obligation be shown as a liability on the lessee's balance sheet.

Here's an example of presentation:

```
Liabilities
Current liabilities
        Accounts payable
        Salaries payable
Noncurrent liabilities
        Bonds payable
        Mortgages
```

Equity is the residual after total liabilities are subtracted from total assets. Additional investment in the entity increases equity as does profit (revenues greater than expenses). Equities are shown in descending order of priority in liquidation. *Liquidation* occurs when an entity is terminated or bankrupt, its assets are sold, and the proceeds pay creditors. Any leftovers are distributed to shareholders. In corporations, there are often two types of capital stock (shares of ownership)—preferred and common. Preferred stockholders receive return of their investment before common stockholders receive theirs. *Retained earnings* are the accumulation of earnings since the entity's inception. In corporations, retained earnings are profits minus dividends paid to the owners (stockholders).

Here's an example of the presentation of equity:

```
Equity
Contributed capital
        Preferred stock
        Common stock
Retained earnings
```

MEASUREMENT CRITERIA

The table below shows the measurement criteria used to place values on the various elements of a balance sheet. Keep in mind that the general guiding principle is historical cost. Some terms may seem confusing. For example, net realizable value and lower-of-cost or market are terms that are not often used but they are in line with conservatism. Net realizable value (NRV) for monetary assets (cash and cashlike assets, such as accounts receivable) is approximately what they would yield if you cashed them in or liquidated them. *Lower-of-cost-or-market value* is used for inventory and recognizes the fact that inventory can lose value over time, particularly if it is not a quick turnover. And so an estimate must be made of current market value and if it is less than the cost, the current market value will be listed on the balance sheet.

Balance Sheet Element	Measurement Criteria
Current Assets	Net realizable value (monetary assets) or lower-of-historical-cost or market
Investments	Market value
Property, Plant, and Equipment	Net book value (cost minus depreciation to date)
Current Liabilities	The amount of the original liability or the amount of cash needed to discharge the liability
Long-Term Liabilities	Discounted present value of future principal and interest payments
Paid-in Capital	Amount of capital raised
Retained Earnings	Accumulated earnings minus all dividends paid

PRESENTATION FORMATS

The format of the balance sheet usually takes two forms, horizontal and vertical.

Sample Company
Balance Sheet
December 31, 2008

Assets

Current assets		
Cash	$20,000	
Accounts receivable	30,000	
Inventories	70,000	
Total current assets	$120,000	
Property, plant, and equipment, net	$400,000	
Intangible assets	30,000	
Total assets	$550,000	

Liabilities and Stockholders' Equity

Current liabilities		
Accounts payable	$30,000	
Salaries payable	12,000	
Total current liabilities	$42,000	
Bonds payable	300,000	
Mortgages	100,000	
Total liabilities	$442,000	
Stockholders' equity		
Common stock	$100,000	
Retained earnings	8,000	
Total liabilities and stockholders' equity	$550,000	

Illustration 3.1. Horizontal Presentation of the Balance Sheet

A horizontal presentation uses a format that presents assets on the left and liabilities and equity on the right.

A vertical presentation uses a format that first presents the assets followed by liabilities and equity directly below the assets.

Sample Company
Balance Sheet
December 31, 2008

Assets

Current assets	
Cash	$20,000
Accounts receivable	30,000
Inventories	70,000
Total current assets	$120,000
Property, plant, and equipment, net	400,000
Intangible assets	30,000
Total assets	$550,000

Liabilities and Stockholders' Equity

Current liabilities	
Accounts payable	$30,000
Salaries payable	12,000
Total current liabilities	$42,000
Bonds payable	300,000
Mortgages	100,000
Total liabilities	$442,000
Stockholders' equity	
Common stock	$100,000
Retained earnings	8,000
Total liabilities and stockholders' equity	$550,000

Illustration 3.2. Vertical Presentation of the Balance Sheet

PERSONAL FINANCIAL BALANCE SHEET

A personal balance sheet can serve individuals in a variety of ways. It can be to obtain loans, enter into various investment transactions, or develop a financial plan. Preparing a personal financial statement often requires the expertise of CPAs who could act as auditors. The American Institute of Certified Public Accountants State of

Position (SOP) 82-1 provides GAAP for personal financial statements, including the personal balance sheet.

The personal balance sheet is very similar to that of a business balance sheet. It lists assets, liabilities, and net worth (Assets – Liabilities = Net). *Net worth* is a concept that is very much like equity in the business world. However, net worth is more of an indication of wealth. One big difference is that accounting standards dictate that assets are shown on a personal balance sheet at their estimated current values. The processes involved in the preparation of these statements are discussed. The *estimated current value* is defined in SOP 82-1 as "the amount at which the item could be exchanged between a buyer and seller, each of whom is well informed and willing, and neither of whom is compelled to buy or sell."

Liabilities on a personal balance sheet are shown at their estimated current amount, which is the discounted amount of cash to be paid. Simply put, the liabilities should be shown at the amount it would take to pay them off as of the date of the balance sheet.

TEST YOURSELF

1. Using the list of assets shown below, determine the total current assets.
    Intangible assets $40,000
    Accounts receivable $100,000
    Inventory $200,000
    Investments (common stock in another company) $225,000
    Cash $45,000
    Property, plant, and equipment $600,000
    Total current assets $_____

2. Determine the balance sheet value for each of the following assets based on the facts that are disclosed.

Asset		Balance sheet value
Cash	$10,000 in the bank with a deposit of $5,000 anticipated next week	$
Accounts receivable	$100,000 owed from customers with $20,000 estimated as uncollectible	$
Inventory	Cost of $200,000 with a market value of $150,000	$
Property, plant, and equipment	Cost of $1,000,000 and accumulated depreciation of $30,000	$
Intangible assets	Cost of patents is $50,000 with $10,000 amortized	$

3. If assets are $500,000 and equity is $270,000, what are the liabilities?

4. What is equity if assets are $900,000 and the liabilities are $520,000?

5. Using the following abbreviations, classify the balance sheet item:

CA = Current   NC = Noncurrent   CL = Current
     asset   asset   liability

LTL = Long-term   INT = Intangible   PPE = Property,
      liability   asset   plant, and
                                              equipment
                     E = Equity

A. _____ Patent

B. _____ Merchandise

C. _____ Retained earnings

D. _____ 30-year mortgage owed by the company

E. _____ Land

F. _____ Current installment due this month on 30-year mortgage

G. _____ Trademark

H. _____ Accounts payable

I. _____ Salaries payable

KEY POINTS TO REMEMBER

- The balance sheet is based on the accounting equation Assets = Liabilities + Equity.

- Classifications are used to make the balance sheet more meaningful.

- Assets are listed in the order of liquidation with cash and cashlike assets shown first and longer term assets such as tangible and intangible assets shown last.

- Liabilities are shown in ascending order of time to maturity. This means that liabilities to be paid soon are shown first and those that are to be paid in a time frame beyond this operating cycle are shown last.

- Equity is a residual concept. Assets – Liabilities = Equity.

- Equity is increased by owner investment and profits (revenues greater than expenses).

- The personal balance sheet that is prepared for individuals and families has one major difference from a business balance sheet: rather than show assets at cost, they are shown at estimated current value.

The Income Statement and Retained Earnings

INTRODUCTION

The results of operations are reported in the income statement, which is also called the statement of income, statement of earnings, or the profit and loss (P&L) statement. Many people still use the term P&L, but this term is seldom found in accounting textbooks anymore. The terms *profits, earnings,* and *income* are used interchangeably. The income statement reports revenues and expenses that happen as a result of the normal operations and gains and losses from other activities.

The income statement recognizes revenues when they are realized (i.e., when goods are shipped, services rendered, and expenses incurred). With *accrual accounting,* the flow of accounting events through the income statement doesn't necessarily coincide with the actual receipt and disbursement of cash; the income statement measures profitability, not cash flow.

The income statement reports net income which is defined as follows:

Net Income = Revenues − Expenses + Gains − Losses

WHAT'S AHEAD

In this chapter, you will learn:

- The elements of an income statement
- The two most common formats of an income statement
- The various types of revenues and expenses that are reported on an income statement

- That earnings per share is a key metric reported on the income statement
- How the statement of retained earnings discloses how accumulated earnings change over the most current accounting period

IN THE REAL WORLD

Cookie jar accounting is a practice, very popular during the 1990s, where a company uses generous reserves from good years against losses that might be incurred in bad years. These kinds of reserves create what is called "income smoothing." Earnings are understated in good years and overstated in bad years. Cookie jar reserves create a false growth curve that is smooth and steady, not like the up and down earnings expected from most companies.

In 1999, the SEC investigated Microsoft for what appeared to be a cookie jar accounting scheme. Profits from successful quarters weren't reported so that less successful quarters could be padded. One published report stated that Microsoft began the practice of utilizing cookie jar reserves with the release of Windows 95 and at one point had over $4 billion in unearned revenue sitting on the books.

According to one report in *USA Today* (June 3, 2002, "Microsoft Settles Accounting Charges with SEC"), the SEC alleged that Microsoft's accounting practices from July 1994 through June 1998 caused its income to be substantially misstated.

One of the reasons that companies could get away with the cookie jar reserve approach is that accounting rules generally allow businesses to set aside funds for potential expenses such as returned products, excessive inventory, and bad debts. A higher estimate of those expenses reduces the amount of reported earnings in one period but may actually help boost earnings in a later period. Under a settlement with the SEC, Microsoft neither admitted to nor denied wrongdoing and no fine was imposed.

KEY CONCEPTS

The income statement and the statement of retained earnings are two required financial statements that focus on profitability (earnings). Both statements cover the same accounting period. While the income statement shows the revenues and expenses for the period and calculates the bottom lines—net income and earnings per share—the retained earnings statement shows a reconciliation of what happened to the accumulated earnings from the start of the period to the end of the period. Retained earnings increase with net income and decrease if there is a net loss and the payment of dividends.

To get a deep understanding of the income statement and statement of retained earnings, you must understand revenue and expense recognition and the components and possible formats of each statement.

REVENUE AND EXPENSE RECOGNITION

The *revenue recognition* principle provides guidelines for reporting revenue in the income statement. The principle generally requires that revenue be recognized in the financial statements when the revenue is realized and earned. Revenues are *realized* when products or services are exchanged or performed for cash or claims to cash (accounts receivable). Revenues are considered *earned* when an entity has substantially accomplished what it must do to be entitled to the benefits represented by the revenues. Revenue recognition normally happens through sales or by providing (performance of) services. Sales and services provide a uniform and reasonable test of realization. There are other limited exceptions to the basic revenue principle, including recognizing revenue during production (on long–term construction contracts) and at the completion of production (for many commodities).

In recognizing expenses, the *matching* principle is the guiding light. It requires that expenses be matched with revenues whenever it is reasonable and practical to do so; for example, matching the cost of goods sold with revenues from the related sales that are reasonable and practical. To match costs when it is difficult to identify some connection with revenues, accountants use a rational and systematic allocation. Depreciation is a good example. Depreciation assigns expenses to the periods during which the related assets are expected to provide benefits. Therefore, if you have a machine, the theory is that you will depreciate it over the period that it helps contribute to the revenue activities of the entity. Some costs are charged to the current period as expenses simply because no future benefit is anticipated and no connection with revenue is apparent, or no allocation is rational and systematic under the circumstances.

ELEMENTS OF AN INCOME STATEMENT

The key elements of an income statement are the following:

- Revenues
- Expenses
- Gains
- Losses
- Net income (or net loss)

Revenues

Revenues are the total amounts earned by an entity by selling its products or by providing its services during a specific period. This may include sales of products (sales), rendering of services (fees), and earnings from interest, dividends, lease income, and royalties. Depending on the type of organization, revenues can take on various names. For a merchant, a majority of the revenues will be in the form of sales of goods. In a law office, most of the revenues will be from fees, just as a school earns its revenues from tuition and fees. In the case of governments, revenues are the gross receipts and receivables from taxes, fees, and other charges.

Nonprofit organizations are distinct from for–profit businesses in various ways, including their ability to collect revenue from a wide variety of sources. Potential sources include those generally available to the private sector such as fees for service, returns on investment, and government contracts. However, nonprofit organizations are also capable of collecting grants and charitable contributions from individuals.

Net sales refer to the value of a company's sales of goods and services to its customers. Even though a company's bottom line (its net income) gets most of the attention from investors, the first line is where the revenue or income process begins.

Expenses

Expenses are the costs an entity incurs for doing business in a specific period, including the cost of materials, supplies, labor, leases, and utilities. In addition, expenses must directly relate to generating revenues for an entity. The following are explanations of typical expenses.

COST OF SALES (A.K.A. COST OF GOODS SOLD OR COST OF SERVICES)

For a manufacturer, cost of sales is the expense incurred for raw materials, labor, and manufacturing overhead used in the production of its goods. It is equal to the cost of goods manufactured adjusted for the change in finished goods. For wholesalers and retailers, the cost of sales is essentially the purchase cost of merchandise used for resale. It is calculated as beginning inventory plus purchases minus ending inventory.

SELLING, GENERAL, AND ADMINISTRATIVE EXPENSES

Often referred to as SG&A, selling, general, and administrative expenses make up a company's operational expenses. General and administrative (G&A) expenses are incurred for the whole of the entity as opposed to some expenses (like selling and manufacturing) that are specific to parts of the entity. G&A expenses include accounting, legal, fees for services, officers' salaries, insurance, wages of office staff, supplies, and office occupancy costs (such as rent, utilities, etc.).

Selling expenses are incurred in selling or marketing. Examples include sales commissions, sales representatives' salaries, rent for the sales department, traveling expenses, advertising, selling department salaries and expenses, the cost of samples given to potential customers, and credit and collection costs.

Financial analysts generally assume that management exercises a great deal of control over this expense category. The trend of SG&A expenses, as a percentage of sales, is watched closely to detect signs, both positive and negative, of managerial efficiency.

Gross Profit

A company's gross profit (also called *gross margin*) does more than simply represent the difference between net sales and the cost of sales. Gross profit provides the resources to cover all of the company's other expenses. Obviously, the greater and more stable a company's gross margin, the greater potential there is for positive bottom line (net income) results.

Gains and Losses

Gains are possible from a variety of events and activities. Gains are from peripheral or incidental transactions of an entity. An example of a gain is when a retailer sells a building and a gain in wealth (selling at a price higher than cost) occurs. Such an event would not be as a result of core business activities (the relating of merchandise). The sale of a building by a retailer of merchandise would be incidental to the everyday business. Other gains can result from investments in stocks and bonds and other financial assets.

Losses are decreases in owners' equity from peripheral or incidental transactions of an entity. Examples are losses on the sale of investments and losses from lawsuits.

There are also many less frequent types of gains or losses. Examples include gains and losses from discontinued operations and extraordinary events. Extraordinary gains and losses are unusual in nature (high degree of abnormality), are unrelated to the ordinary and typical activities of the entity, and are infrequent in occurrence, meaning that such events would not be reasonably expected to happen in the foreseeable future.

Net Income

Net income, or the bottom line as it is often called, is the excess of all revenues and gains for a designated period over all expenses and losses of that period. A net loss is the excess of expenses and losses over revenues and gains for a designated period.

INCOME STATEMENT FORMAT

The income statement is typically prepared using one of two formats: single–step and multiple–step. Each format has its advantages. The advantage of the multiple–step income statement is that it clearly displays important financial and managerial information

Revenues	
Net sales	$2,000,000
Gains	150,000
Total revenues	$2,150,000
Expenses	
Cost of goods sold	$1,100,000
Selling and administrative expenses	600,000
Interest expenses	11,000
Losses	9,500
Income tax expenses	160,000
Total expenses	$1,880,500
Net income	$269,500

Illustration 4.1. Single–Step Income Statement

Net sales	$2,000,000
Cost of goods sold	1,100,000
Gross profit	$900,000
Selling and administrative expenses	600,000
Operating profit	$300,000
Other revenues and gains	150,000
Other expenses and losses	20,500
Pretax income from continuing operations	$429,500
Income taxes	160,000
Net income	$269,500

Illustration 4.2. Multiple–Step Income Statement

that the user would have to calculate from a single–step income statement. The single–step format has the advantage of being relatively simple to prepare and to understand.

In the single–step presentation, the gross and operating income figures are not stated; nevertheless, they can be calculated from the data provided.

In the multistep income statement, four measures of profitability are revealed at four critical junctions in a company's operations: gross profit, operating profit (or operating income), pretax income, and after tax net income.

EARNINGS PER SHARE

Generally accepted accounting principles (GAAP) require the disclosure of earnings per share (EPS) on the income statement of all publicly held companies. EPS is the amount of earnings per each share of the entity's common stock. Common stock is held by the owners of the entity; it is evidence of ownership. The basic EPS for net income is calculated as follows:

$$\text{EPS} = (\text{Net Income} - \text{Preferred Stock Dividends}) / \text{Weighted Average Number of Common Shares}$$

Preferred stock is a class of ownership in a corporation that has a higher claim on the assets and earnings than common stock. Preferred stock generally has a dividend that must be paid out to preferred stockholders before dividends to common stockholders are paid, and that is why preferred stock dividends are deducted from net income. In other words, EPS reflects earnings potentially available to be paid to common stockholders in the form of dividends.

EPS is an important metric for investors, potential investors, management, directors, and others. It indicates profits behind each share of common stock. It is considered to be an important variable in determining a share's price, and therefore EPS estimates and actual EPS are watched very carefully by participants in the financial markets.

When a company is profitable and has enough earnings so as to give back to shareholders in the form of a dividend, a dividend payout ratio can be calculated as follows:

$$\text{EPS} / \text{Dividend per Share}$$

Income Statement Measure	Formula
Gross Profit	Net Sales – Cost of Sales
Operating Profit (or Operating Income)	Gross Profit – Selling and Administrative Expenses
Net Income	Operating Profit + Other Revenue and Gains – Other Expenses and Losses – Income Taxes
Earnings per Share	(Net Income – Preferred Stock Dividends) / Weighted Average Number of Common Shares

Illustration 4.3 Income Statement Measures and Formulas

EPS not paid out in the form of dividends is placed into the retained earnings—which then become a source of money or capital that can be used to help fund the growth of a company.

STATEMENT OF RETAINED EARNINGS

Prepared after the income statement, the statement of retained earnings explains the changes in a company's retained earnings over the reporting period. Retained earnings are also reported on the balance sheet under "stockholders' equity," and are affected by net income earned (or net loss) during a period of time minus any dividends paid to the company's owners/stockholders. *Retained earnings* are earnings that have accumulated over the period the entity has been in existence.

The equation can be expressed as followed:

Ending Retained Earnings = Beginning Retained Earnings + Net Income – Dividends Paid

The statement of retained earnings covers the same accounting period as the income statement. It gives the reader of the financial statements full disclosure of the effect of earnings, losses,

Statement of Retained Earnings

Retained earnings, January 1, 2009	$1,300,000
Add net income for the year	230,000
	$1,530,000
Less dividends paid to stockholders	110,000
Retained earnings, December 31, 2009	$1,420,000

Illustration 4.4 Statement of Retained Earnings

and dividends on stockholders' equity. From time to time, an adjustment called *prior period adjustment* may also be shown on the statement of retained earnings. This is done to clearly show that the item pertains to a past period or periods rather than the current period. Two examples of prior period adjustments are the correction of an error made in a prior year and the recognition of a tax loss carryforward benefit arising from a purchased subsidiary.

TEST YOURSELF

1. Which of the following are revenues to be reported for the current period? (Put a check mark next to the transaction to be reported as revenue.)
   A. _____ Collected $10,000 from last year's sales.
   B. _____ This week, performed $1,500 of services for a client, but the client won't pay until next year.
   C. _____ Received $10,000 retained for work to be performed in the next accounting period.
   D. _____ Today, sold and delivered $15,000 of products to customers.
   E. _____ This week, the town government collected $300,000 in current–quarter real estate taxes from its citizens.

2. Calculate gross profit based on the following numbers:
   Sales: $500,000
   Selling expenses: $50,000

Legal fees: $3,000

Cost of goods sold: $230,000

Gross profit $_____

3. Based on the following information, prepare a single–step income statement.

Net sales: $2,000,000

Cost of goods sold: $1,100,000

Selling and administrative expenses: $600,000

Gains: $150,000

Interest expense: $11,000

Losses: $9,500

Dividends paid: $25,000

Income tax expense: $160,000

4. Using the same numbers from question 3, prepare the income statement using the multiple–step format.

5. Based upon the following facts, calculate earnings per share (EPS).

Net income: $2,500,000

Preferred stock dividend: $600,000

Common stock shares outstanding at the start of the period: 800,000

Common stock shares outstanding at the end of the period: 700,000

EPS $_____

6. Based on the following facts, calculate the ending retained earnings balance.

Retained earnings, January 1, 2009: $500,000

Dividends for the period January 1 through December 31, 2009: $200,000

Net income for the 12 months ending December 31, 2009: $350,000

Retained earnings, December 31, 2009 $_____

KEY POINTS TO REMEMBER

- The matching principle guides the reporting of revenues and expenses on the income statement.

- The income statement equation is Revenues – Expenses = Net Income.

- Key components of the income statement include revenues, expenses, gains, losses, and net income (net loss). Also, depending on the format used, an income statement can also include gross profit, operating income, and earnings per share.

- Revenues can include sales of products, fees for services, earnings from investments, lease income, and royalties. In the case of nonprofits and government entities, revenues can include taxes and other appropriations, grants, and charitable donations.

- Expenses are the cost of doing business and include the cost of sales, selling, general, and administrative costs, taxes, and interest.

- The income statement can take one of two commonly used formats: single–step or multiple–step.

- Earnings per share are disclosed on the income statement and are an important metric for all types of financial statement users. They indicate the amount of net income (after deducting preferred dividends) behind each share of stock.

- The statement of retained earnings is another financial statement required by GAAP. It discloses the amount of earnings that have accumulated since the entity was founded. Retained earnings are also reported on the balance sheet, as they are key components of the equity of a corporation.

The Statement of Cash Flows

INTRODUCTION

Cash is the lifeblood of an entity. Managing cash flow is critical to the long-term survival and prosperity of any entity. The *statement of cash flows* is the only one of the financial statements that shows what has happened to cash during the accounting period. The income statement does not shed light on cash flow; in fact, an income statement can be a bit misleading when considering cash. A business can make a profit, as reported on the income statement, and still not have enough cash available to meet its obligations.

WHAT'S AHEAD	
In this chapter, you will learn: • The three classifications of cash flow reported on the statement of cash flows • The types of investing activities that produce cash flow • The kinds of financing activities that impact cash flow	• The two acceptable methods of presenting operating cash flow • How to calculate free cash flow

IN THE REAL WORLD

Long John Silver's, Inc., (*www.ljsilvers.com*) based in Louisville, Kentucky, is the world's most popular quick-service seafood chain, specializing in a variety of seafood items. Inspired by Robert Louis Stevenson's classic novel *Treasure Island*, Long John Silver's was founded in 1969 in response to growing consumer demand for quick-service seafood. Today, there are more than 1,250 Long John Silver's, Inc., restaurants worldwide serving nearly 4,000,000 customers each week.

Long John Silver's, Inc., is a subsidiary of YUM! Brands, Inc., the world's largest restaurant company in terms of system units, with approximately 33,000 restaurants in more than 100 countries and territories.

Things were not always so rosy for Long John Silver's Inc. In June of 1998, the company sank into bankruptcy and closed 72 of its worst-performing restaurants. Cash flow problems, exacerbated by high interest payments, made it difficult for the company to upgrade its facilities and to develop new products that would spur sales.

The company had become debt burdened as a result of a management-led leveraged buyout almost 10 years earlier. A *leveraged buyout* is the acquisition of a company, often by management, by using a significant amount of borrowed funds. In a leveraged buyout, the assets of the company are used as collateral for the funding (debt) to acquire the company. The new debt appears on the balance sheet of the acquired company, and the company's cash flow is used to repay the debt. Leveraged buyouts are interesting and creative ways to acquire a company when funds are short; however, as was the case with Long John Silver's, leveraged buyouts can lead to high interest debt that stress the cash flow of the company.

In March 2002, YUM! Brands, Inc., acquired Long John Silver's and A&W All-American Food from a restaurant investment holding company that had owned the restaurant chains since 2000.

YUM! Brands had the capital and sufficient cash to not only upgrade operations and develop new products but also to develop multibranding opportunities with successful YUM! brands such as KFC.

KEY CONCEPTS

Understanding cash flow means you must learn how to read the statement of cash flows. Accounting rules require that cash flows be categorized in three ways: cash flows from operating activities, investing, and financing. Investors are attracted to entities that produce sufficient cash flow from operations. A metric called *free cash flow* is carefully monitored by management, investors, and creditors.

STATEMENT OF CASH FLOWS

The primary purpose of a statement of cash flows is to provide information about the cash receipts and cash payments of an entity during a period. The statement of cash flows reports the cash effects of the following:

- Operations
- Investing
- Financing

The FASB requires a statement of cash flows as part of the set of financial statements. It is the only financial statement that presents a summary of cash inflows and outflows (sources and uses of cash). Cash flow is an important concept because without it, an entity cannot survive. Creditors examine the statement of cash flows because they are concerned about the risks of being paid on time. Cash flow from operating activities gets a great deal of focus when a company is examined by investors and creditors. Relatively large amounts of cash flow produced by operating activities reveal that an entity is able to generate sufficient cash internally. When operating cash flow is not enough, then a company must borrow, sell assets, or issue stock (equity) to acquire enough cash to keep things running.

The statement of cash flows helps complete the picture. High levels of net income do not always indicate a solvent company. Financial analysts agree that along with traditional financial analysis (ratios), it is important to examine the statement of cash flows to assess financial liquidity, flexibility, and free cash flow. Free cash flow is found by subtracting capital expenditures and dividends from cash flow provided by operating activities. The primary purpose of the statement of cash flows is to provide information about the cash inflows and outflows of an entity. The secondary purpose is to give the financial statement user some insights into the operating, investing, and financing activities of the entity.

When reviewing a statement of cash flows, a user might ask the following questions:

- How well does the entity generate cash from its operations?
- What trends in net cash flow exist when examining cash generated by operations over time?
- What are the major reasons for positive or negative cash flow?

CLASSIFICATION OF CASH FLOWS

The statement of cash flows reports the cash effects of its activities. It does this by classifying cash effects in three ways: cash effects of operating activities, investing, and financing. To fully comprehend the messages that spring forth from the statement of cash flows, you must understand the types of activities categorized under the three types of cash flows, as explained in the sections that follow.

Cash Flow from Operating Activities

It would almost make sense to discuss cash flow from operating activities last because it includes all those activities that bring in cash or cause outflows of cash except investing and financing activities. However, since it is the first classification of cash flows on the statement of cash flows, it is covered first.

This section of the cash flow statement shows how much money the company received from its actual business operations. The term *net cash provided by operating activities* is used to show how net income is adjusted to derive net cash provided. The adjustments are necessary because of accrual accounting rules—net income and cash flow are not synonymous. Cash flow from operating activities includes cash received from sales and fees, interest on loans and dividends on equity securities, and cash payments to suppliers for inventory and other goods and services, employees for services (salaries and wages), taxes, and payments made to lenders for interest. A good rule of thumb to remember when trying to understand cash flow from operations: it is the cash effects of transactions that enter into the determination of net income.

Cash Flow Investing Activities

Cash flow from investing activities reports the change in an entity's cash position resulting from any gains (or losses) from investments in the financial markets and operating subsidiaries, as well as changes resulting from amounts spent on investments in capital assets such as plant and equipment. When you examine this section of a statement of cash flows you will see activities such as making and collecting loans, acquiring and disposing of debt or equity instruments, and acquiring and disposing of property, plant, and equipment and other productive assets.

When analyzing an entity's statement of cash flows, it is important to consider each of the various sections and how they contributed to the change in cash position. Sometimes an entity may have negative overall cash flow for a given period. But if the company can generate positive cash flow from its business operations, the negative overall cash flow may be a result of heavy investment expenditures, which could be a very good thing as investing activities help renew the organization and improve the productivity.

Here's a list of investing activities:

- Sale of property, plant, and equipment
- Purchase of property, plant, and equipment
- Sale of debt or equity securities of other entities
- Purchase of debt and equity securities of other entities
- Collection of loans to other entities
- Loans made to other entities

Cash Flow from Financing Activities

This section of the statement of cash flows measures the flow of cash between the entity and its owners and creditors. The activities include obtaining resources from owners and providing them with a return on investment, as well as a return of investment and borrowing money from creditors and repaying the amounts borrowed. Negative numbers can mean the company is servicing debt, but it can also mean the company is making dividend payments and stock repurchases.

Here's a list of financing activities:

- Issuance of equity securities
- Issuance of debt (bonds and notes)
- Payment of dividends
- Redemption of debt
- Reacquisition of capital stock

Illustration 5.1 shows an example of the cash flow statement prepared with what is called the indirect method.

STATEMENT OF CASH FLOWS

For the Year Ended December 31, 2009

Cash Flows from Operating Activities

Net Income	$39,000	
Decrease in inventory	400	
Increase in accounts payable	1,000	
Depreciation expense	1,250	
Loss on disposal of land	100	
Increase in accounts receivable	(1,000)	
Gain on sale of equipment	3,000	
Net cash flow from operating activities		$43,750

Cash Flows from Investing Activities

Cash flow from the sale of equipment	9,000	
Purchase of equipment	(20,000)	
Cash flow from sale of land	1,500	
Net cash flow from investing activities		($9,500)

Cash Flows from Financing Activities

Repayment of long-term debt	(1,000)	
Dividends	(1,800)	
Net cash flow from financing activities		($2,800)
Net increase in cash		$31,450
Plus: beginning cash balance		2,800
Ending cash balance		$34,250

Illustration 5.1. Example of Statement of Cash Flows

METHODS OF PRESENTING OPERATING CASH FLOWS

The statement of cash flows is really a type of reconciliation. It shows what happened to cash during a particular accounting period. For purposes of the cash flow statement, cash normally includes cash equivalents. Cash equivalents are short-term, temporary investments that can be readily converted into cash, such as marketable securities, short-term certificates of deposit, treasury bills, and commercial paper. *Commercial paper* is short-term debt investment issued by large corporations. Other corporations purchase commercial paper much like individuals purchase certificates of deposit from their banks. However, the denominations of commercial paper are in the average millions of dollars and can be for a few days and up to 270 days under SEC rules. A major benefit of commercial paper is that it does not need to be registered with the SEC, making it a very cost-effective means of financing.

The cash flow statement shows the opening balance in cash and cash equivalents for the reporting period, the net cash provided by or used in each one of the categories (operating, investing, and financing activities), the net increase or decrease in cash and cash equivalents for the period, and the ending balance.

There are two methods of presenting the statement of cash flows, and the difference lies in the way the operating cash flows are shown. The two methods—the direct method and the indirect method—yield the same result, but different procedures are used to arrive at the cash flows.

Direct Method

Under the direct method, you are basically analyzing your cash accounts to identify cash flows during the period. Under the direct method, you report the following in the cash flows from the operating activities section of the cash flow statement:

- Cash receipts from customers
- Cash payments for inventory
- Cash paid to employees
- Cash paid for operating expenses
- Taxes paid
- Interest paid
- Equals net cash provided by (used in) operating activities

Indirect Method

In preparing the cash flows from the operating activities section under the indirect method, you start with net income per the income statement, reverse out entries to income and expense accounts that do not involve a cash movement, and show the change in net working capital. Entries that affect net income but do not represent cash flows could include income you have earned but not yet received, depreciation, amortization of prepaid expenses, and accrued expenses. Under this method you are basically analyzing your income, expense accounts, and working capital and making adjustments to net income to derive the changes in cash.

The following is an example of how the indirect method would be presented on the cash flow statement:

- Net income per the income statement
- Minus entries to income accounts that do not represent cash flows
- Plus entries to expense accounts that do not represent cash flows
- Equals cash flows before movements in working capital

Add or subtract the change in working capital, as follows:

- An increase in current assets (excluding cash and cash equivalents) would be shown as a negative figure because cash was spent or converted into other current assets, thereby reducing the cash balance.

- A decrease in current assets would be shown as a positive figure because other current assets were converted into cash.

- An increase in current liabilities (excluding short-term debt, which would be reported in the financing activities section) would be shown as a positive figure since more liabilities mean that less cash was spent.

- A decrease in current liabilities would be shown as a negative figure because cash was spent in order to reduce liabilities.

The net effect of the above would then be reported as cash provided by (used in) operating activities.

Investors and Cash Flow

Investors are attracted to companies that produce free cash flow (FCF). *Free cash flow* is an indication of an entity's ability to pay its debts and dividends, buy back stock, and fuel the growth of the enterprise. Free cash flow is the excess cash produced that can be returned to shareholders or invested in new growth opportunities without hurting the existing operations. This is the most common method of calculating free cash flow:

Cash Flow from Operations
 − Capital Expenditures
Free Cash Flow

What an entity does with its free cash flow is just as important as generating sufficient free cash. For example, companies that simply hoard cash or spend it foolishly may have lots of free cash but are frivolous with it.

TEST YOURSELF

1. Which of the following would be classified as cash flows from investing activities? (Put a check mark next to your choices.)

    A. _____ Sold equipment used in the factory

    B. _____ Cash sales of merchandise

    C. _____ Raised $1,000,000 by issuing common stock

    D. _____ Paid $50,000 in cash dividends

    E. _____ Collected $100,000 from a loan made to a supplier

    F. _____ Advanced $55,000 of cash to a supplier and accepted a note payable due in two years

    G. _____ Issued $2,000,000 in bonds

    H. _____ Acquired $10,000,000 (cash) of the entity's own common stock

    I. _____ Acquired $10,000,000 of bonds by trading company common stock

2. Which of the following would be classified as cash flows from financing activities? (Put a check mark next to your choices.)

    A. _____ Sold equipment used in the factory

    B. _____ Cash sales of merchandise

    C. _____ Raised $1,000,000 by issuing common stock

    D. _____ Paid $50,000 in cash dividends

    E. _____ Collected $100,000 from a loan made to a supplier

    F. _____ Advanced $55,000 of cash to a supplier and accepted a note payable due in two years

    G. _____ Issued $2,000,000 in bonds

    H. _____ Acquired $10,000,000 (cash) of the entity's own common stock

    I. _____ Acquired $10,000,000 of bonds by trading company common stock

3. Assume the following:

    Net cash flow from operations $100,000

    Net cash flow from investing activities ($11,000)

Net cash flow from financing activities $9,000
Ending cash $115,000

What was the beginning cash balance? $_____

4. Using the same information from problem 3, but ignoring the ending cash balance, what would be the ending cash balance if the beginning cash balance was $25,000?

Ending cash balance $_____

5. If you assume the same facts as problem 3, if capital expenditures totaled $55,000, what is the amount of free cash?

Free cash $_____

KEY POINTS TO REMEMBER

- The statement of cash flows is the only one of the financial statements that shows what has happened to cash during the accounting period.

- There are three classifications of cash flow reported on the statement of cash flows: cash flow from operations, investing, and financing.

- Cash flow from operations is all those activities that impact cash flow except investing and financing activities.

- Cash flow from investing activities includes sales and purchases of financial instruments and property and the granting and collections of loans.

- Cash flow from financing activities measures the impact of the flow of cash between the entity and its owners and creditors.

- The statement of cash flows can take two forms: direct or indirect.

- Free cash flow is calculated by subtracting capital expenditures from the cash flow from operations.

Working Capital

INTRODUCTION

W*orking capital* is a term synonymous with current assets. The ability to manage working capital will improve the rate of return on the entity's assets and will minimize the risk of running short on cash—the most important working capital asset. Managing working capital means a variety of things, including cash management, prudent investment, good credit decisions and strong collection efforts, and effective inventory management. But before you can practice effective and efficient working capital management, you must understand the various components of working capital and how it is reported on the entity's balance sheet.

WHAT'S AHEAD	
In this chapter, you will learn: • The critical issues related to cash reporting and cash management • How receivables are valued for balance sheet reporting • The four basic methods for valuing inventory	• How the lower-of-cost-or-market value is applied to inventory • The three basic classifications of investments on the balance sheet

IN THE REAL WORLD

Working capital investment is necessary for a thriving enterprise. Working capital is the resource base that is required by the entity to finance operations on a day-to-day basis. However, too much working capital is not a good thing because it could mean that opportunities are lost. There is an opportunity cost for having working capital. Working capital, which includes cash, accounts receivable, and inventory, is a necessary investment but it does carry a cost. For example, too much inventory ties up funds and incurs a carrying cost, as space is needed to store the inventory, and resources are consumed as inventory is moved and insured.

Just-in-time inventory (JIT) is part of a production system whereby a company greatly reduces its investment in inventory and the costs associated with carrying inventory so that utilization of production inputs, storage of inventory, and delivery of finished products are accomplished without incurring significant holding costs. "Just in time" is a phrase that originated at Toyota. Originally, it described how material should be processed and moved in order to arrive just in time for the next operation. In recent years, JIT was utilized by Dell Computers to give it a competitive advantage.

In the case of Dell Computers, JIT means fewer finished computers in inventory and a smaller chance that Dell will lose money on them, as they risk becoming obsolete sitting on a shelf in a warehouse somewhere. Dell makes each machine to order and maintains only 12 days of inventory.

Dell locates its manufacturing facilities near its customers in Europe. The European manufacturing plant is located in Limerick, Ireland. Through the Ireland facility, Dell's just-in-time, build-to-order manufacturing system produces computers for customers throughout Europe, the Middle East, and Africa.

Dell's build-to-order model enables the company to have much smaller investment in working capital than its competitors. Dell grew its business quickly and was able to finance that growth internally by its efficient use of working capital and its profitability. A study of Dell's strategy and its working capital management reveals the importance of working capital management in a rapidly growing firm.

KEY CONCEPTS

The assets near the top of the balance sheet are usually cash and cashlike assets, including investments, receivables, and inventory. All these assets are utilized through the operating cycle. Inventory is sold, many times on credit, and therefore a receivable is created. Receivables are collected and excess cash is invested. Balance sheet users know that a good portion of current assets consists of these liquid and near liquid assets. They also know that cash management techniques and strong internal controls are necessary to help assure that enough liquidity is in place to keep the entity afloat.

Accounting principles require that receivables, investments, and inventory be conservatively valued. In the case of receivables, an allowance account is used to estimate uncollectible amounts and to offset them against receivables to derive a conservative carry value of the asset. Investments and inventory are also monitored and reported in ways that keep overbloated values in check. Without such principles, tools, and techniques, balance sheet users would quickly lose faith and the confidence that solvency could be accurately assessed. *Solvency* is simply the ability to meet financial obligations in a timely manner with available cash.

CASH AND CASH EQUIVALENTS

The asset section of every balance sheet starts with the cash account. Cash is the most liquid of assets and one of the toughest to safeguard, as it can be transferred easily in physical and electronic form.

In the accounting word, cash is a broad term. Cash includes cash on hand (currency) and also money on deposit in the bank—including both demand deposits (checking accounts) and time deposits (savings accounts), as well as checks received but not yet cashed or deposited—and other negotiable instruments including money orders, certified checks, and travelers checks. Cash is a current asset.

There must be sufficient cash to keep an entity vital. Corporate finance experts say that each entity should determine its own appropriate cash level. Too little cash is a bad thing and the same could be said for too much cash, as cash does not increase in value unless it is invested. Entities should keep just enough cash to cover their interest, expenses, and capital expenditures, plus some amount in case of emergencies.

The cash account is usually a control account with a subsidiary ledger of accounts for each bank account. However, on the balance sheet, only one cash account is presented. A subsidiary ledger contains the detail on each of a number of items that collectively make up a single general ledger account, called the *control account*. Other control accounts are accounts receivable, plant and equipment, and accounts payable.

Cash equivalents are highly liquid investments that are easily converted to cash and are often grouped with cash on the balance sheet. They are investments that are so liquid and so safe that they are nearly the same as cash. These are assets that are so close to maturity (the day they become cash) that there is very little risk. They have an original maturity of three months or less. Cash equivalents include treasury bills, money market funds, and commercial paper. Commercial paper is issued by large corporations as an alternative to acquiring short-term loans.

Compensating Balances

A *compensating balance* is a minimum amount that must be on deposit per a loan or other borrowing arrangement. For example, if ABC Corporation signs a loan agreement with First Trust Bank for $2,500,000, the agreement could require ABC Corporation to maintain a minimum balance of $100,000 on hand at all times or be in default of the loan agreement.

A compensating balance is cash since it is funds on deposit at a financial institution. However, since the amount is not available for immediate withdrawal or use, it must be segregated and reported separately from other cash and cash equivalents on an entity's balance sheet. Depending on the length of the borrowing agreement, the compensating balance may be show as either short-term (less than 12 months) or long-term (more than 12 months).

CASH MANAGEMENT

Cash needs to be managed. Enough cash must be available to pay the bills and make the payroll. Cash budgeting is extremely important. Management must predict the cash inflows and outflows, month by month and in some cases, week by week. Cash budgeting alerts management to resource needs and helps keep payments on time and credit histories strong.

If a future month's cash budget predicts a shortfall (deficit), then plans must be put in place to establish a line of credit or to borrow working capital loans. If the budget shows a surplus, then plans must be made to decide how excess (surplus) cash will be invested.

Cash in a checking account typically earns no interest and if it does, it is meager. Often called a nonearning asset, cash should be held in minimal amounts—just enough to support ongoing operations.

Cash management also involves sturdy cash controls. Management must find ways to safeguard cash against theft and other abuses. Periodic bank reconciliations are a critical internal control and need to be prepared for each individual bank account as soon as the bank statement is received. Bank reconciliations reconcile the cash balances per the general ledger (entity's records) to the bank records (the bank statement). Reconciliations can disclose errors and fraudulent activities on both sides—the entity's operations and the bank.

Cash controls also involve tools and techniques like proper credit and collections policies and procedures. Internal auditors test cash controls. They review practices such as cash budgeting, bank reconciliations, and collection procedures to ensure that cash controls are working. Auditors test to ensure that policies and procedures governing cash receipts and disbursements make sense and are adhered to consistently. All departments that are involved in cash collections (currency/coin, personal checks, bank drafts, money orders, travelers' checks, cashiers' checks, and credit/debit card transactions) should establish a procedure to document all such receipts.

Another important internal control aspect of managing cash is the separation of duties. To the extent staffing levels permit, the duties of collecting, recording, depositing, and reconciling cash receipts should be separated among different individuals to help guard against theft. Where staffing levels do not permit separation of duties, compensating controls such as strict individual accountability and thorough management review and supervision should exist.

RECEIVABLES

Receivables are amounts owed to the entity and can take two basic forms: accounts receivable and notes receivable. If the receivable arises from the sale of goods or services, it is an *account receivable*. Accounts receivable can be a major asset for companies that extend credit to their customers. Credit managers make their living on their ability to manage accounts receivable, an important component of working capital. They evaluate character, capacity, capital of the customer, and the economic conditions to decide whether credit should be extended and a new receivable set up on the books.

An account receivable begins its life as revenue. For example, if $1,000 of goods is sold to a customer on credit, both a sale (revenue) and a receivable (asset) are recognized in the accounting records. Most of the time, an account receivable is a current asset since collection is reasonably expected to happen within the year or the entity's normal operating cycle.

Notes receivable are written contracts, evidenced by a promissory note that is a promise to pay specified amounts on specified dates, and usually includes interest and possibly late penalties. A note receivable may result from a customer transaction that was initially an accounts receivable that could not be paid within the agreed upon time. Thus, a note receivable would be created to formalize the credit agreement and stipulate interest and late penalties, terms that are often not part of accounts receivable arrangements. While an account receivable is mostly an undocumented contract, a note receivable is a document, signed by the debtor—a true written promise.

Receivables can arise from other transactions. For example, a tax refund due to an entity would be a tax receivable. Other examples of receivables include amounts owed to an entity because of leases; advances (loans) to shareholders, directors, officers, and other employees; claims for insurance proceeds; or amounts arising from litigation, interest, dividends, or royalties.

Uncollectible Accounts

Although accounts receivable are recorded when a sale is made and are initially entered into the books of the company at a value equal to the sale, the principal valuation factor is an estimation of the uncollectible accounts. The book value, also called the net realizable value or the net recoverable amount of receivables, is the total amount owed minus the estimated uncollectible amount.

There are two approaches for determining the uncollectible amount: direct write-off method and the allowance method. Both methods result in an amount that must be recognized as an uncollectible account expense. It is what accountants call a *loss contingency*, but it is simply the recognition of a reality: no matter how good you are at evaluating the four Cs of credit (character, capacity, collateral, and conditions), ultimately some customers will not pay. Nonpayment is an expense of doing business.

DIRECT WRITE-OFF METHOD

The direct write-off method is not acceptable under GAAP. However, it is used by a lot of smaller entities that do not have to strictly adhere to GAAP. With the direct write-off method, a bad debt expense (uncollectible account expense) is recognized when it is established that a particular account will not be collected.

There are various ways that an accountant could determine that an account will not be collected. For example, it could be known that the debtor has entered into bankruptcy or that a person owing money could die with a very small estate. In both cases, the likelihood of collection would be small and a write-off of the account would occur. The term *write off* means to remove the balance from the books so that in the case of receivables, the asset would be reduced by the amount owed. For example, assume that ABC Corporation owed your firm $10,000 for goods purchased on credit. The ABC account receivable is part of a total of $200,000 of receivables owed. Subsequently, ABC Corporation declares bankruptcy and by all accounts has very little chance of settling its debts. The write-off would be for $10,000 of uncollectible account expenses and a reduction of the total receivables by $10,000. Therefore, the income of the entity would be reduced by $10,000, and the accounts receivable would be valued at $190,000 ($200,000 minus the $10,000 write-off of the ABC Corporation account).

ALLOWANCE METHOD

The allowance method is an acceptable method under GAAP. This method attempts to match the bad debt expense with the related revenue in an attempt to determine the net realizable value of accounts receivable. The allowance method utilizes an account called the *allowance for doubtful accounts*, a *contra-asset account* that is subtracted from accounts receivable to derive the net realizable value.

Accounts Receivable – Allowance for Doubtful Accounts = Net Realizable Value of Accounts Receivable

Assume that a company has $200,000 of accounts receivable but has estimated that $15,000 will not be collected. Here's how it would be shown on the company's balance sheet:

Accounts receivable	$200,000
Less: Allowance for doubtful accounts	(15,000)
Net realizable value	$185,000

There are a number of ways of estimating uncollectible accounts. One popular way is to utilize a percentage of sales that is usually based on past bad debt losses. For example, if last year the company experienced $15,000 of bad debts (uncollectible accounts receivable) on credit sales of $300,000, then a bad debt estimate of 5 percent of sales could be used to estimate this year's uncollectible accounts expense.

Another popular method for estimating bad debt expense is to age the accounts receivable and to apply different percentages to blocks or groups of receivables according to age. Larger percentages would be used for the older receivables. As you can see in the example shown in Illustration 6.1, a very low percentage is used to estimated the uncollectible amount of receivables not yet due (1 percent). But for those receivables that are over 90 days past their

Customer	Not Yet Due	1–30 Days Past Due	31–60 Days Past Due	61–90 Days Past Due	Over 90 Days Past Due	Total
Adams Drug Store	$10,000	$5,000	$2,000			$17,000
Ashmont	4,000	5,000			9,000	18,000
Arlans Department Store					10,000	10,000
Beacon Lumber Yard					4,000	4,000
Causeway Cleaners			2,000			2,000
Dalton Floors		5,000				5,000
Everlasting Works	1,000					1,000
Fall River Chevy		500	600	800		1,900
Griffin Industries		1,000				1,000
Hallmark Motors					15,000	15,000
Total	$15,000	$16,500	$4,600	$800	$38,000	$74,900
Estimated Uncollectible	1%	3%	6%	10%	25%	
Estimated Uncollectible Accounts	$150	$495	$276	$80	$9,500	$10,501

Illustration 6.1. Aging of Accounts

due date, the estimated uncollectible percentage is much higher (25 percent), which is in line with the credit manager's assumption that the older the receivable, the greater the likelihood that if will not be collected. Also notice that in the example, the total accounts receivable amount is $74,900 with the total uncollectible amount estimated at $10,501. That means that the net realizable value for the receivables reported on the balance sheet is $64,399.

INVENTORY

Inventory consists of tangible personal property that is held for sale in the ordinary course of business. It can be composed of finished goods—items that are immediately available for sale—or those in various stages of production. For example, in a manufacturing concern, inventory can consist of raw materials, parts, work in progress (not yet completely converted to a finished good), and finished goods.

In retailing, inventory usually begins its life as a purchase—an item that will be resold without any significant modification. Take a sporting goods store for example. The baseball gloves are purchased and put on the shelf as inventory available to be sold. Once inventory is sold, it becomes cost of goods sold, an expense.

The cost of inventory for a merchandiser (retailer or whole-saler) is quite straightforward; it is the cost of the purchase (plus the cost of any modifications—which are usually small or nonexistent). Also included in cost are any freight charges incurred by the buyer in shipping the inventory to the place of business, the cost of insurance taken out during the time the inventory is in transit, the cost of storing the inventory before it is sold, and the various types of inventory-related taxes such as excise and sales tax. The cost of inventory for a manufacturer is a bit more complicated.

There are three distinct types of costs for a manufactured inventory: direct materials, direct labor, and manufacturing overhead. There is more on manufacturing costs in chapter 9, Managerial and Cost Accounting.

Cost Flows and Valuation

Understanding how cost flows happen and how value is added when it comes to inventory are key prerequisites to deriving a value for inventory. There are four basic methods, also called cash flow assumptions, for valuing inventory. They are the following:

1. Specific identification
2. First in, first out
3. Last in, first out
4. Average cost

The specific identification method tracks cost flows exactly the way they happen. In other words, this system tracks which units are sold and which units are on hand. Serial numbers (such as for automobiles) and other tagging systems—including bar coding—make specific identification possible, but because of the practical difficulty of keeping track of individual items sold, many companies choose to use other methods.

With the first-in, first-out (FIFO) method, the assumption is made that the first goods purchased are the first sold and that the ending inventory consists of the most recent purchases. Cost of goods sold includes goods purchased at the beginning of the current period and possibly prior periods.

The last-in, first-out (LIFO) method is a cost flow assumption that is exactly opposite of FIFO. Under LIFO, the assumption is that the most recent purchases are sold first. In times of inflation, LIFO reduces taxable income because it results in the highest cost of goods sold.

The average cost method, also called *weighted average cost*, is a relatively easy approach to costing inventory. It assigns the same unit cost to all units available for sale during the period. The weighted average cost is calculated as follows:

Cost of Goods Available for Sale / Units Available for Sale =
Average Cost per Unit

Ending inventory is found by multiplying the number of units in the ending inventory by the average cost per unit. The cost of goods sold is then found by subtracting the ending inventory from the cost of the goods available for sale.

Lower-of-Cost-or-Market (LCM) Method

Inventory is the least liquid of the working capital accounts. To convert it to cash it must be sold. Inventory that doesn't move rapidly can lose value. Computers, for example, can lose as much as 1 percent of their value per week as they sit in inventory. Perishable inventory can quickly lose value and in the fashion business, changes in consumer tastes could signal new styles that might make older inventory items obsolete. In cases where inventory is losing value, a departure from cost basis might be necessary when valuing inventory for the balance sheet. That departure is called the *lower-of-cost-or-market* (LCM) method.

With the LCM, the cost of inventory is compared to the market price of the inventory. If the market price is lower than the cost, then the inventory is written down to the lower amount. Such an adjustment not only lowers assets (reduction in inventory value), but net income is reduced as the reduction in inventory value is recognized as a loss (*loss on decline in value of inventory*).

The *market price* is defined as replacement cost subject to a couple of limitations. Market value should not exceed a ceiling equal to net realizable value (NRV). NRV is the estimated sales value reduced by cost of completion and disposal. Market value should not be less than a floor equal to NRV minus an allowance for an approximately normal profit.

Here is a simple example:

Replacement cost	$23
Cost	24
Selling price	40
Disposal (selling) costs	6
Normal profit	17

Ceiling NRV = Selling Price $40 − Disposal Costs $6 = $34

Floor NRV = Ceiling NRV $34 − Normal Profit $17 = $17

The market is replacement cost of $23 subject to a ceiling NRV of $34 and a floor NRV of $17. Since the replacement cost is within the range ($34–$17), it equals the market value. Market is therefore lower than the $24 cost, and therefore the LCM is $23.

INVESTMENTS

Excess cash is a nonearning asset and therefore should be invested. Investments can take many forms; some are highly liquid like treasury bills and short-term notes, while other investments are made in stocks and bonds. Stocks are called equities since they represent an ownership interest. Alternatively, bonds are debt securities and are issued by corporations and governments. The term of a bond can be relatively short, such as 5 years, or for much longer, such as 20 or 30 years.

There are a few issues related to the manner in which investments are shown on the balance sheet. Accountants classify investments into three categories:

1. Held-to-maturity securities
2. Trading securities
3. Available-for-sale securities

Held-to-Maturity Securities

Held-to-maturity securities are investments in bonds of other entities when the investor has the intent and the ability to hold the securities to maturity. Held-to-maturity securities are reported at their cost. Investments that could be sold because of such factors as a need for liquidity, changes in market rates, and changes in foreign currency risk are not classified as held-to-maturity securities. Held-to-maturity securities are noncurrent assets.

Trading Securities

Trading securities are certain debt securities that are not classified as held-to-maturity and certain equity securities with readily determinable values. These are stocks and bonds that are bought and held for the purpose of selling them in the near future. Usually the objective of trading securities is short-term profits from price appreciation. They are purchased and sold frequently. Trading securities are classified as current assets.

Available-for-Sale Securities

Available-for-sale securities include equity securities with readily determinable values that are not classified as held-to-maturity or trading securities. Available-for-sale securities can be reported as either current or noncurrent assets, depending on the nature of the investment.

Bonds and Carrying Amounts

Bonds are a very common investment. A *bond* is a promise to pay an amount of money (called face value) at a maturity date, and usually bonds (with the exception of zero coupon bonds) pay periodic interest. Bonds are recorded at their cost with adjustments made for discounts or premiums. A discount occurs when a bond is purchased for less than its face value. For example, if a company purchases 100 bonds ($100,000 face value) for $90,000 there would be a $10,000 discount. With the carrying value for the bonds on a balance sheet being face value minus the discount or plus the premium, here is how the bonds would be carried on the balance sheet:

Bonds	$100,000
Less discount	(10,000)
Carrying value	$90,000

A premium is recorded and reported if the bond is purchased at a price greater than its face value. For example, if the bonds in the above example cost $1,200 each and 100 bonds were purchased, the premium would be $20,000, and the asset would be reported on the balance sheet as follows:

Bonds	$100,000
Plus premium	20,000
Carrying value	$120,000

Over time, the discount or premium is amortized. This means that as the bond moves closer to its maturity date (and will be redeemed for cash), less of the premium and discount will be reported.

In the case of a bond issued at a premium, as the years go by the premium will be reduced until the day of maturity when the carrying value of the bond will be equal to its face value. The same is true of a bond with a discount. Discounts and premiums are amortized over the remaining life of the bond.

TEST YOURSELF

For problems 1 and 2, use the following information:

- Customers owe the company $500,000 as the result of $750,000 of credit sales.

- One customer owes $10,000 but has filed for bankruptcy and shows no evidence of ever paying the bill.

- Last year's bad debt experience equaled 3 percent of credit sales, and management assumes a similar bad debt experience for this current year.

1. Under the direct write-off method, what is:

    Net realizable value $_____

    Uncollectible accounts expense $ _____

2. Under the allowance method for accounting for accounts receivable, what is:

    Net realizable value $_____

    Uncollectible accounts expense $ _____

3. Complete the aging of accounts receivable analysis below. Based on your analysis, what is:

    Net realizable value $_____

    Uncollectible accounts expense $ _____

Customer	Not Yet Due	1–30 Days Past Due	31–60 Days Past Due	61–90 Days Past Due	Over 90 Days Past Due	Total
Adams Drug Store	$20,000	$5,000	$15,000			$40,000
Ashmont	4,000	5,000	$6,000		9,000	$24,000
Arlans Department Store					10,000	10,000
Beacon Lumber Yard					4,000	4,000
Causeway Cleaners		$20,000				$20,000
Dalton Floors		5,000				5,000
Everlasting Works	1,000			$5,600		$6,600
Fall River Chevy		500	600	800	$900	$2,800
Griffin Industries		1,000				1,000
Hallmark Motors					15,000	15,000
Total	$25,000	$36,500	$21,600	$6,400	$38,900	$128,400
Estimated Uncollectible	1%	4%	8%	10%	30%	
Estimated Uncollectible Accounts						

4. Based on the inventory activity shown below, what is the value of the ending inventory under each of the following methods:

FIFO $ _____

LIFO $_____

Average cost $_____

	Units Purchased	Units Sold	Cost per Unit
Day 1	100		$10
Day 2		30	
Day 3	90		$11
Day 4		75	
Day 5	110		$12
Day 6		50	

5. Consider the following bond information and complete the table.

Face Value	Cost	Premium or Discount (Label P or D)	Carrying Amount
$100,000	$90,000		
$120,000	$150,000		
$110,000	$135,000		

KEY POINTS TO REMEMBER

- Cash and cash equivalents are always listed first on the balance sheet, as they are the most liquid of assets.

- Cash management involves not only managing cash flow through budgeting and other tools but also the safeguarding of cash flow through strong internal controls.

- Receivables are promises to pay made by customers (accounts receivable), employees (advances and loans), shareholders, tax authorities (tax refunds), and others.

- Receivables must be analyzed and revalued to estimate uncollectible accounts.

- Various techniques are utilized to estimate uncollectible account (bad debt) expenses, including using a historical percentage and aging of the accounts.

- Inventory is the least liquid of the working capital items and must be carefully monitored and managed to minimize holding costs and write-downs of loss of value (as a result of obsolescence, changing styles, and spoilage).

- Several methods are used to value inventory and each assumes a different cost flow; however, in the end, the guiding light is lower-of-cost-or-market value.

- Investments help turn excess cash into a productive, return-generating asset.

- Depending on the nature of the investment and the intent of management on how long to hold or how to use the funds, investments are categorized into three classifications for the balance sheet: held-to-maturity, trading, and available-for-sale securities.

Property, Plant, and Equipment, and Intangible Assets

INTRODUCTION

The productive capacity of an entity is in part due to the investment that is made in long-term assets—the operating assets of the concern, also called property, plant, and equipment. Other long-term assets, which are not tangible in nature (they are called intangible assets), such as patents, copyrights, and other forms of intellectual property, can also prove critical to the long-term success of the entity. Intangible assets, like all assets, provide future economic benefits.

WHAT'S AHEAD

In this chapter, you will learn:

- How property, plant, and equipment are initially recorded
- That the cost for long-term assets (tangible and intangible) includes all the costs that are normal and necessary to acquire the asset and prepare it for use
- How depreciation is calculated on all personal property, plant, and equipment (except for land) and how the asset's book value is adjusted as a result of depreciation

- The basics of three depreciation methods
- How intangible assets are amortized: a cost allocation very similar to straight-line depreciation

IN THE REAL WORLD

Led by a wealthy businessman named John Henry, a man who had made his fortune in futures and foreign exchange trading, a group of investors purchased the Boston Red Sox in 2002 for a reported $700,000,000. They were the only prospective buyers who wanted to keep the ballpark, citing both sentimental and economic reasons. Other suitors wanted to build a new ballpark with all the modern features. The new ownership group knew that to make their investment in the Red Sox a great success, the property, plant, and equipment, most specifically Fenway Park, would need to be upgraded.

Small improvements were undertaken at first. The Red Sox owners put up turnstiles on Yawkey Way, a street that runs along one side of the ballpark. The turnstiles created a game-day area with food vendors and other attractions that could help fuel additional revenue streams.

The owners also added Green Monster seats upon the famous left-field wall. This created more seating and therefore more revenue and a new buzz about probably the most unique spectator seats in all of professional baseball.

Many more improvements followed. In April 2006, State Street Chairman and Chief Executive Officer Ronald E. Logue and Red Sox President and CEO Larry Lucchino unveiled the new State Street Pavilion. Formerly the top half of the .406 Club, an outdated, enclosed area above home plate, the State Street Pavilion became the newest major improvement to Fenway Park, featuring 2,224 open-air seats and new concession stands. State Street Corporation (NYSE: STT), the world's leading specialist in providing institutional investors with investment servicing, investment management, and investment research and trading services, became one of several corporations purchasing naming rights to sections of Fenway Park.

New seating areas like the State Street Pavilion allowed the Red Sox to give their fans what they had asked for—newer, wider seats, extra legroom, new food and beverage options, improved access, and additional restrooms and club lounges without compromising the integrity, character, beauty, and charm that distinguish the historic park.

In 2008, another major seating area was added. The new 412-seat Coca-Cola Corner was introduced opening day. The seats cost $75 (2008 dollars) a pop. Above the seats sits a 42-by-15-foot red and white sign with 1,059 LED lights that will scroll through the Coca-Cola logo. Coca-Cola's new sign replaces the older Coke bottles that encircled one of Fenway's light towers for more than a decade, and according to published reports, Coca-Cola's sponsorship deal with the Sox was extended past 2012. The Coke sponsorship is expected to bring as much as $4,000,000 to $5,000,000 a year for the team.

These improvements to the old ballpark not only add new fan experiences but also offer new revenue streams, as they create new opportunities for branding and naming rights and additional revenue streams for the ball team. In April of 2008, *Forbes* magazine estimated that the Boston Red Sox franchise was worth $816,000,000.

KEY CONCEPTS

Long-term assets are held for a period longer than one year or one operating cycle. They include tangible and intangible assets and are recorded at cost. On the balance sheet, long-term assets are shown at book value. In the case of tangible long-term assets, such as property, plant, and equipment, book value equals cost minus accumulated depreciation. For intangibles like intellectual property and goodwill, the book value is cost minus the amortization.

Various methods are acceptable to calculate depreciation. Usually, amortization of intangible assets is done using the straight-line method, which results in equal amounts of amortization each period.

Initial Measurement

Assets that are classified as property, plant, and equipment (PPE) are initially recorded at acquisition cost, also called historical cost. Acquisition cost includes all the costs that are normal and necessary to acquire the asset and prepare it for use.

> Purchase price
> + Sales taxes
> + Transportation charges
> + Installation costs
> = Acquisition cost

The cost of land includes not only the amount that is paid for the land but also related legal fees, broker's commissions, title insurance, and surveying costs. Site preparation costs such as clearing, draining, leveling the property, and razing existing buildings are also included in the cost of the land.

Types of PPE

PPE can include a variety of tangible assets, including personal property (property that can be moved from one location to another) and real property (land and buildings). Improvements to land such as landscaping, drainage, streets, street lighting, sewers, sidewalks, parking lots, driveways, and fences are also part of PPE. Furniture, fixtures, and vehicles are also classified as PPE.

Depreciation

All property, plant, and equipment, with the exception of land, have a limited life and generally decline in usefulness over time. Accounting rules require that the decline in usefulness be estimated and recognized as an expense. This is an allocation of the acquisition cost in a manner that is consistent with the decline in usefulness and that results in a matching of expenses and revenue. The economic value of the loss of usefulness of property, plant, and equipment is depreciation, and it must be systematically and rationally allocated.

Many factors contribute to the loss of usefulness of a tangible, long-term asset. Depreciation occurs because of physical deterioration. Wear and tear that results from heavy use or exposure to the elements may cause loss in usefulness. Some long-term assets, such as computers, become obsolete over time. With obsolescence, usefulness declines, as the asset is surpassed in performance by new and more technologically advanced assets.

Whether it is because of physical deterioration or obsolescence, tangible long-term assets must be depreciated using one of several acceptable methods. The three common methods are *straight line, units of production,* and *double-declining balance.* All depreciation methods are based on the asset's original acquisition cost, and all require an estimate of two other important factors: the life of the asset (useful life) and its residual value. The residual value, which is sometimes called the salvage value, is an estimate of the amount of money that could be obtained from selling the asset at the end of its useful life. It could be that the residual value is estimated to be zero, and it is often the case that the long-term asset has a small value at the end of its useful life. After all, at the end of its useful life it is no longer useful, and long-term assets derive their value from the utility they provide.

Depreciation is recognized as an expense and an increase in an account called *accumulated depreciation,* a contra-asset account. When you look at a balance sheet, if you see the entry "Property, Plant, and Equipment—Net," it is referring to the fact that the company has deducted accumulated depreciation from the figure presented.

METHODS OF DEPRECIATION

The simplest and most commonly used depreciation is straight-line depreciation. Straight-line depreciation is calculated by taking the purchase or acquisition price of an asset minus the salvage value divided by the total useful life—the number of years the asset can be reasonably expected to benefit the company.

Here's an example. A company buys a new piece of equipment for $5,000. The expected residual value is $200. The company has upgraded its equipment every three years, so a realistic estimate of useful life is three years.

($5,000 Purchase Price – $200 Approximate Salvage Value) /
3 Years Estimated Useful Life

Therefore the annual depreciation under the straight-line method is $1,600, the depreciation charges your business would take annually if you were using the straight-line method.

The double-declining-balance depreciation method is an accelerated method, which means it results in more depreciation expense in the early years than the straight line. To use it, first calculate depreciation as if you were using the straight-line method. Then calculate the percentage of the asset's depreciable cost (cost minus the residual value) that is depreciated the first year and double it. Each subsequent year, that same percentage is multiplied by the remaining balance to be depreciated. At some point, the value will be lower than the straight-line charge, at which point, the double-declining method will be scrapped and straight-line used for the remainder of the asset's life.

For example, in the previous example using the straight-line method, it was calculated that a $5,000 piece of equipment with a $200 salvage value and an estimated useful life of three years would be depreciated by $1,600 annually. Dividing $1,600 by $4,800 (the depreciable amount), the straight-line depreciation charge is 33.33 percent of the total depreciation amount. With the double-declining-balance method, you double the rate (33.33% × 2 = 66.67%) to derive the double-declining-balance rate of 66.67 percent.

In the first year, the depreciation under the double-declining method would be found by multiplying $5,000 by .6667 to get a total depreciation charge of approximately $3,333. In the second year, we would take the same percentage (66.67 percent) and multiply it by the remaining amount to be depreciated. Continuing with the example, we find that $1,667 is the remaining amount to be depreciated at the start of the second year ($5,000 − $3,333 = $1,667). Multiply $1,667 by .6667 to get $1,111.

The units-of-production method is a usage-centered depreciation method. This method calculates depreciation as a function of an asset's use rather than the time it has been held. For a piece of equipment, as production varies, so too will the equipment's depreciation.

The first step in calculating depreciation under the units-of-production method involves calculating a depreciation amount per unit.

Depreciation per Unit = (Acquisition Cost − Residual Value) / Total Number of Units in Asset's Life

Here is a simple example. Assume our original example of equipment with a cost of $5,000, estimated residual value of $200, and a useful life of three years. In this case, an estimate must be made for the number of units produced over the useful life. Assume that 1,000 units will be produced during this asset's life.

($5,000 − 200) / 1000 = ($4,800) / 1000 = $4.80 Depreciation per Unit

If year 1 production equals 400 units, then the depreciation for year 1 would be:

$4.80 × 400 = $1,920 Depreciation in Year 1

If year 2 usage drops to 300 units, then the depreciation expense would also drop to $1,440:

$4.80 × 300 = $1,440 Depreciation in Year 2

Depreciation would continue to be recorded until 1,000 units are produced.

Depletion

Natural resources such as mineral deposits, oil and gas reserves, timber, coal mines, and stone quarries are other types of long-term assets. As natural resources are used (e.g., extracting of minerals or cutting of timber), the expense that is recognized is *depletion*.

There are many industry-specific accounting measurements attributable to such assets. As a general rule, natural resources are initially entered in the accounting records at their cost plus related costs like legal fees, surveying costs, and exploration and development costs. Once the cost basis is established, it must be allocated over the periods benefited through depletion. Depletion is to a natural resource as depreciation is to property, plant, and equipment.

To calculate depletion, the cost of a natural resource (minus any expected residual value) must be divided by the estimated units in the resource deposit; the resulting amount is depletion per unit. If all of the resources extracted during a period are sold, then depletion expense equals depletion per unit times the number of units extracted and sold. If a portion of the extracted resources are unsold resources, then the cost of those units (i.e., number of units times depletion per unit) should be carried on the balance sheet as inventory.

For example, assume that a mine site is purchased for $9,000,000, and another $3,000,000 is spent on developing the site for production. Assume the site is estimated to contain 5,000,000 tons of the targeted ore. At completion of the operation, the site will be water flooded and sold as a recreational lake site for an estimated $2,000,000. The depletion rate is $2 per ton, with the calculations as follows:

Initial cost	$9,000,000
Development cost	3,000,000
Less: residual value	− 2,000,000
Base for depletion	$10,000,000
Estimated units	÷ 5,000,000
Depletion per unit	$2.00

If 1,000,000 tons of ore are extracted in a particular year, the cost would be $2,000,000 (1,000,000 tons × $2.00). But where does that cost go? If 600,000 tons are sold and the other 400,000 tons are held in inventory of extracted material, then $1,200,000 would go to cost of goods sold and the other $800,000 would be shown on the balance sheet as inventory.

INTANGIBLE ASSETS

Intangible assets are long-term assets with no physical properties. As our economy has become knowledge based, intangible assets—in particular, intellectual property—have become a large percentage of total assets. Copyrights to a publisher, patents to a manufacturer, and a trademark for a brand name to a national consumer product marketer are extremely valuable assets—assets that provide current and future economic benefits. The balance sheet shows the acquisition costs of intangible assets—net of amortization. Intangible assets that have a finite useful life are amortized over that useful life. That means a portion of the cost is recognized as an expense, and the intangible asset's book value is adjusted downward by the amount of the annual amortization.

Intangible Asset	Description
Patent	Right to use, manufacture, or sell a product. A patent is granted by the U.S. Patent Office. Patents have a legal life of 20 years.
Goodwill	The excess of the purchase price to acquire a business over the value of the net assets acquired.
Copyright	Right to reproduce or sell a published work. Copyrights are granted for 50 years plus the life of the creator.
Franchise	Exclusive right to sell products or perform services in certain geographic areas. Franchises are usually granted (sold) by businesses to help expand their markets.
Trademark	A symbol or name that allows a product or service to be identified; provides legal protection for 20 years plus an indefinite number of renewal periods.

Accounting for Intangible Assets

The cost of an intangible asset includes all the costs to acquire the asset and prepare it for its intended use. The costs include all legal costs. For example, to acquire a patent from the U.S. Patent Office, legal costs and filing fees are normally incurred. Those costs are capitalized as an intangible asset.

Intangible assets are reported on the balance sheet at acquisition cost minus accumulated amortization. Amortization is very much like depreciation. It involves allocating the acquisition cost of the intangible asset to the periods benefited by the asset. For example, if a patent costs $8,000 it would be amortized by $400 per year ($8,000 / 20 years = $400). After year 2, the asset would be carried at $7,200 on the balance sheet ($8,000 − 400 − 400) and most likely labeled as follows:

Intangible Asset net of amortization = $7,200

TEST YOURSELF

1. A company purchased a new sign to be erected in front of its retail store. The sign company had a list price on the sign of $25,000 but granted a 20 percent discount. In addition, the sign company paid $500 of the freight costs to deliver the sign, and the company was responsible for paying the shipping. An electrician was hired by the company to wire the sign at a cost of $600. The city required an inspection of the sign for a fee of $250, and an annual permit will be required beginning in year 2 for a cost of $75 per year. The first year electricity for the sign is estimated at $127.

    Determine the cost to be recorded for the sign and shown on the balance sheet (please ignore depreciation for the purposes of this problem).

    Initial cost to be recorded: $_____

2. A printer purchases a copy machine for $3,000. It cost $250 to deliver and install the machine. It has an estimated useful life of five years, at which time it is estimated that it can be sold for $200. Assuming the straight-line method, complete the table below:

Years	Annual Depreciation	Accumulated Depreciation	Book Value at End of Year
1			
2			
3			
4			
5			

3. Complete the table below, using the same facts as in problem 2, assuming the double-declining-balance method of depreciation.

Years	Annual Depreciation	Accumulated Depreciation	Book Value at End of Year
1			
2			
3			
4			
5			

4. ABC Bus Company purchases a used passenger bus (28-passenger capacity) for $40,000. It has a useful life of 160,000 miles and a residual value of $8,000. Complete the table below based on annual miles of:

- Year 1: 15,000 miles
- Year 2: 22,000 miles
- Year 3: 20,000 miles
- Year 4: 18,000 miles
- Year 5: 20,000 miles

Years	Annual Depreciation	Accumulated Depreciation	Book Value at End of Year
1			
2			
3			
4			
5			

5. A copyright cost $15,000 for the company to acquire. Show how the asset would be listed on the balance sheet at the end of year 3. Assume 50 years of useful life.

KEY POINTS TO REMEMBER

- Property, plant, and equipment are initially recorded at the purchase price plus all the costs that are normal and necessary to acquire the asset and prepare it for use.

- Depreciation is calculated on all personal property, plant, and equipment (except for land), and the asset's book value is adjusted as a result of depreciation.

- The three basic depreciation methods are straight line, double-declining balance, and units of production.

- Straight-line depreciation is simple; it results in the same amount of depreciation expense each year (except for partial years when a prorated amount is used).

- The double-declining-balance method is an accelerated method resulting in more depreciation expense in the early years than the straight-line depreciation method.

- The units-of-production method results in depreciation expense that is correlated with the usage of the asset: more usage, more depreciation.

- Natural resources owned by an entity are initially reported at cost but are reduced over time by the amount of depletion that takes place. Depletion results in expense when the resources are sold.

- Intangible assets are initially listed at cost and are amortized—a cost allocation very similar to straight-line depreciation.

Liabilities

INTRODUCTION

The balance sheet presents items in categories to make it easier for the user to analyze the report. Liabilities are presented in two categories: current and long term. Current liabilities finance a major portion of the working capital. Payables, such as accounts payable, taxes payable, and accrued liabilities, help finance the cash, accounts receivable, and inventories of the entity. Therefore, the classification of liabilities into current and long term helps the user understand liquidity.

WHAT'S AHEAD

In this chapter, you will learn:
- About the various types of payables that are part of the current liabilities of most entities
- How warranties are recorded as liabilities and recognized as expenses
- How employee benefits result in liabilities

- About the different types of long-term debt that appear on the balance sheet
- The issues related to the accounting for bonds
- How leases impact the balance sheet

IN THE REAL WORLD

Gift cards are a great way to answer the question: "What to buy for Uncle Mike this holiday season?" And gift cards are everywhere. You can buy them at major retailers, supermarket chains, and most restaurants. Just during the 2006 and 2007 holiday shopping season (November and December), gift card sales were estimated at $80 billion and $100 billion respectively. The advantage of gift cards is that they offer the buyer an easy way out and allow the recipient of the card many more product choices. Some experts even contend that gift cards help smooth demands on inventory, in that most cards are sold during holiday seasons when inventories are falling and are redeemed during slow seasons.

According to SEC accounting bulletins, sales of gift cards do not result in revenue until merchandise or services are exchanged for the gift card. That means deferred revenue (liability) must be maintained on the balance until the gift card is redeemed.

Gift cards also create what retailers call *breakage*—the tendency of consumers to not use gift cards or to leave unspent balances on the cards. According to a 2007 article in the *Journal of Accountancy*, breakage can occur in 10 to 19 percent of gift card sales. How long should the gift card liability remain on the books if breakage can run as high as 19 percent and in some cases, many cards are never redeemed? Sometimes the handling of breakage can mean a significant impact on the bottom line. For example, it has been reported that Best Buy, Inc., added $43,000,000 of unredeemed gift card proceeds to its February 2006 sales revenue.

KEY CONCEPTS

Liabilities are debts and other obligations of an entity. At any point in time, amounts are owed to third-party creditors, employees, and government authorities (such as the IRS) that require something of value, usually cash, to be transferred to the creditor to settle the debt. Most obligations are known amounts based on invoices and contracts; some liabilities are estimated because the value that changes hands is not fixed at the time of the initial transaction, such as warranties and other contingent liabilities.

Liabilities are reported in the balance sheet as current (short term) or long term, based on when they are due to be paid. Current liabilities are those obligations that will be paid within the next year.

PAYABLES AND CURRENT LIABILITIES

Short-term financing is a major concern for many entities. Accounts payable and accrued payables, such as taxes payable and payroll liabilities, are a type of spontaneous financing, happening in tandem with increases in revenue. Accounts payable—money owed to vendors as a result of purchases of goods and services—increase with increases in revenues. As demand for an entity's products and services increases, the need to purchase more inventory increases, with suppliers willing to provide credit in the form of accounts payable.

Accounts payable are an inexpensive form of financing since interest charges are normally not part of established agreements. In fact, accounts payable usually carry an opportunity for savings, with terms structured to motivate the creditor to pay early and take a discount. For example, an accounts payable arrangement for a $5,000 purchase might carry terms of 2/10, n30, which means if the payable is paid in 10 days a 2 percent discount can be taken, otherwise the full amount is due in 30 days. On a $5,000 purchase, the 2 percent discount would be $100 and only $4,900 would be paid.

Salaries and wages payable are another type of current liability that is commonly found on balance sheets. Usually, the salaries and wages payable account needs to be adjusted to reflect the liability owed to employees as of the financial statement date. This is the case unless the financial statement date falls exactly on a payday and all employees have received wages owed to them. For example, assume that the employee payroll is $1,000 per day and that the employees are paid weekly. Also assume that payday is a Friday and the financial statement date happens to be a Wednesday. To reflect reality, the balance sheet should show a wages payable amount of $3,000 (3 days × $1,000), and an additional wages expense of $3,000 would need to be recognized as part of the wages expense reported on the income statement. This example ignores other payroll liabilities such as payroll taxes and fringe benefits that also may accrue with each pay period.

Amounts owed to employees for work performed are recorded separately from accounts payable. Expense accounts such as salaries or wages expenses are used to record an employee's gross earnings, and a liability account such as salaries payable, wages payable, or accrued wages payable is used to record the net pay obligation to employees.

Additional payroll-related liabilities include amounts owed to third parties (IRS, state revenue departments, Social Security Administration) for any amounts withheld from the gross earnings of each employee and the payroll taxes owed by the employer.

Examples of withholdings from gross earnings include the following:

- Federal, state, and local income taxes
- FICA (Federal Insurance Contributions Act): Social Security and medical taxes
- Investments in retirement and savings accounts
- Health-care premiums
- Other possible deductions such as union dues, stock purchase plans offered by employer, and charitable contributions
- Employer payroll taxes including Social Security and medical taxes (same amount as employees), federal unemployment tax, and state unemployment tax

Federal unemployment tax and the employer's share of FICA taxes are expenses, but since they are only paid periodically, they are often listed as payables as of the date of the balance sheet.

Other taxes that may show up as payables on a balance sheet are property taxes and sales taxes. Property taxes are owed on real estate owned by the entity and in some cases on personal property such as inventory and equipment. Sales taxes are levied on certain types of merchandise sales in most states. The tax is paid by the customer purchasing the merchandise but is collected and later remitted by the seller. Income taxes payable by the entity are covered in a later section of this chapter.

CONTINGENT LIABILITIES AND WARRANTIES

A warranty (also called a product guarantee) is agreement by the seller of goods or services to satisfy for a stated period of time deficiencies in the item's quality or performance. Warranty terms may be included on the buyer's receipt or in a separate document. The warranty usually provides for repair or replacement of the item in the case of malfunctioning or poor workmanship. Typically, there is no additional charge during the warranty period.

The seller records warranty expenses and related estimated liability in the year of sale. A warranty percentage is usually based on prior experience.

Here's an example. Assume sales for the year are $100,000. Estimated warranty cost is 2 percent of sales. Warranty expenses for the year would be $2,000 ($100,000 × 2%), and a warranty payable would be recognized, also for $2,000.

When actual warranty services are performed, the cost of the service and parts would be recognized and the warranty payable would be reduced. Here's a simple example: Assume that a particular product under warranty needed to be repaired, and the entity paid a vendor to perform the service for $50. The liability for the warranty (warranty payable) would be reduced by $50, and cash for payment of the services would also be reduced.

Warranties are a common contingent liability. A contingent liability is an obligation that involves an existing condition for which the outcome is not known with certainty and depends on some event that will occur in the future. Like any contingent liability, the actual amount of the liability must be estimated, and therefore judgment calls on how to best predict the value of a contingent liability must be made. Choosing a warranty cost percentage (such as the 2 percent in the example above) is another example of how accounting can be as much of an art as a science. Contingent liabilities, like those for warranties, are based on likelihoods.

The FASB uses terms such as *probable, reasonably possible*, and *remote* to identify three areas within a range of possibilities (likelihoods) that a contingent liability should be recorded. An estimated loss from a situation should be accrued by a charge to expense, and a liability should be recorded only if both of the following conditions are met:

- Information available before the issuance of the financial statements indicates that it is probable that a liability has been incurred at the date of the financial statements.
- The amount of the loss can be reasonably estimated.

INCOME TAX ACCOUNTING

Sole proprietorships and partnerships are not tax entities. The sole proprietor and the members of the partnership are subject to personal income taxes on their share of the entity's taxable income. Therefore, income tax liabilities do not appear on the balance sheet of a sole proprietorship or partnership.

Income taxes do appear as an expense and a liability on the financial statements of profit-seeking corporations. In addition, most corporations make estimated quarterly income tax payments to the IRS and state income tax authorities.

Many companies report different amounts of income on their income statement and on their income tax return. This difference occurs because the definition of income is not the same under GAAP and IRS regulations. GAAP requires income tax expenses to be calculated on income before taxes on the income statement, while the tax return calculates taxes due based on taxable income per the income tax return. That difference results in deferred income taxes.

If the differences between GAAP and IRS regulations are considered temporary, in other words, if certain revenues and/or expenses are reported in different years on income statements and on income tax returns, an asset or liability called *deferred income tax* is created. If deferred income tax represents the portion of the income tax expense that will be paid in future years, a long-term liability called *deferred taxes* is recorded on the balance sheet.

PENSION BENEFITS AND OTHER POSTRETIREMENT BENEFITS

A pension is a payment made by a company to a retired employee and is usually a percentage of the employee's former salary. As part of a pension, an entity may provide insurance and other benefits as well. A company that is obligated to provide pension benefits to its employees upon their retirement must periodically have an actuary determine the company's updated projected pension obligation in present value terms. To the extent that the company's projected obligation exceeds the amount that the company has contributed to or set aside for the plan, the company must record a liability for the remainder of this obligation that it has yet to fund.

For example, assume that an actuary calculates the present value of the pension obligation to be $500,000, and the company has invested only $200,000 in a pension plan. The difference of

$300,000 would be listed as a liability to reflect the unfunded part of the pension. A similar analysis is also required if there are other postretirement employee benefits (other than the pension). The accounting for postretirement benefits is too complex for discussion here; however, the basic concept is that if employees have been promised postretirement benefits, the present value of those benefits is calculated using reasonable assumptions, and the amount is listed as a liability.

NOTES PAYABLE

A liability is created when an entity signs a note for the purpose of borrowing money or extending its payment period credit. A note is sometimes created for an overdue invoice (an account payable). Therefore, an account payable becomes a note payable. More commonly, notes payable are created when the company borrows cash or in exchange for an asset.

Notes payable are classified as current liabilities when the amounts are due within one year of the balance sheet date. When the debt is long term (payable after one year) but requires a payment within the 12-month period following the balance sheet date, the amount of the payment is classified as a current liability on the balance sheet. The portion of the debt to be paid after one year is classified as a long-term liability. More on that issue in the next section.

LONG-TERM DEBT

Long-term debt can take many forms, such as bank loans, bonds (both secured and unsecured), and capital leases. Capital leases are covered in the next section. Bank loans are called notes payable, or in the case of long-term loans, they are backed by real estate deeds: mortgage notes payable. Equipment and other types of property can serve as collateral for loans and bonds, and these are called *secured debts.* Mortgages can be obtained from a bank, life insurance company, or other financial institutions.

Unsecured debt is not backed by collateral but rather the faith that the borrower has the ability and the character to pay. When a lender loans money, whether it is a bank or investors who purchase debentures (unsecured bonds), without the security that an underlying asset provides, the unsecured debt carries more risk for the lender. This in turn makes the loan more expensive. The more risk that a lender must take on, the higher the rate of interest a borrower must pay, making unsecured loans subject to higher rates than mortgages.

Whether the long-term debt is secured or unsecured, the current portion of the liability (the amount due within the current year or current operating cycle) is reported on the balance sheet as a current liability. For example, if a 30-year mortgage for $200,000 has $10,000 due this year, the liability would be reported as follows:

Current Liabilities:
Current portion of mortgage payable $10,000
Long-Term Liabilities:
Mortgage payable $190,000

Bonds

Bonds are another long-term liability, usually only showing up on the balance sheet as fixed interest investments, which provide regular interest payment during the term of the bond, and then return your upfront investment at the fixed end date or maturity. They usually have a face value of $1,000. The *face value* is also called the principal value or the denomination, and it is stated on the bond certificate. A bond is governed by a contract known as an indenture. An *indenture* is a promise to pay a sum of money (face value) at a designated maturity date plus periodic interest at a specified rate. Bond interest is usually paid twice a year—semiannually.

The *selling price* of a bond is set by supply and demand of buyers and sellers and is a function of risk, market conditions, and the economy. The difference between the face value and the selling price of the bond is either a discount or a premium. If the price is less than the face value, the bond is selling at a discount, and if it is priced above the face value, it is called a premium.

The rate of interest that is earned by the bondholders is called the effective yield or market rate. When bonds sell at a discount, the effective yield is higher than the stated rate. If the bonds sell at a premium, the reverse is true: the effective yield is lower than the stated rate.

Bond discounts and premiums are amortized over the life of the bond. The amortization has an impact on bond interest expense. Bond interest expense is increased by amortization of a discount and decreased by amortization of a premium.

Here's an example: Assume that the amortization of a discount is $600 for this year, while the interest paid to the bondholder is $4,000, and the carrying value of the bond is $92,000. After the payment of the interest, the following would be true:

Cash paid: $4,000
Interest expense: $4,600
Discount amortization for the period: $600
Carrying value of bond: $92,600

If another bond is listed on the balance sheet at a premium of $100,800, interest paid is $4,000, and the amortization of the premium is $600, the following would be true after the payment of interest:

Cash paid: $4,000
Interest expense: $3,600
Premium amortization for the period: $600
Carrying value of the bond: $100,200

Some bonds have one or both of two features: they can be convertible and callable. *Convertible bonds* can be exchanged at the option of the bondholder for a specified ownership interest—either common stock or preferred stock. The issuing company benefits from the convertible feature because bondholders are willing to accept a lower interest rate because of the conversion feature. Bondholders are attracted to convertible bonds because the convertible feature offers some possible price appreciation, an opportunity normally lacking in traditional bonds. If the market value of the underlying stock increases, the bondholder can increase wealth by converting to the stock. If the stock price doesn't increase, the bondholder is still promised interest payments, priority claims in a bankruptcy, and maturity value of the bond.

Callable bonds allow the issuing entity to redeem (pay off) the bond before the maturity date. If interest rates fall, the issuing entity can issue lower-cost bonds and call (pay off) higher-cost bonds. To encourage investors to purchase callable bonds, the call price usually exceeds the face value of the bonds. For example, if the face value is $1,000, the call price might be $1,080. The difference between the face value and the call price is called the call premium. In this example, the call premium is $80.

LEASES

Leases give the right to use the property of another entity for a certain periodic payment over a prescribed amount of time. Leases are contracts and if the contract is long term, then it is possible that the lease will be listed as a long-term liability—if it meets the test of a capital lease.

A capital lease means that the risks and benefits of the property are substantially transferred to the lessee company. There are specific criteria that accountants apply to determine if a lease is a capital lease. The lessee balance sheet shows the capital-leased property as if it was purchased, using an asset account and also a lease liability account for the amount of the asset.

An operating lease is considered an arm's length transaction in which the lessee is merely borrowing the use of the property, while substantial control and benefit continue to reside with the lessor. The lessee company accounts for this transaction by recognizing lease expense for all lease payment, but it does not record an asset or liability to reflect the lease asset. Operating leases are often called off-balance-sheet financing because they do not have to be listed as an obligation on the balance sheet of the lessee.

TEST YOURSELF

1. The current balance sheet of Acme Watch, Inc., has a liability of $3,000 for warranties before any adjustment for this year's sales. Watch sales for 201X (the current year) are $1,200,000. Estimated warranty cost is 7 percent of sales. After accounting for the warranty expense for this year, what would be the following:

   Warranty expense 201X $_____

   Warranty payable as of the year end 201X $_____

2. A company's mortgage of its office building is $500,000. Payments (principal) for the next 12 months total $15,000. How would this obligation be shown on the balance sheet?

3. Consider the following facts for a bond issue with a $1,000,000 face value and a carrying value of $930,000:

   • Interest payment in cash $60,000
   • Interest expense $66,000

   What is the amount of discount amortized as a result of the interest payment? $_____

   What is the carrying value of the bond issue after the interest is paid? $_____

4. Consider the following facts for a bond issue with a $1,000,000 face value and a carrying value of $1,100,000:

    • Interest payment in cash $60,000

    • Interest expense $53,000

    What is the amount of premium amortized as a result of the interest payment? $_____

    What is the carrying value of the bond issue after the interest is paid? $_____

KEY POINTS TO REMEMBER

- Payables, such as amounts owed to suppliers (accounts payable), taxes owed to governments (e.g., income tax payable), and payroll-related obligations (FICA, income, and unemployment taxes) are types of spontaneous, short-term financing, shown as current liabilities on the balance sheet.

- Warranties and other contingent liabilities are estimated and shown as liabilities on the balance sheet.

- Income tax accounting involves estimating the current period's income tax expense and any remaining liability and tax owed as a result of timing differences attributed to differences between tax regulations and generally accepted accounting principles.

- Obligations as a result of employee benefits, such as pensions and postretirement health benefits, must be estimated and listed as liabilities.

- Long-term liabilities include bonds, capital leases, and loans to be paid in periods beyond the current one.

- Operating leases do not appear on the balance sheet as liabilities and are therefore called off-balance-sheet financing.

PART

MANAGEMENT ACCOUNTING

Managerial and Cost Accounting

INTRODUCTION

Cost accounting supports both financial accounting and managerial accounting. Measuring, analyzing, and reporting cost information is necessary to keep track of inventory values and also allows management to make good decisions.

WHAT'S AHEAD

In this chapter, you will learn:

- The connection between managerial accounting and financial accounting and the contrasts between the two disciplines
- The list of management accounting tasks and activities that support management decision making
- Cost concepts that form the basis for both managerial accounting and its subset, cost accounting
- That a job cost system tracks the utilization of resources and the stage of production of inventory
- The basics of process costing and how it differs from job costing
- How activity-based costing is a cost system refinement to encourage more accurate and relevant cost information
- How absorption cost, a requirement of GAAP, is used to value inventory and cost of goods sold

IN THE REAL WORLD

Sun Life Financial is a leading international provider of insurance and wealth accumulation products and services to individual and corporate customers. The Sun Life group of companies has offices in 22 countries serving millions of customers.

The company was founded in 1865 and is headquartered in Toronto, Canada. Sun Life Financial, Inc., is a public company and trades on the Toronto, New York, and Philippine stock exchanges. The financial services business is a very competitive one. Despite the introduction of cost-saving new technologies, Sun Life experienced decreasing margins and in response looked at strategies to better manage if not cut costs.

According to published reports, Sun Life looked to implement an activity-based costing system in its claims division as one of the cost management strategies. *Activity-based cost accounting* (ABC) is a method of assigning the organization's resource costs through activities to the products and services provided to its customers. It is generally used as a tool for understanding product and customer cost and profitability.

At Sun Life, teams were formed to conduct activity analysis—a way of understanding how the work is done and what drives the incurrence of costs. Activity analysis can reveal inefficient steps, also called nonvalue-added activities, which become candidates for elimination and therefore opportunities for cost savings. Other Sun Life value-added activities were redesigned as a result of ABC to produce further savings. Benchmarking is also something that Sun Life examined to determine how its claim processing centers stacked up against industry standards and the performance levels of outsource partners.

ABC is a costing system that is effective at drawing management's attention to the things that matter most. At Sun Life, ABC helped focus management's attention on the importance of accurate measures and the management of those measures. ABC yields data regarding time, quality, and cost drivers that are not tracked and reported in a traditional costing system.

KEY CONCEPTS

Managerial and cost accounting are closely aligned. In fact, accounting scholars will say that cost accounting is a subset of managerial accounting. *Managerial accounting* is one of the major disciplines within accounting; the others being financial and tax accounting. *Managerial accounting* serves the information needs of those within the organization, while *financial accounting* exists to provide external parties with the information they need to make investing and credit decisions.

Cost accounting helps us track costs and perform cost analysis for inventory valuation, cost of goods sold calculations, and a variety of decisions including pricing. In recent years, the traditional methods of cost accounting have come under scrutiny as questions have been raised about the relevance of cost data, especially overhead allocations. Refinements such as activity-based costing have helped make cost data more useful.

MANAGERIAL VERSUS FINANCIAL ACCOUNTING

Financial statements are used by both external users and internal management and provide general information about the entire company. For example, the balance sheet reports total inventories, and the income statement reports cost of goods sold, but the costs of individual products are not disclosed to the public. Detailed cost data is critical for internal decision making and is key input for budgets and pricing models.

Internal management needs detailed information to make decisions about its business. Managerial accounting exists to meet the needs of management. The guiding light of managerial accounting is usefulness. A comparison of managerial and financial accounting can help you to understand managerial accounting. The table below shows the differences between the two disciplines.

	Managerial Accounting	Financial Accounting
Users	Internal managers and staff	Creditors, investors, potential investors, investment analysts, and other external users
Guidelines for preparation	Flexible since usefulness is the only guiding principle	GAAP
Purpose	Decision making, pricing, budgeting, and other control and performance information	General information for credit and investment decisions
Frequency of preparation	As needed	Annually and quarterly
Independent review or opinion	None required since the information is only examined by internal managers and staff	External auditor's opinion

In contrast to financial accountancy information, management accounting information is usually confidential and used by internal management. Managerial accounting reports are kept within the organization instead of made publicly available. Management accounting reports can be forward looking: they can help forecast, predict, and budget for future events. Contrast that to financial accounting data, which is based on some type of historical evidence. Finally, management accounting information is pragmatically computed: commonsense and reasonable procedures are utilized instead of complying with accounting standards, rules, and regulations.

Management accounting is a bit harder to define than financial accounting, which is geared so tightly to the financial statements. To get a better idea of the kinds of activities that fall under the umbrella of management accounting, examine this list of management accounting tasks and activities:

- Variance analysis
- Rate and volume analysis
- Development of business metrics
- Pricing modeling
- Product profitability reporting
- Product and service costing
- Client profitability analysis
- Cost analysis
- Cost benefit analysis
- Capital budgeting
- Buy versus lease analysis
- Strategic planning
- Sales and financial forecasting
- Budget preparation
- Cost allocation

INSTITUTE OF MANAGEMENT ACCOUNTANTS

Financial accounting has the American Institute of Certified Public Accountants (AICPA) to help guide the profession. The AICPA is the national, professional organization for Certified Public Accountants. Its mission is to provide members with the resources, information, and leadership that enable them to provide valuable services in the highest professional manner to benefit the public as well as employers and clients.

In the world of management accounting, there is the Institute of Management Accountants (IMA). The IMA's mission is to provide a dynamic forum for management accounting and finance professionals to develop and advance their careers through certification, research and practice development, education, networking, and the advocacy of the highest ethical and professional practices.

Management accountants can carry a variety of different job titles, including the following:

- Staff accountant
- Cost accountant
- Senior accountant
- Corporate or division planner
- Financial analyst
- Budget analyst
- Internal auditor
- Finance manager
- Controller
- Vice president, finance
- Treasurer
- Chief financial officer (CFO)

The IMA awards the Certified Management Accountant (CMA®) designation, which according to the IMA "represents a broad business competency and mastery of the management-level skills required to add value, drive business performance, and build quality financial practices within organizations. The program objectively tests and validates expertise in areas essential to analyzing, managing, and evaluating business solutions that contribute to the success of an organization."

COST ACCOUNTING

A subset of management accounting is *cost accounting.* Modern day cost accounting has its roots in the textile industries of England and New England soon after the industrial revolution. Much of the traditional cost accounting techniques, procedures, and policies utilized today were customary in the early 1900s. Johnson and Kaplan claimed in their book, *Relevance Lost,* that "by 1925, American industrial firms had developed virtually every management accounting procedure known today."

How do you define cost? According to Concept Statement No. 6 (SFAS6) of the Financial Accounting Standards Board (FASB), cost is an economic sacrifice. The National Association of Accountants, the predecessor to the Institute of Management Accountants, defined cost as "the cash or cash equivalent value required to obtain an objective . . ." (1983). Cost is certainly an important input to the financial accounting system. Many costs are matched to revenue as expenses.

Cost accounting is the set of procedures to determine costs, especially production costs.

Cost Concepts

Cost accounting allows managers to perform a number of tasks that are critical to managing the enterprise, including the following:

- Calculating the cost of products, services, departments, divisions, and customers
- Using cost data to prepare bids and proposals
- Obtaining information for planning and control (including budgeting) and performance evaluation
- Analyzing relevant cost data for a variety of different decisions, including capital expenditures

A cost is a resource sacrificed or foregone to achieve a specific objective. Cost accumulation occurs because we need to calculate the cost of a product, service, project, department, or other important cost object. There are a variety of reasons why you would need to calculate the cost of an object. One obvious reason is the balance sheet and income statement. We calculate costs of assets to report them on the balance sheet. Expenses have to be calculated so that we can compute gross profit, operating profit, and net income. Costing is necessary when bidding on a project or when determining the feasibility of a new business or a capital expenditure.

When calculating costs, it is often useful to also classify the costs. One common classification is direct costs. The direct cost of an object is related to the particular object and more importantly, can be traced (associated) with the object accurately and in an economically feasible way. We can trace direct costs back to a particular object with ease. An example would be the major parts of a bicycle. It is easy to see with your eyes that the cost of wheels and the frame are direct materials, as is the cost of the laborer who assembled the parts into a finished product, ready to roll out of the store or warehouse.

On the other hand, it is not so easy to trace the cost of the machines used to make the parts or the exact cost of the paint on the bike. Those costs are indirect costs—costs that are related to a particular object but not traceable to it in an accurate, cost-effective manner. Indirect costs are not ignored, even though they are difficult to track accurately. Instead, they are allocated. *Cost allocation* means that some costs are estimated and associated with a cost object. More will be discussed on cost allocation in the section on absorption costing.

Classifying costs as direct or indirect can be influenced by materiality and technology. The smaller the amount of the cost, the less we worry about tracking it accurately. If a cost is immaterial, the less likely we will want to spend the time and money tracking it. For example, if it cost $1 per unit to track a 40-cent item in an accurate manner, it would be more cost-effective to estimate the cost per unit and save the $1.

Available information technology and the cost of that technology can also play a factor. If information technology is suddenly available that allows you to track more traditionally indirect cost items to a cost object, especially if it is cost-effective, then you will do it. However, the cost-benefit equation must always be considered.

When discussing the costs related to manufactured goods, the classification of costs between inventory and period costs must be made clear. *Inventoriable costs* are all costs of a product that are first considered assets on the balance sheet and eventually costs of goods sold on the income statement. All production costs (manufacturing costs) are inventoriable. That means the cost of materials, labor, and all the overhead costs (utilities, rent of the factory, property taxes on the factory, indirect wages, etc.) must be assigned to inventory. It is simple logic: all the costs of creating a product must be classified as inventory. In a merchandising company, such as retailers and wholesalers, the cost of inventory is the cost of purchasing the goods plus any incoming freight costs, insurance, and handling costs.

Some costs are period costs; they are treated as an expense when incurred. In a manufacturing entity, all nonmanufacturing costs are period costs, such as salaries of nonfactory personnel, office supplies for the headquarters, distribution costs, marketing, accounting, and finance costs.

Absorption Costing

GAAP requires *absorption costing*. This means that for manufactured products, direct materials, direct labor, and overhead must be incorporated in inventory costs. *Direct materials* are the parts and raw materials that go into a product. *Direct labor costs* are labor costs that can be identified with a specific product or service. *Overhead* includes all the manufacturing costs that cannot be traced (accurately attributed to) the product. Overhead costs include indirect labor and materials, plant depreciation, insurance, property taxes, and management salaries.

In cost accounting, a cost object must be identified. A *cost object* is simply anything for which management desires a cost measurement. The obvious cost objects are products and services. However, a cost object can be anything including an activity, department, or customer.

In manufacturing where absorption costing is prevalent, the cost object is the manufactured product. Absorption costing principles are used to calculate the cost of goods manufactured, value of inventory, and the cost of goods sold.

There are various types of systems to manufacture products, including job shops and continuous flow, also known as processing. To keep things simple, the focus will be on absorption costing with the content of job shops.

A *job shop* or a *job system* involves customized production to customer specifications. A print shop is an excellent example of a job system, where every job is unique with activities and processes designed to meet the specific needs of the customer. One day the focus might be on the printing of a brochure, while the next day the focus and resources will be dedicated to a catalog. Distinct jobs require a different mix of materials and labor. The cost of each job in this type of system is tracked separately, as opposed to mass production within a process (continuous flow) environment. In a process environment, every unit is the same, and therefore there is no need to track the cost of each job, but rather the average unit costs can be calculated and justifiably relied upon. Soft drinks, corn flakes, and motor oil are all examples of products that are produced in a continuous flow and tracked by a process cost system.

In a job order costing system, the amount of direct materials used (and their costs), the direct labor, and an allocation of overhead are done on a job-by-job basis. For example, assume that job number 1001 used the following resources:

- $10,000 of raw materials
- $15,000 of direct labor
- Overhead allocated at a rate of 150 percent of direct labor

The cost of job 1001 would be $47,500 ($10,000 + $15,000 + 1.5(15,000)). Other jobs would have other costs depending upon how much raw material was used for a particular job, the amount of direct labor, and the amount of overhead applied to the job (which in this example is a function of direct labor cost).

Overhead cost allocations are the tricky parts of absorption costing. It is very possible to accurately track direct labor (via payroll records and logs) and direct material utilization (through inventory record keeping, bar codes, etc.). But accurately associating the cost of machines, electricity, depreciation, heat, supplies, and indirect labor (such as custodians, repair personnel, etc.) to a particular job is virtually impossible. Therefore, allocation bases are used to estimate overhead utilization.

In the example above, the allocation base is direct labor. The 150 percent factor would have been estimated using the following formula (with the denominator representing the allocation base):

Budgeted Overhead Costs for the Year / Budgeted Direct Labor Costs for the Year

For example, if the organization estimated that the total cost of overhead—rent, utilities, management salaries, other indirect labor costs, supplies, plant and equipment depreciation, etc.—to be $750,000 and that direct labor costs would be $500,000, then the allocation rate would be 150 percent:

$750,000 / $500,000 = Overhead Allocation Rate of 150% of Direct Labor Costs

Allocating overhead involves management judgment as to what makes sense for an allocation base and how to best predict the costs. If all resource consumption, including the traditional overhead items, could be traced directly to products, then cost accounting would be straight and simple arithmetic. However, that is not the case, and therefore a part of cost accounting—specifically indirect cost allocation—is an art. Common allocation bases used by U.S.-based manufacturers include the following:

- Direct labor hours
- Direct labor cost
- Machine hours
- Number of parts
- Time in a manufacturing area
- Units produced

As goods are being manufactured, value is being added; hence the expression "value added activities." As value is added, the inventory accounts of the entity are updated to reflect the work being done. Raw material and parts accounts are reduced when those assets are put into play (placed into the manufacturing process). As work is being done, an asset called *work in process* is increased by amounts, attributed to the following:

- Direct materials
- Direct labor
- Allocated overhead

When the goods are completed, they move from the work in process account to finished goods—just as the physical goods move from a production area to a storage or shipping area. When the finished goods are sold, their costs are moved into cost of goods sold. Therefore, cost accounting keeps track of the transformation or conversion of inventory, and that phenomenon is tracked between the following inventory related accounts:

- Direct materials (e.g., raw materials and parts)

- Work in process (goods and projects that are being worked on but are not finished)
- Finished goods (goods that are available for sale because they are in completed form)
- Cost of goods sold

PROCESS COSTING

In a process costing system, the cost object is masses of identical or very similar units of product or service. Computer chips, orange juice, and the cost to open a checking account at a bank are all examples of products that are mass produced with resource consumption tracked by a process costing system. Since the output of mass production is identical or very similar products, the assumption can be made that each unit has consistent amounts of materials, labor, and overhead. Process costing systems divide the total cost of producing a product or providing a service by the total number of units produced to obtain a per-unit cost. Using an average unit cost, the process costing system can then assign values to the ending inventory and the cost of goods sold.

One complicating factor to the process costing formula is the units produced. Not all units will be completed by the end of an accounting period. Some units will be fully completed but some units will most likely be physically incomplete. Therefore, when using process cost accounting, equivalent units of production need to be derived.

Equivalent unit is a derived amount of output that takes into account the quantity of input (e.g., materials and labor) in units completed and in the incomplete units of work in process. Then the accountant must convert the quantity of input into the amount of completed output units that could have been produced with that quantity of input.

Here's an example: Assume that 500 units of product (electric golf carts) have been worked on during the period and that 200 units were fully completed with 300 units still in process. Assume further that the 300 units in process have had 100 percent of the materials put into production but only 60 percent with respect to the labor. The question is what do the 300 unfinished units represent in equivalent units (EUs)?

The answer is found in two parts: EUs with respect to the materials and EUs with respect to the labor. The EUs of the 300 units of work in process, with respect to materials, is 300 because 100 percent of the materials have been added. There is enough material to complete the 300 units. It is the labor, in this example, that is keeping the units from being complete. The work in process equivalent units, with respect to the labor, is equal to 180 units (60 percent of 300). There has been enough labor to complete 180 units (although the reality is that there are 300 units, 60 percent complete as to labor).

Keeping it simple, assume that production costs for the period were $760,000, broken out as follows:

- $600,000 materials
- $160,000 labor

The unit cost for the golf carts would be found as follows:

- Materials of $600,000 / 500 = $1,200
- Labor of $160,000 / 380 = $421.05
- Total cost per equivalent unit = $1,621.05

Here's how the inventory cost would be allocated:

$$\text{Finished goods} = 200 \times \$1,621.05 = \$324,211$$

Work in process:

$$\text{Materials } 300 \times \$1,200 = \$360,000$$
$$\text{Labor } 180 \times \$421.05 = \$75,789$$

Therefore, the work in process would total $435,789 and the finished goods would be valued at $324,211, accounting for the $760,000 of production costs.[1]

ACTIVITY-BASED COST ACCOUNTING

Robin Cooper and Robert Kaplan introduced ABC in a number of articles published in the *Harvard Business Review* beginning in 1988. Cooper and Kaplan described ABC as an approach to solving the problems of traditional cost management systems. These traditional costing systems are often unable to determine accurately the actual costs of production and of related services. A big part of the reason for inaccurate costing is overhead (indirect costs). As is demonstrated in the section entitled Absorption Costing, indirect cost allocations are educated guesses at best. As product diversity and complexity increase in companies and as indirect costs become a larger cost pool (as has been the case with increased automation and computer-aided processing), a greater degree of the cost of any object has been the result of almost arbitrary allocation. Consequently, in many organizations, managers were making decisions based on inaccurate data, especially where there are multiple products.

Instead of using broad arbitrary percentages to allocate indirect costs, ABC seeks to identify cause-and-effect relationships to objectively assign costs. Once costs of the activities have been

---

[1] Rounding was used. Also, this example assumes that the finished goods were started and completed during the period; in other words, all costs (materials and labor) were incurred during the period. For simplicity's sake, overhead costs were not considered. In the real world, an estimate for equivalent units with respect to overhead costs would also need to be made, or at least an estimate of equivalent units with respect to conversion costs. Conversion costs are direct labor and overhead; they are all production costs other than direct material.

identified, the cost of each activity is attributed to each product to the extent that the product uses the activity. In this way, ABC often identifies areas of high overhead costs per unit and so directs attention to finding ways to reduce the costs or to charge more for costly products. Sounds logical, but ABC isn't possible without technologies that can help keep track of volume, monitor usage, and provide information—both financial and nonfinancial—about activities.

TEST YOURSELF

1. Complete the table below:

Characteristic	Managerial Accounting or Financial Accounting
The users are internal managers and staff	
The guidelines are spelled out in GAAP	
The purpose is to provide information for credit and investment decisions	
No independent review or opinion is required since the information is only examined by internal managers and staff	

2. Two jobs are summarized below:

Job Number	Direct Material Used	Direct Labor Cost	Machine Hours
100	$1,000	$3,000	10
101	$2,000	$4,000	25

The firm assigns overhead to jobs using machine hours as the allocation base. The budgeted overhead cost for the year is $1,500,000 with machine hours estimated at 50,000. Calculate the total cost of both jobs.

Job 100 $_____

Job 101 $_____

3. Use the same facts as in problem 2, except assume that the company utilizes an overhead application rate of 130 percent of direct labor. Calculate the total cost of both jobs.

Job 100 $_____

Job 101 $_____

4. A company manufactures wheel barrows. There is only one model, and therefore each unit is exactly the same. The following production data is attributed to the month of January 20XX.

- 1,000 units started and completed during January
- 300 units started but incomplete as of the end of the month, January 31, 20XX

With regards to the 300 units that are still work in process, all the direct material has been added to the process but only 40 percent of the conversion costs have been added. There was no beginning inventory on January 1, 20XX. Product costs for January were as follows:

- Direct materials: $56,000
- Conversion costs: $32,400

What was the equivalent cost per unit? $_____

5. Continuing with the facts from problem 4, what is the value of:

    *   Finished goods $_____

    *   Work in process $_____

        If 300 units are sold in January 20XX, what is the cost of goods sold? $_____

        If the sales price for the wheel barrow is $179, what is the gross profit per unit? $_____

KEY POINTS TO REMEMBER

*   Managerial accounting serves the information needs of managers and staff.

*   Management accountants will produce any type of report, both financial and nonfinancial, provided that it is cost-effective and useful information that supports management decision making and control.

*   Cost accounting is a subset of managerial accounting and focuses on the tracking, analysis, and management of cost data.

*   Absorption costing, which is required by GAAP, assigns overhead costs to the cost of products and services.

*   Job costing systems are principles used to track the cost of unique or customized products and services.

*   Process costing systems use average cost data to allocate production costs to products and services.

*   Activity-based costing is a cost system that introduces refinements, possibly because of technology, to the traditional costing of goods and services.

Cost Behavior

INTRODUCTION

Cost behavior is the relationship between costs and activities, such as production and sales. Understanding cost behavior can help managers build mathematical models and formulas that allow analysis of the potential impact of managerial decisions. One such model is cost-volume-profit (CVP) analysis, which examines the behavior of revenue and costs (and therefore profit) as we change assumptions such as volume (units sold), selling price, variable costs, and fixed costs. CVP analysis helps us play "what if" so we can make informed decisions.

WHAT'S AHEAD

In this chapter, you will learn:

- The behavior of variable, fixed, and mixed costs
- The formula for total costs
- How to calculate the contribution margin
- How the contribution margin differs from gross margin

- How to prepare an income statement based on the contribution margin format
- The break-even formula and how to use it to perform cost-volume-profit analysis
- How to calculate the volume needed to achieve a target operating income
- How to calculate the break-even point when multiple products are involved

IN THE REAL WORLD

When managers contemplate cost-cutting techniques, they must consider cost behavior and the fallout from the cost cutting moves, such as loss of employee morale and revenue. It seems as though state and municipal governments are always battling budget crises in which the only solution is cost cutting. On the nonprofit side, sometimes the answer to falling revenues seems simple: no choice but to cut back on services, as they seem to drive costs. But in both governments and nonprofits, cost cutting by reducing services may not net the amount of cost savings anticipated. Factors to consider when cutting costs are both the mix of costs and the behavior of costs.

The simple view of cost mix is that it is two parts: fixed and variable. *Fixed costs* are constant; they do not vary depending on production, sales levels, or service levels. Examples of fixed costs are salaries, rent, property tax, insurance, and interest expense. *Variable costs* include the cost of labor, material, or overhead that change in concert with the change in the volume of production units.

Understanding how much of your cost structure is fixed and how much is variable is important when considering cost-cutting measures. Financial managers and management accountants must build models that take into account the nature of the various costs and how they react (cost accountants use the term *behave* to describe how costs change in response to certain events) to changes in other variables.

For example, reducing the number of beds in a hospital might be a strategy in tough budget times, the thinking being that a reduction in patients served will reduce operating costs. But such a strategy may be of limited effectiveness because of the relatively low variable cost of medical care. Variable costs (for medication and supplies) are saved if a facility does not provide a service, but reduction in service has no impact on significant fixed costs (for salaried labor, buildings, and equipment). Very little cost savings can be realized over the short term when a health-care facility reduces service. The same is true with other labor and infrastructure-intensive industries, such as education and entertainment.

In many service-oriented industries, such as health care, entertainment, and education, significant cost cutting cannot be accomplished through cutting variable costs. To produce substantial cost savings, it might mean cutting significant fixed costs, a strategy that is often more painful than cutting variable costs and in some cases, much more dramatic and newsworthy.

Then there is the nonfinancial side of cost cutting—especially when jobs are involved. In 2008, heavy layoffs of staff were reported at television stations owned and operated by CBS in the

United States. In those highly publicized layoffs were 30 staffers at WBZ Boston, 17 at WBBM Chicago, 14 at KPIX San Francisco, and about one dozen at KCBS Los Angeles. Some of those affected had been longtime, on-air, popular personalities. In Boston, a popular sports reporter and a longtime arts and entertainment reporter were let go, along with several other well-known television personalities.

WBZ Boston, channel 4, was the hardest hit. The *Boston Herald* reported that "the layoffs were across the board, 'hitting the newsroom, the Web unit, sales, the engineering department, and promotions. Some employees were swiftly escorted out the door by security,' sources said." Management of a station like channel 4 Boston must wonder what impact cutting popular personalities might have on ratings and on revenues that are so dependent on viewer ratings.

KEY CONCEPTS

The manager who wants to understand the cost structure of the firm must classify costs into two categories: fixed and variable. Sometimes that is not so easy. Some cost objects have mixed costs, but even in those cases management must separate the one part that is fixed and the part that is variable.

One tool that helps us sort out the cost behavior of a business is the *contribution margin*: the value from each sale that will help cover fixed costs and ultimately provide for a profit. The contribution margin is different from gross margin (revenues or cost of sales). The contribution margin is revenues minus total variable costs—a useful financial concept.

Understanding cost behavior can lead to a firm grasp of the break-even point and can help managers create mathematical representations of the business model that can be used to assist them when contemplating the bottom-line impact of decisions.

HOW COSTS BEHAVE

Cost behavior is a concept that all managers must master. The ability to predict how costs will respond to changes in activity is critical for making decisions and for other major management functions. In a black-and-white world, costs fall into two categories: fixed and variable; but in the real world, there are three major classifications of costs: *variable, fixed,* and *mixed*.

Mixed costs consist of a mixture of variable and fixed elements. The annual cost of operating an automobile is a mixed cost. Some of the costs of car ownership are fixed, because they do not change in total as the number of annual miles change. For example, your cost of automobile insurance is not dependent on the amount of use of the car. Other car-related expenses are variable, because they will increase when the miles driven increase (and will decrease when the miles driven decrease). The variable cost of your car includes the cost of gas, oil, tires, and to some extent, depreciation.

The algebraic formula for a mixed cost is $y = a + bx$, where:

y is the total cost
a is the fixed cost per period
b is the variable rate per unit of activity
x is the number of units of activity

For the annual cost of operating an automobile, the fixed cost, a, might be $3,000 per year; the variable rate, b, could be $0.40; and the number of units of activity, x, might be 15,000 miles per year.

$y = a + bx$
At 15,000 miles, the cost to operate the car is $9,000
$y = \$3,000 + .4(15,000) = \$9,000$
At 10,000 miles, it is $7,000

Managers use costs classified by behavior as a basis for many decisions. To facilitate this use, the income statement can be prepared in a contribution format. The contribution format classifies costs on the income statement by cost behavior (i.e., variable versus fixed) rather than by the functions of production, administration, and sales. This requires a careful, almost line-by-line examination of all costs (expenses) while asking the question, is this cost fixed, is it variable, or is it mixed? If it is mixed, a deeper examination must be made—a decomposition of sorts—to determine which part of the mixed cost is fixed and which is variable.

CONTRIBUTION MARGIN

The contribution margin is a useful financial concept. It can be calculated on a per unit basis or on a gross—or total—company-wide basis. When calculating on a company-wide basis, it is found by subtracting all variable expenses from revenues. It indicates the amount available from sales to cover the fixed expenses and profit. For example, if a company has sales of $1,000,000 and variable expenses of $750,000, its contribution margin is $250,000, an amount that is available to cover fixed costs and perhaps provide for a profit.

The contribution margin can also be calculated on a per unit basis. For example, if a product sells for $25 and its variable cost per unit is $15, then its contribution margin per unit is $10. Once again, the contribution margin represents an amount that can help contribute to covering fixed costs and perhaps providing a profit. In this example, each time one unit of product is sold, a $10 amount is free and clear of variable costs, and if all fixed costs are already covered (from past sales), the contribution margin per unit would represent pure profit.

There is also the contribution margin ratio. This ratio is the percentage of each revenue dollar that is available to cover a company's fixed expenses and profit. The ratio is calculated as follows:

Contribution Margin / Sales

For example, assume that sales are $1,000,000 and that variable costs are $750,000. The contribution margin would be $250,000, and the contribution margin ratio would be 25 percent. This means that on average, for every $100 of revenue, there will be $25 of contribution margin.

INCOME STATEMENT: CONTRIBUTION FORMAT

It is useful to recast the income statement into a contribution margin format. Instead of calculating gross margin, the contribution margin format calculates contribution margin. The two concepts are different:

$$\text{Gross Margin} = \text{Revenues} - \text{Cost of Sales}$$
$$\text{Contribution Margin} = \text{Revenues} - \text{Total Variable Cost}$$

Revenues	$100,000
Variable Costs	40,000
Contribution Margin	$60,000
Fixed Costs	10,000
Operating Income	$50,000

Illustration 10.1. Income Statement Based on Contribution Margin Format

One of the advantages of the contribution margin format is that it can provide data for break-even point calculations and cost-volume-profit analysis. Both concepts are covered in the sections that follow.

BREAK-EVEN POINT

An important question to contemplate when starting a new venture is: "At what level of revenue will my company make a profit?" Another question is: "At what level of revenue will I cover all costs?" The answer to that last question is the break-even point—the amount of revenues or units sold that will result in exactly covering all costs—a point of no profit but no loss. At the break-even point, total revenue is exactly equal to total costs. Many people think of the break-even point as a type of hurdle; one that once cleared opens the door to profitability and wealth building.

Business plans often include break-even analysis, as potential investors and creditors will factor the break-even point into their analysis as they contemplate the viability of the business and the plausibility of the assumptions upon which the business plan is based. For an entity that is already up and running and operating above the break-even point, the break-even point can represent a margin of safety, as it allows you to answer the question: "How far can the output or revenue level fall before the entity reaches its break-even point?"

The break-even point model makes some basic assumptions. For example, it assumes that you can clearly segregate costs into two categories—fixed and variable—and that the behavior of these costs will remain unchanged over a relevant range of activity (a range of production and sales). It also assumes that the quantity of goods produced is equal to the quantity of goods sold.

In multiproduct entities, the break-even point model assumes that the relative proportions of each product sold and produced are constant. The relative proportion of products sold is called the *sales mix*. In spite of these limitations and assumptions, the break-even point model is a useful tool for investors, creditors, and managers. A derivative of the break-even point model is used to perform cost-volume-profit (CVP) analysis—a tool that allows you to ask "what if" with regards to cost alternatives, varying sales and revenue volumes, and profit targets.

Break-even quantity is calculated by this equation:

Total Fixed Costs / (Selling Price – Average Variable Costs)

In other words,

Total Fixed Costs / Contribution Margin per Unit = Break-Even Point in Units

For example, if the fixed costs are $500,000, the selling price is $25, and the variable cost per unit is $15, the break-even point would be:

$500,000 / ($25 − $15) = $500,000 / $10 = 50,000 Units

At the heart of break-even point or break-even analysis is the relationship between expenses and revenues. It is critical to know how expenses will change as sales increase or decrease. Some expenses will increase as sales increase, whereas some expenses will not change as sales increase or decrease. Variable expenses increase when sales increase. They also decrease when sales decrease. Fixed expenses do not increase when sales increase; they are constant— at least over the short run. Fixed expenses do not decrease when sales decrease.

COST-VOLUME-PROFIT ANALYSIS

Cost-volume-profit (CVP) analysis examines the behavior of total revenues, costs, and operating income as changes occur in the units sold, selling price, variable costs, and fixed costs. CVP is a model that can be used to play "what if." What if we sell more units? What will happen to profits if we cut variable costs by 10 percent per unit? If fixed costs are slashed by 80 percent, what will happen to the break-even point?

The basic formula for CVP is the formula for operating income:

Revenues − Variable Costs − Fixed Costs = Operating Income

When working with CVP analysis, it is helpful to break the operating income into its main components:

[(Selling Price × Quantity Sold) − (Variable Cost per Unit × Quantity Sold)] − Fixed Costs = Operating Income

For example, assume the following financial variables:

Selling price: $10
Quantity sold: 10,000
Variable cost per unit: $4
Fixed costs: $10,000
Operating income would be $50,000 as shown in illustration 10.2.

What if sales volume could be increased to 20,000 units but would require a significant investment in fixed assets and as a result, fixed costs increased to $30,000?

By playing with the assumptions within the CVP model, you can see the impact of decisions on the bottom line. However, CVP is a decision model and as such, it has limitations and simplifying assumptions:

- The number of units sold is the only revenue driver and the only cost driver (for the variable costs). A revenue driver is any factor that affects revenues, while a cost driver is any factor or activity that causes a cost to be incurred.

Revenues	$100,000
Variable Costs	40,000
Contribution Margin	$60,000
Fixed Costs	10,000
Operating Income	$50,000

Illustration 10.2. Operating Income

Revenues	$200,000
Variable Costs	80,000
Contribution Margin	$120,000
Fixed Costs	30,000
Operating Income	$90,000

Illustration 10.3. Operating Income at Twice the Volume and Three Times the Fixed Costs of the Original Scenario (Illustration 10.2)

- Costs can be separated into two components: fixed and variable.

- Selling price, variable cost per unit, and total fixed costs are known and constant within a relevant range and time period. This means that each time you run the model (populate it with your assumptions), the selling price per unit, unit variable cost, and total fixed cost will be constant.

PROFIT PLANNING AND CVP

The CVP model can also be used to plan for profit. To factor a target profit (operating income) into the CVP (break-even) model, you can simply modify the formula:

(Total Fixed Costs + Target Operating Income) /
(Selling Price – Average Variable Costs)

Simplified, the formula is as follows:

(Total Fixed Costs + Target Operating Income) /
Contribution Margin per Unit

For example, assume the following variables:

Selling price: $10
Variable cost per unit: $4

Fixed costs: $10,000
Target profit: $250,000
($10,000 + $250,000) / ($10 − $4)
($260,000) / $6 = 43,333.33 units

Therefore, about 43,333 units sold will produce an operating profit of $250,000.

Alternatively, you can factor income taxes into this model by using the following formula:

$$(\text{Total Fixed Costs} + \text{Target Operating Income} / (1 - \text{Tax Rate})) / \text{Contribution Margin per Unit}$$

Assuming a tax rate of 40 percent:

$$\$260,000 / (1 - .4) / \$4 = 72,222.22 \text{ Units}$$

Therefore, if you want to achieve a target income after taxes of $250,000, you must sell about 72,222 units if the income tax rate is 40 percent. Certainly, tax rates put a greater burden on an entity. More needs to be produced and sold to achieve target net income when tax rates are relatively high.

BREAK-EVEN WITH MULTIPLE PRODUCTS

One of the assumptions of the basic break-even model is that one product is sold or that an average price and average variable cost per unit can be reasonably estimated. If the entity sells multiple and diverse products and services, a more complex model of the break-even point should be used. However, in the case of multiple products, a sales mix assumption must be made.

The sales mix is the proportion of the various products (or services) that make up the total unit sales of the company. For example, if a company has two products, A and B, the proportions can be determined by examining the sales forecast. If it is projected that 100,000 units of product A will be sold while 300,000 units of product B are projected as sales, the sales mix would be 1:3. In other words, for every three units of B that are sold, the company will sell one unit of A.

Sales mix assumptions need to be made in the break-even or CVP model because different products have different contribution margins. With different contribution margins, products contribute to cover fixed costs and provide for a profit at different rates. If product A has a contribution margin of $10 while B has a $15 contribution margin, the sales mix assumption will be critical in determining the amount of volume needed to break even.

Here is an easy way to work the break-even model when multiple products are involved:

1. Set the lowest product volume to N (the unknown). In this case, product A volume would be equal to N.

2. Set the other product volumes to a multiple of N. In this example, product B volume would be equal to 3N (because the sales mix assumption has B's sales at three times the sales of A).

3. Plug into the break-even formula by multiplying the projected contribution margins by the projected volume. Here's an example using product A and B numbers and assuming total fixed costs of $300,000:

$$\$10N + \$15(3N) - \$300,000 = 0 \text{ (No Profits at}$$
$$\text{the Break-Even Point)}$$

Solving for N:

$$N = 5454.545455$$

Therefore, assuming a 1:3 sales mix (A versus B), approximately 5,454 units of A will need to be sold, while about 16,364 units of B (three times the number of units of A) will need to be sold to break even.

TEST YOURSELF

1. A company is looking at cell phone pricing plans which are all mixed costs. One particular plan has a flat rate of $39.99 per month with 8 cents per minute over 500 minutes. If the typical monthly use is 2,100 minutes, what would be the total monthly cost?

   Total monthly cost $_____

2. Convert the following income statement into one based on the contribution margin format. Assume that one-half of the cost of sales are fixed costs and that $7,000 of the operating costs are also fixed.

Revenues	$100,000
Cost of Sales	35,000
Gross Margin	$65,000
Operating	37,000
Expenses	$28,000

   What is the contribution margin ratio?
   Contribution margin ratio _____%

3. If fixed costs are $300,000, the selling price is $50, and the variable cost per unit is $17, what is the break-even point?

4. Using the same information as problem 3, what is the volume of sales (in units) needed to achieve a $50,000 profit (ignore taxes)?

5. If a company has three products (A, B, C) and the sales mix is 1:3:4 respectively, what would be the break-even point, assuming the following financial variables:

	A	B	C
Selling price	$10	$15	$20
Variable cost per unit	$4	$5	$6

   Total fixed cost = $500,000

KEY POINTS TO REMEMBER

- The formula for total costs is fixed cost plus total variable costs.

- The contribution margin per unit is the selling price minus variable costs per unit.

- The contribution margin ratio is found by dividing the contribution margin by total revenue.

- The break-even point is the volume (sales) needed to cover the total costs. It is the point (i.e., sales volume) where total revenue exactly equal total costs.

- CVP utilizes the contribution margin income statement format to play "what if." "What if" analysis can greatly aid management when making decisions.

- To calculate the break-even point with multiple products (or services), you must determine a sales mix; the proportion of sales volume for each product or service sold.

PART

FINANCE

Financial Statement Analysis

INTRODUCTION

Financial statement analysis can be performed by calculating financial ratios, interpreting those ratios, and by utilizing other techniques such a horizontal analysis and common-size financial statements. Financial statement analysis and its tools and techniques provide messages that are not revealed simply by reading the financial statements.

WHAT'S AHEAD

In this chapter, you will learn:

- The four key areas addressed by financial ratio analysis

- Profitability ratios measure income relative to sales and resources

- Asset utilization ratios help financial statement users to evaluate levels of output generated by assets

- Liquidity ratios help measure the adequacy of a firm's cash to meet near-term obligations

- The limitations of financial ratio analysis

- How horizontal analysis reveals additional information about a company's financial strengths and weaknesses

- How to prepare a common-size balance sheet

IN THE REAL WORLD

Financial ratios are an excellent way to fully understand the financial strengths and weaknesses of a company. When analyzing a loan request, credit analysts at a bank will "run" financial ratios and compare them to industry standards. The same is true for investment analysts who perform fundamental analysis before recommending a stock to investors. Fundamental analysis involves analyzing its financial statements, its management and competitive advantages, and its competitors and markets.

After calculating a ratio, it is compared to a standard. There are many established sources listing the industry standards for financial ratios. *Robert Morris Annual Statement Studies* is published by Robert Morris Associates (RMA). Banks use this annual as a standard to evaluate businesses applying for financing. RMA provides balance sheet and income statement data and financial ratios compiled from financial statements of more than 100,000 commercial borrowers, classified into five income brackets in over 400 different industry categories.

Dun and Bradstreet publishes an annual called *Industry Norms and Key Business Ratios*. It covers over 800 types of businesses arranged by industry categories, presenting typical balance sheets, income statements, and 14 key ratios for the median, upper, and lower quartiles for each industry.

Prentice Hall publishes the *Almanac of Business and Industrial Financial Ratios*. It lists 24 key financial ratios for 180 industries, based on data from the IRS in the United States.

KEY CONCEPTS

Financial statements are the raw material of financial analysis. Profitability, liquidity, debt burden, and efficiency and effectiveness can be revealed through ratio analysis. Ratios show financial relationships and important concepts of risk and return that are of great interest to creditors, investors, and management. This chapter covers some of the basic analytical concepts that help provide a more complete picture so that well-informed decisions can be made. However, the lessons of financial analysis should include a cautionary note: there are limitations to ratio analysis, horizontal, and vertical (common-size) analysis.

FINANCIAL RATIOS

Financial ratios are tools to help you interpret the numbers found in financial statements. Ratios, which show financial relationships by dividing one financial item by another, help to answer critical questions, such as whether the business is carrying excess debt or inventory, whether customers are paying according to terms, whether the operating expenses are too high, and whether the company assets are being used properly to generate income. Potential and current investors and security analysts use ratios to determine the financial strengths of a company. The banker or credit analyst uses financial ratios to judge creditworthiness. Ratios are also important tools for management. All functional areas of a company can benefit from ratios. They have strategic value; ratios are a diagnostic tool that tells management whether they are properly executing their plan. In that way, ratios can help aid not only planning but control.

There are four key areas addressed by financial ratios:

- Profitability
- Utilization of assets
- Liquidity
- Debt burden

When computing financial ratios and analyzing them against benchmarks and in light of trends, a company's financial strengths and weaknesses become clear. Examining these ratios over time provides some insight as to how effectively the business is being operated.

Many industries compile average industry ratios each year. Average industry ratios offer the means of comparing a company with others within the same industry.

PROFITABILITY RATIOS

How much profit is enough? To measure the ability of a company to earn a profit and an adequate return on sales, assets, and invested capital, profitability ratios must be calculated. An important grouping of ratios, *profitability ratios* are financial metrics that determine a business's ability to generate earnings and effective employment of resources.

If a profitability ratio has a higher value relative to a competitor's ratio or the same ratio from a previous period, it is indicative that the company is doing well. There are four profitability ratios examined in this chapter:

- Gross profit margin
- Profit margin
- Return on assets
- Return on equity

Gross Profit Margin

The *gross profit margin* is a measure of the gross profit earned on sales. It's a leading indicator of profitability and cash flow, especially in the retail industry. The gross profit margin is a critical element in measuring how productive you are at managing the costs of your inventory investment. It is found as follows:

Gross Profit Margin = Sales − Cost of Goods Sold / Sales

Gross margin erosion can occur if companies don't monitor and manage their markup percentages. Several factors can cause overall margins to erode, including the following:

- Competitive price pressures forcing below-standard markups
- Vendor price increases pushing retail prices up against natural price points
- Unanticipated shifts in sales mix toward lower-priced and lower-margin merchandise

Gross profit margins can vary widely, depending on the industry or type of company within an industry. For example, according to U.S. Census Bureau information, the average retail gross margin in 2006 was 28.6 percent; however, sporting goods, hobby, book, and music stores had average profit margins greater than 50 percent. Gas stations, which are also part of the retail sector, had an average profit margin of 16.4 percent. Grocery stores are known to have relatively low gross margins (29 percent in 2006), but high volume operations can be even lower. In 2006, discounter Costco's gross margin was 12.2 percent.

Net Profit Margin

The net profit margin tells you what percent of profit is made from sales (revenues). Just as is the case with gross profit margins, net profit margins vary by industry and can vary for firms within an industry. A good example is the consumer sector. According to Yahoo! Finance, in 2008, the average net profit margin for the consumer sector was 7.45 percent, but within the sector there is variation. The sporting goods industry, a part of the consumer sector, has a net profit margin of 2.5 percent, while beverages–soft drinks, also a part of the consumer sector, had a net profit margin of 10 percent.

The general rule is that the higher a company's net profit margin compared to its competitors, the better. Here is how it is calculated:

$$\text{Net Income After Taxes / Revenue}$$

Return on Assets

Return on assets (ROA) is a measure of how effectively the company's assets are being used to generate profits. It helps capture an important idea of trying to convert investment (assets) into profit. ROA is a percentage. It is found as follows:

$$\text{Return on Assets} = \text{Net Income / Total Assets}$$

Once again, the ROA will vary widely across different industries. Return on assets gives an indication of the capital intensity of the company. Companies that require large initial investments will generally have lower return on assets.

Return on Equity

Return on equity (ROE) measures the rate of return on the ownership investment (i.e., shareholders' equity). ROE is viewed as one of the most important financial ratios, as it appeals to the information needs of investors (owners) and potential investors. It measures a firm's efficiency at generating profits from every dollar of net assets (assets minus liabilities), and it shows how well a company uses investment dollars to generate earnings growth.

It is calculated as follows:

$$\text{Net Income / Equity}$$

ASSET UTILIZATION RATIOS

Asset utilization ratios (also sometimes called activity ratios) are used to determine how well a company is managing its assets. Speed and time are important aspects of utilization ratios. How fast we can collect bills and sell inventory are part of the focus. So too is how well a company can squeeze revenues out of its assets.

Like most financial ratios, the asset utilization ratios are especially useful when compared to standards such as industry averages or a particular company (such as a competitor who is thought to be not only a peer but a good benchmark). Below is the list of asset utilization ratios:

- Accounts receivable turnover
- Average collection period
- Inventory turnover
- Fixed asset turnover
- Total asset turnover

Accounts Receivable Turnover

The accounts receivable turnover indicates how quickly the company collects its accounts receivables. It can be used to determine whether the company is having trouble collecting on sales it provided customers on credit.

The accounts receivable turnover is calculated as follows:

Accounts Receivable Turnover = Annual Credit Sales / Accounts Receivable

Since many companies do not disclose how much of the sales were made on credit, investors often use total sales as a shortcut. When this is done, it is important to remain consistent if the ratio is compared to that of other companies.

Average Collection Period

The average collection period is the average amount of time it takes for outstanding invoices to be paid in full. This ratio shows how quickly the customer base as a whole is remitting payments. The average collection period not only helps monitor the effectiveness of credit management policies and practices, it also helps the company budget for cash flows.

The average collection period is calculated as follows:

$$\text{Average Collection Period} = \text{Accounts Receivable} /$$
$$(\text{Annual Credit Sales} / 365)$$

Inventory Turnover

Inventory is an asset that must be managed. The goal, of course, is to sell inventory as fast as possible, as older inventory tends to lose value. The inventory turnover ratio is a metric that gives financial statement users an indication of how effective the company is at managing inventory. A low turnover is usually a bad sign because products tend to deteriorate, go out of style, or spoil as they sit in a warehouse. Companies selling perishable items should have very high turnover.

The formula for inventory turnover is as follows:

$$\text{Inventory Turnover} = \text{Sales} / \text{Inventory}$$

Or it can be calculated as:

$$\text{Inventory Turnover} = \text{Cost of Goods Sold} /$$
$$\text{Average Inventory}[1]$$

---

[1] Average Inventory = ((Beginning Inventory + Ending Inventory) / 2). Using an average helps smooth out seasonality effects.

Fixed Asset Turnover

The fixed asset turnover indicates how well the business is using its fixed assets to generate sales.

The fixed asset is calculated as follows:

$$\text{Fixed Assets} = \text{Sales} / \text{Fixed Assets}$$

Generally speaking, the higher the fixed asset turnover ratio, the better, because a high ratio indicates the company has relatively less money tied up in fixed assets for each dollar of sales revenue. A declining ratio may indicate that the business is over-invested in plant, equipment, or other fixed assets.

Total Asset Turnover

Asset turnover measures a firm's efficiency at using its assets in generating sales or revenue—the higher the number the better.

The total asset turnover is calculated as follows:

$$\text{Total Asset Turnover} = \text{Sales} / \text{Total Assets}$$

LIQUIDITY RATIOS

Liquidity ratios give financial statement users a glimpse at a company's ability to pay off short-term obligations as they come due. A company's ability to convert short-term assets into cash to cover debts is of great importance to creditors who are seeking payment (or attempting to judge creditworthiness).

Since cash (and cash flow) are the lifeblood of a business, liquidity ratios are used to determine whether a company will be able to continue as a going concern. The higher the value of a liquidity ratio, the larger the margin of safety that the company possesses to cover short-term debts. There are two key liquidity ratios:

- Current ratio
- Quick ratio

Current Ratio

The current ratio gives the financial statement user an idea of the company's ability to pay back its short-term liabilities (debt and payables) with its short-term assets (cash, inventory, receivables). The greater the current ratio, the more capable the company is of paying its obligations. A ratio under one suggests that the company would be unable to pay off its obligations if they all came due immediately.

The formula for the current ratio is as follows:

$$\text{Current Ratio} = \text{Current Assets} / \text{Current Liabilities}$$

Quick Ratio

The quick ratio is quite similar to the current ratio in that it is an indicator of a company's ability to meet short-term debt and liability obligations, but it takes a more conservative view of liquidity. The quick ratio measures a company's ability to meet its short-term obligations with its most liquid assets by subtracting inventory (the least liquid of the current assets) from total current assets. The higher the quick ratio, the better the position of the company.

The quick ratio formula is calculated as follows:

$$\text{Quick Ratio} = (\text{Current Assets} - \text{Inventory}) / \text{Current Liabilities}$$

DEBT RATIOS

The debt ratio focuses on the use of debt to finance the company, and therefore puts an emphasis on the capital structure and gives some insight into issues related to long-term risk management. It shows financial statement users and management how much debt the company is using and how well that debt is managed.

Debt-to-Total Assets

The debt-to-total assets ratio is expressed as a percentage. It shows the proportion of assets financed by debt. For example, a debt-to-total assets ratio of 55 percent means that a bit more than half of the assets are financed with debt.

The formula for the debt-to-total assets ratio is as follows:

$$\text{Debt-to-Total Assets} = \text{Total Debt} / \text{Total Assets}$$

Times Interest Earned

A measure of safety, times interest earned reveals how many times earnings before interest and taxes (EBIT) cover interest expenses. It is expressed as a multiplier (times). For example, if the times interest earned is seven times, then EBIT could cover interest expense seven times. In that example, if interest expense is $1,000,000, then EBIT would be $7,000,000.

The times interest earned ratio is calculated as follows:

$$\text{Times Interest Earned} = \text{Income before Interest and Taxes} / \text{Interest Expense}$$

Fixed-Charge Coverage

The term *fixed charge* means any expense associated with financing the operation that is fixed, including bank loans, leases, and bonds. The fixed-charge coverage ratio gives an indication of a firm's ability to satisfy fixed financing expenses, and it is expressed as a multiple (times). For example, if the ratio is calculated at six, it means that income can cover the fixed charges six times.

The fixed-charge ratio is calculated as follows:

$$\text{Fixed-Charge Coverage} = \text{Income Before Fixed Charges and Taxes} / \text{Fixed Charges}$$

LIMITATIONS OF RATIO ANALYSIS

Ratio analysis can be a powerful tool for a financial statement user attempting to fully interpret a set of financial statements. However, there are limitations to ratio analysis. Many of these limitations relate to the shortcomings inherent in accounting data. Inflation has harshly distorted some balance sheets. Recorded values (values used in financial analysis) are often immensely unlike the true economic value. Inflation has also had an impact on net income since it can distort inventory costs (and therefore the cost of goods sold) and depreciation expense. Seasonality can also distort comparative analysis—comparing the ratios of one period to another—so that even within one firm's operations, financial ratios can vary greatly within a period of time. An example of this is apparent in the toy industry when inventory balances are extremely high just prior to the holiday rush.

The diversity of a firm's operations can also present a deceiving picture when performing comparative analysis. A firm that is well diversified has no peer for comparative purposes. The classic example is a company like Textron (TXT), a Providence, Rhode Island–based corporation with stock traded on the New York Stock Exchange. Textron's business is very diverse. They manufacture helicopters and aircrafts, have a large division dedicated to defense and intelligence, produce golf carts, own a company that produces wire and cable tools, manufacture high-quality lawn-care equipment, and run a large finance company. It is very difficult to compare the ratios of Textron to another company. Companies like General Electric and United Technologies are also diversified and compete in some of the industries that Textron competes in, but they also operate in markets and industries that Textron does not.

Ratios can sometimes be too good. A firm with very good liquidity ratios could be too heavy in cash and marketable securities, neglecting a greater profit potential realizable through investment in inventory and long-term investments. Finally, since ratios are based on accounting data, they are subject to the limitations of accounting data. Different accounting methods yield different results.

HORIZONTAL ANALYSIS

Another commonly used financial analysis tool is *horizontal analysis*. It is the comparison of ratios or financial line items in a company's financial statements, over different periods of time. For example, if you were to compare all the ratios for a particular company as of the year-end for three years, you would be performing horizontal analysis. If you hear an analysis that revenues increased 20 percent this past year, once again, that analyst would be performing a type of horizontal analysis. Horizontal analysis can be used on any item in a company's financials (from revenues to earnings per share).

Using horizontal analysis to review changes from one period to another can involve percentage changes. For example, if you were reviewing a comparative balance sheet—one that shows more than one balance sheet as of the end of some time period (e.g., end of year, end of quarter, etc.)—you could calculate the percentage change in cash from one period to the other. If cash was $50,000 on December 31, 2007, and $65,000 on December 31, 2008, the percentage increase would be 30 percent, found as follows:

$$\text{Percentage Change} = \text{Change} / \text{Base Period Amount}$$
$$30\% = \$15,000 / \$50,000$$

Illustration 11.1 shows an example of a comparative balance sheet. The percentage change column is an example of a type of horizontal analysis.

ASSETS

	12/31/2007	12/31/2008	Change	% Change
Current assets				
Cash	$50,000	$65,000	$15,000	30%
Accounts receivable	224,000	250,000	26,000	12%
Inventories	1,310,000	1,413,200	103,200	8%
Prepaid expenses	52,000	42,000	(10,000)	−19%
Total current assets	$1,636,000	$1,770,200	$134,200	8%
Fixed assets				
Property, plant, and equipment	$956,400	$860,000	($96,400)	−10%
Less: Accumulated depreciation	600,000	550,000	(50,000)	−8%
Net fixed assets	356,400	310,000	(46,400)	−13%
Total assets	$1,992,400	$2,080,200	$87,800	4%

| | **LIABILITIES AND OWNERS' EQUITY** | | |
	12/31/2007	**12/31/2008**	**Change**	**% Change**
Current liabilities				
Notes payable—bank	$60,000	$55,000	($5,000)	-8%
Current portion of long-term debt	7,000	5,000	(2,000)	-29%
Accounts payable	600,000	640,000	40,000	7%
Notes payable	140,000	135,000	(5,000)	-4%
Accrued expenses	50,000	48,000	(2,000)	-4%
Total current liabilities	$857,000	$883,000	$26,000	3%
Long-term debt				
Notes payable—bank	$80,000	$75,000	($5,000)	-6%
Total liabilities	$937,000	$958,000	$21,000	102%
Owners' equity				
Common stock	$100,000	$125,000	$25,000	25%
Retained earnings	955,400	997,200	41,800	4%
Total equity	1,055,400	1,122,200	66,800	6%
Total liabilities and equity	$1,992,400	$2,080,200	$87,800	4%

Illustration 11.1. Comparative Balance Sheet

COMMON-SIZE FINANCIAL STATEMENTS

Financial statement users also like to work with data that expresses relationships within a single accounting period. This type of analysis, which is commonly referred to as vertical analysis, involves preparing common-size financial statements. A common-size financial statement shows each item as a percentage of some other financial item. For example, in illustration 11.2, every account balance is expressed as a percentage of total assets (based on account balances from illustration 11.1).

The main advantages of analyzing a financial statement in this manner are that the financial statements of businesses of all sizes can easily be compared. It also makes it easy to see relative annual changes in one business.

ASSETS

	12/31/2007	Common-Size Ratio
Current assets		
Cash	$50,000	3%
Accounts receivable	224,000	11%
Inventories	1,310,000	66%
Prepaid expenses	52,000	3%
Total current assets	$1,636,000	82%
Fixed assets		
Property, plant, and equipment	$956,400	48%
Less: Accumulated depreciation	600,000	30%
Net fixed assets	356,400	18%
Total assets	$1,992,400	100%

LIABILITIES AND OWNERS' EQUITY

Current liabilities		
Notes payable—bank	$60,000	3%
Current portion of long-term debt	7,000	0%
Accounts payable	600,000	30%
Notes payable	140,000	7%
Accrued expenses	50,000	3%
Total current liabilities	857,000	43%
Long-term debt		
Notes payable—bank	$80,000	4%
Total liabilities	$937,000	47%
Owners' equity		
Common stock	$100,000	5%
Retained earnings	955,400	48%
Total equity	1,055,400	53%
Total liabilities and equity	$1,992,400	100%

Illustration 11.2. Common-Size Balance Sheet

TEST YOURSELF

1. Using the following data, calculate the profitability ratios:

    - Sales: $1,200,000
    - Cost of goods sold: $900,000
    - Net income: $84,000
    - Total assets: $600,000
    - Total liabilities: $180,000

    Gross profit margin _____%   Net profit margin _____%

    Return on assets _____%   Return on equity _____%

2. Based on the following data, calculate the asset utilization ratios:

    - Annual sales: $2,500,000
    - Accounts receivable: $327,500
    - Cost of goods sold: $1,625,000
    - Inventory 12/31/08: $35,000
    - Inventory 12/31/07: $40,000
    - Total assets: $1,200,000

    Accounts receivable turnover _____   Average collection period _____

    Inventory turnover _____   Fixed asset turnover _____

    Total asset turnover _____

3. Based on the following data, calculate the liquidity ratios:

    - Current assets: $2,300,000
    - Inventory: $500,000
    - Current liabilities: $1,000,000

    Current ratio _____   Quick ratio _____

4. Based on the following data, calculate the debt ratios:

- Total debt: $1,500,000
- Total assets: $3,200,000
- Net income: $500,000
- Tax expense: $100,000
- Interest expense: $75,000
- Lease payments: $45,000

Debt-to-total assets _____   Times interest earned _____

Fixed-charge coverage _____

5. Evaluate the ratios shown below by comparing the company's ratios to those of the benchmarks (industry average). Specify as "good" or "needs improvement."

Ratios	Industry Average	Company Ratio	Comment: "Good" or "needs improvement"
Gross profit margin	21.58%	30%	
Net profit margin	9.6%	5%	
Average collection period	37	32	
Inventory turnover	23.5	12	
Times interest earned	6	10	
Current ratio	1.38	2	

KEY POINTS TO REMEMBER

- Financial analysis involves using financial ratios and other techniques to gain a deeper understanding of the financial strengths and weaknesses revealed through the numbers of a company's financial statements.

- Financial ratios belong to four groups: those that measure profitability, asset utilization, liquidity, and debt burden.

- Profitability ratios measure a company's ability to generate earnings and effectively employ resources.

- Asset utilization ratios show how well the company is managing its assets.

- Liquidity ratios reveal a company's ability to meet its short-term obligations.

- Debt ratios measure the debt burden of a company in two dimensions: principal owed relative to assets and cash flow dedicated to the cost of debt.

- Horizontal analysis allows for comparison of financial balances between periods.

- Vertical analysis, done by preparing common-size financial statements, allows for analysis within a single accounting period.

Budgeting and Responsibility Accounting

INTRODUCTION

Major businesses and nonprofit organizations usually require some sort of structure comprised of subunits, such as departments and divisions. Each subunit, to help contribute to the mission of the organization, has its own objectives and goals—controlled by budgets. Monitoring subunit performance is the responsibility of the accountant and financial managers. A budget and responsibility accounting system traces costs, revenues, and profits to the individual managers who are responsible for making decisions about them and can take actions that impact these financial variables. Responsibility accounting works well when top management has delegated authority to make decisions. The idea is that each manager's performance should be judged by how well he manages those financial resources under his control.

WHAT'S AHEAD

In this chapter, you will learn:

- The budget principles that guide managers
- How the budgeting process works
- The components of the operating and financial budgets

- The principles of variance analysis and how management uses it as a learning tool and to identify corrective actions
- How to calculate price and efficiency variances
- The basics of responsibility accounting

IN THE REAL WORLD

Budgeting by a government was established in Great Britain in the late 17th century. The enactment of the 1689 Bill of Rights gave taxing authority to Parliament as opposed to the king. Parliament gradually established formal spending programs and by the 1820s, began publishing detailed annual financial statements showing revenues and expenditures and projected surpluses or deficits.

The United States government did not begin using budgets until 1800, when a law was passed requiring the secretary of the treasury to submit an annual financial report to Congress. The budget of a government is a summary or plan of the intended revenues and expenditures of that government.

In the United States, the federal budget is prepared by the Office of Management and Budget (OMB) and submitted to Congress for consideration. The OMB is a cabinet-level office and is the largest office within the executive office of the president of the United States.

In addition to overseeing the preparation of the federal budget, the OMB is concerned about the efficient spending of appropriations. According to OMB regulations, federal departments and agencies are required to use value engineering (VE) as a management tool, where appropriate, to reduce program and acquisition costs. VE is an organized effort directed at analyzing the functions of systems, equipment, facilities, services, and supplies for the purpose of achieving the essential functions at the lowest life-cycle cost consistent with required performance, reliability, quality, and safety.

Value engineering began at General Electric Co. during World War II. Because of the war, there were shortages of skilled labor, raw materials, and component parts. VE helped GE managers look for acceptable substitutes; those substitutes often reduced costs, improved the product, or both.

KEY CONCEPTS

Budgets set goals that guide the organization and give it direction and focus. A great budget process is participatory—it involves all managers. Past performance is certainly considered when preparing a budget, but equally important is anticipation of future developments that impact the allocation of resources. Budgets not only help plan the operation, they also help with the control part. Through comparisons between budgeted performance and actual performance, variances can be researched and analyzed and correct action taken to get the enterprise back on track.

BUDGETING PRINCIPLES

A budget is many things, all of which are important to the success of an organization. It is a blueprint for the future operations of the firm and, therefore, is a planning mechanism. It can help reveal efficient and inefficient uses of resources and, thus, is an important management control. It is a communication device in that it expresses the company strategy—its objectives and how they translate into the goals of the divisions and departments. If done properly, there is also a motivational slant to the budget. It can function to inspire employees, especially when they are part of the budgetary process.

Business success depends on goal setting and the constant striving for goal realization. A budget, above all, sets forth goals that give an enterprise direction and focus. A budget takes the vision of what the company should be and articulates that vision through specific operating objectives. Budgets make day-to-day efforts evolve into the realization of objectives. Yet a budget is not enough to assure the success of a business.

All types of organizations and businesses need budgets. Budgets help managers estimate the resources necessary to achieve goals and objectives. In carrying out the business and activities of an organization, managers use a budget system to measure current financial performance, discover significant variances from the plan, and detect substantial changes in circumstances or business conditions.

For budgets to work, they must be realistic, reasonable, and attainable and be based on a thorough analysis that includes a comprehensive assessment of the unit's financial needs in order to fulfill its goals. They must include a plan to increase resources or modify goals and objectives, if current resources fall short of meeting a unit's needs. Budgeting is most useful when it is integrated with an organization's strategy. *Strategy*, also called strategic management or strategic planning, matches an organization's strengths with opportunities.

Organizations prepare mission statements, set objectives, and move forward to prepare budgets that will allocate resources in such a way as to achieve the objectives and the mission. Once a budget has been established, the next step is to accumulate actual financial results and to periodically compare those results to the budget. That is how variances are disclosed. A *variance* is the difference between actual results and expected performance, also called budgeted performance—a point of reference for making comparisons.

Budgets help measure financial performance and help assure that unnecessary costs are being avoided, that expenditures are reasonable and necessary to accomplish the unit's goals, and that all transactions are adequately supported. This is particularly the case in government, where a budget is also the way that spending is authorized. Approval of the budget by the voters in local government or the legislature in state and federal governments is how expenditures are authorized and controlled.

There is a compliance aspect to budgeting. All expenditures must comply with all relevant policies, rules, and regulations. Expenditures should not violate company policies and rules, and in the case of governments and nonprofits, expenditures must comply with laws and the stipulations of funding, such as grants and government subsidies.

BUDGET PROCESS

The budget process for the approaching fiscal year begins months before the end of the current fiscal year. In many organizations, budget development is assigned to a committee. The makeup of the committee is purposely diversified and includes such people as the budget director, sales manager, production manager, controller, and treasurer. The committee energizes and guides the process. Here are some typical functions of a budget committee:

- Request and collect budget estimates
- Review and evaluate budget estimates and assumptions
- Suggest modifications to budget estimates and assumptions
- Approve budgets

Whether or not a budget committee is used, participation is important. All subunits must be involved. Those who participate in the budget process understand the basis upon which it was developed. Working together, personnel should plan the performance of the company as a whole and the performance of its subunits. Taking into account past performance and anticipated changes in the future, managers at all levels reach a clear understanding of what is expected.

TYPES OF BUDGETS

The main budget of the organization is called a static budget or master budget. The term *static budget* means that the plan is based on one level of revenue (output). The *master budget* contains the financial expression of the operating and financial plans for a future fiscal year. As an example, a master budget for a manufacturer would include the following budgets:

- Revenue (or sales) budget
- Production budget (including budgets for materials, labor, and overhead)
- Cost of goods sold budget
- Research and design budget
- Marketing budget
- Capital expenditures budget
- Pro forma income statement, balance sheet, and statement of cash flows

The revenue, production budget, cost of goods sold, research and design, and marketing budgets are all part of the operating budget, while the capital expenditures and the pro forma financial statements are part of the financial budget.

Of the budgets listed above, the capital expenditures budget needs some explanation. The capital expenditures budget identifies the amount of cash an organization plans to invest in significant projects and long-term assets. The process of capital budgeting includes a financial evaluation to determine if the company's return on investment targets can be met.

As the year plays out, many organizations prepare a flexible budget as a comparison point with the static/master budget. A *flexible budget* is adjusted (flexed) to adapt to the actual output level of the budgeted period. When preparing a flexible budget, you ask the question: "If we had known at the beginning of the period what the output volume would be, what would the budget have looked like?" The comparison of the master budget to the flexible budget to the actual results leads to variance analysis, the subject of the next section.

VARIANCE ANALYSIS

Often, actual results are different from the budget. That's when a variance exists. Variances are judged as favorable or unfavorable with regards to net income. Favorable variances arise when actual results exceed those budgeted, and therefore there is a positive impact on net income. Higher-than-anticipated revenue and lower expenses result in favorable variances.

Unfavorable variances arise when actual results fall below budgeted results and therefore have a negative impact on net income. Lower-than-expected revenues and higher-than-expected expenses result in unfavorable variances.

Below is a table that helps summarize variances:

	Net Income	**Revenue**	**Expenses**
Actual greater than budgeted	Favorable variance	Favorable variance	Unfavorable variance
Actual less than budgeted	Unfavorable variance	Unfavorable variance	Favorable variance

Management only cares about significant (also called material) variances. If a variance is significant, a manager must do the following:

- Determine the cause
- Evaluate the activity
- Take corrective action

Units must operate within their budget; that assumption is at the heart of budgeting. Where expenditures exceed budget, justification for such excess must be provided. In many organizations, when a subunit experiences a significant variance, the subunits must develop a formal plan to eliminate the variance from future periods.

Variance analysis is extremely important because it helps managers control operations. Variances offer early detection of problems, allowing management to evaluate performance and take corrective action. Analysis of variances can involve a decomposition of the variance by drilling down to find what caused the variance. For example, an unfavorable material cost variance might be caused by higher-than-expected prices or inefficient use of materials, or both. Efficiency is the degree to which inputs are used in relation to a given level of outputs.

An unfavorable operating income variance could be caused by lower revenues, higher-than-expected material costs, labor costs, and overhead costs. Management must determine whether variances happen because of poor forecasting or because of internal problems such as inefficient use of resources.

STANDARDS

Standards are developed by management and are important inputs to the preparation of the budget but also serve as comparisons when performing variance analysis. A standard cost in a manufacturing company consists of per-unit costs for direct materials, direct labor, and overhead. The per-unit costs can be further divided into the expected amount and cost of materials per unit, the expected number of hours and cost per hour for direct labor, and the expected total overhead costs and a method for assigning those costs to each unit.

Within the expected amount of materials, waste or spoilage must be considered when determining the standard amount. For example, if a product requires more material than is actually needed, it could be because of waste. The cost of the full piece of material is used as the standard cost because the waste has no other use.

A standard is a carefully determined price, cost, or quantity used as a benchmark for performance. For example, if management determines that one square foot of leather should be used to manufacture a wallet, that's a standard.

If management predicts that the leather should cost $12 per square foot, that is also a standard. Therefore, if variance analysis shows that a typical wallet uses 1.2 square feet of leather at a cost of $13 per square foot, the variance is $3.60 per wallet ($15.60 − $12.00 = $3.60). Is it because of price or efficiency? Price and efficiency variances can be calculated for materials and labor (price being wages and efficiency related to the use of labor hours). The point is that there are often multiple causes of variances. The answer is both; the actual cost of the leather was higher than expected, and the amount of leather used was more.

A price variance is calculated as follows:

$$\text{Price Variance} = (\text{Actual Price of Input} - \text{Budgeted Price of Input}) \times \text{Actual Quantity of Input}$$

A price variance can be calculated on materials and also labor. For example, if you assume that the budgeted hourly rate of workers is $20, while the actual rate was $22 and 5,000 hours were actually worked, the variance would be $10,000 unfavorable ($10,000 = ($22 − $20) × 5,000).

An efficiency variance is calculated as follows:

$$\text{Efficiency Variance} = (\text{Actual Quantity of Input}$$
$$\text{Used} - \text{Budgeted Quantity of Input Allowed for Actual}$$
$$\text{Output}) \times \text{Budgeted Price of Input}$$

For example, if the standard is one square foot of leather per wallet, and 100 wallets are produced using 120 feet of leather, the efficiency variance would be $240 unfavorable.

$$\$240 = (120 - 100) \times \$12 \ (\$12 \text{ is the budget cost per square}$$
$$\text{foot of leather})$$

Efficiency variances can also be calculated for labor so that instead of quantities like square feet or pounds, the quantity is labor hours and the price is an hourly wage.

Variance analysis is part of an effort of organizational learning. Managers learn why variances arise and use that information to improve operations. These lessons help in the current period as well as to adapt strategies, activities, and other efforts to achieve optimal performance in future periods.

MONITORING AND EVALUATING FINANCIAL DATA

Good budget systems for monitoring and evaluating financial data produce periodic reports (i.e., monthly reports) that are appropriate and accurate. These reports must be clear, concise, and detailed, and they must identify all sources of revenue and expenditure, provide variances (budget versus actual comparisons), and clearly identify trends and special areas of concern.

Reviews by management of periodic budget reports should be timely so that appropriate action can be taken before variances become worse. Sometimes variances require new control procedures that must be implemented to correct the situation.

Finally, effective budgeting systems involve good documentation of the corrective actions. That documentation should include the following:

- Why the variance occurred
- How the budget was revised
- What accounts were affected
- When the actions were taken and who authorized the actions

RESPONSIBILITY ACCOUNTING

Budgeting assists management in controlling the operations of a decentralized organization. Budget performance reports—the output of a responsibility accounting system—are the control part of budgeting. A budget performance report compares actual results to planned results. *Responsibility accounting* is an information system. It arranges financial information into areas of responsibility in an organization. A key requirement of a responsibility accounting system is that reports should include only those items that are controllable by managers, since managers are held accountable for only the items of expense, revenue, and investment they can influence.

In a responsibility accounting system, management establishes a responsibility center for each area or level of management responsibility. The firm's accounting system generates a performance report for each center. These centers fall into four categories:

- Cost centers
- Revenue centers
- Profit centers
- Investment centers

A *cost center* is responsible for costs (expenses) only. An example of a cost center is a maintenance department. Such a subunit only causes costs and does not bring in revenues.

A *revenue center* is responsible for revenues only. An example of a revenue center is the sales department of a car dealership. A *profit center* is responsible for both revenues and expenses, such as a unit in a retail establishment like the sporting goods department. An *investment center* is responsible for revenues, expenses, and invested capital. A good example of an investment center is a branch sales office where the manager has control over investment decisions.

Performance evaluation is critical to the responsibility accounting system. An effective budgetary system includes procedures that will compare actual results with expectations so that the performance of managers can be judged, and it also takes into account the behavioral aspects of budgeting.

The design and maintenance of a responsibility accounting system should allow for behavioral factors. Managers should have input into the goals and standards of their areas of responsibility. If a manager works to set her goals, motivation is maximized. If a manager believes a target is unrealistic or that the plans were developed without her participation, motivation is minimized.

There should always be an opportunity for management to respond to the variance analysis of performance reports. Only controllable expenses and revenues should be the focus. Holding someone accountable for events outside his control will destroy the integrity of the responsibility accounting system and could lead to demoralized managers.

Reports from a responsibility accounting system are the essence of management by exception. Management by exception calls for managers to focus on the problems. It is especially effective and efficient to report only those items with significant variances from budget, for this heightens awareness of areas that need immediate attention.

TEST YOURSELF

1. Complete the analysis below. Calculate the variance for each line item and note whether it is favorable (F) or unfavorable (U).

Problem 1

Income Statement

	Actual	Budget	Variance	Favorable or Unfavorable
Sales in units	22,000	23,500		
Sales	$484,000	$505,250		
Cost of goods sold	264,000	282,000		
Gross profit	$220,000	$223,250		
Selling expenses	28,000	26,400		
General and administrative expenses	19,700	21,000		
Operating income	$172,300	$175,850		
Interest expense	11,000	9,000		
Income before income taxes	$161,300	$166,850		
Income taxes	48,390	50,055		
Net income	$112,910	$116,795		

2. Prepare a flexible budget based on the actual volume level. Assume the following:

   • Cost of goods sold is variable.

   • Selling and general and administrative expenses are fixed.

   • The income tax rate is 30 percent.

Problem 2

Income Statement

	Actual	Flexible Budget
Sales in units	22,000	
Sales	$484,000	
Cost of goods sold	264,000	
Gross profit	$220,000	
Selling expenses	28,000	
General and administrative expenses	19,700	
Operating income	$172,300	
Interest expense	11,000	
Income before income taxes	$161,300	
Income taxes	48,390	
Net income	$112,910	

3. A company makes a product that requires two yards of material per unit at a projected cost of $3 per unit. During the year, 10,000 units are produced and 19,000 yards of material are used. The actual cost of the material was $3.25. What is the price variance? What is the efficiency variance?

Price variance $_____ (favorable or unfavorable)

Efficiency variance $ _____ (favorable or unfavorable)

4. A company makes a product that should take 1.5 hours of direct labor at a budgeted wage of $15 per hour. During the year, it produces 5,500 units over 8,500 hours at a wage cost of $125,375. What is the price variance? What is the efficiency variance?

Price variance $_____ (favorable or unfavorable)

Efficiency variance $ _____ (favorable or unfavorable)

KEY POINTS TO REMEMBER

- Budgets articulate goals in quantitative terms to give an organization direction and focus and to promote the efficient use of resources.

- Budgeting is an important part of the implementation of strategic plans.

- A good budget process involves all managers and takes into account past performance and anticipates future developments.

- A typical budget is initially static but is adapted and updated as the year plays out in what is referred to as a flexible budget.

- Variance analysis helps managers determine significant departures from the plan and where management attention should be focused for corrective action.

- Each variance is judged as favorable or unfavorable with regards to the impact on net income.

- Standards are developed by management and provide important benchmarks for planning and control.

- Responsibility accounting establishes accountability for variables controllable by management.

Time Value of Money: The Math of Finance

INTRODUCTION

Many financial decisions cannot be made without utilizing time value of money concepts. Time value of money has been called the math of finance. It is used when computing compounding of interest on a savings account, when calculating the annual rate of return on an equity mutual fund, and when evaluating the projected cash flows from a capital project. Loan amortizations, lease payments, and bond interest rates are all related to the principles of the time value of money. Both future and present values are important inputs into financial decision making, both in personal finance and business finance.

As you follow along with the time value of money examples in this chapter and as you work on the test yourself problems, you can refer to the time value of money tables provided in Appendix A.

IN THE REAL WORLD

How does an appraiser estimate a value on income-producing commercial properties, such as apartment complexes, shopping centers, hotels, and industrial property? Certainly, recent sales of similar properties can be useful inputs to a real estate appraisal of income-producing property, but that is only one approach. Usually lenders and investors want at least two approaches to value.

One approach to value is discounted cash flows: a method which uses future free cash flow projections and discounts them (using an assumed cost of capital) to arrive at a present value which is an estimate of the market value of the property. Assumptions are extremely important when using this method. The appraiser must choose a discount rate; a key variable. Also, assumptions must be made about occupancy rates in multiunit income-producing properties.

Once the cash flows have been projected and a discount rate applied, an estimated present value for the property can be established. Lenders can take that value into account when considering the property as collateral on a mortgage. Investors can consider the discounted cash flow when deciding whether to invest in the real estate.

KEY CONCEPTS

Time value of money is the math of finance. Four basic approaches are used: future value of a single amount, the future value of an annuity, the present value of a single amount, and the present value of an annuity. These basic calculations form the basis for a variety of computations used in accounting and finance to do such things as value investments, invest to reach goals, fund pensions, and calculate loan payments.

COMPUTATIONAL TOOLS FOR TIME VALUE OF MONEY

A number of computation tools can be used to calculate future values, present values, annuities, and rates of return. The most basic are financial tables. Spreadsheet functions, like those of Microsoft Excel, are probably the easiest to use.

There are also financial calculators that can help you compute time value of money, such as the popular HP-12C by Hewlett-Packard, a standard handheld calculator in use for more than 25 years.

Financial calculators contain numerous preprogrammed financial routines with financial keys for number of periods, interest rate per period, present value, future value, and amount of payment (for annuity arrangements)—in essence, all the possible variables involved in time value of money calculations.

PV: Solves for the present value of cash flows

FV: Solves for the future value of cash flows

NPER: Solves for the number of periods for an investment

NPV: Solves for the net present value of a series of cash flows

PMT: Solves for annuity payment, such as a monthly loan payment

IRR: Solves for the internal rate of return for a series of cash flows

RATE: Solves for a periodic interest rate (rate of return)

Illustration 13.1. The Basic Time Value of Money Functions in Microsoft Excel

FUTURE VALUE—SINGLE AMOUNT

Money can grow in value over time because of interest or other types of returns (e.g., dividends or price appreciation). A dollar received today is really worth more than a dollar received a year from now because of the ability to earn a rate of return. Practical applications of future value of a single amount include estimating the value of an investment on the day you retire or when a child starts school, the amount that a U.S. savings bond will be worth in 10 years, and the estimated value of your home five years from now when you think you may relocate.

Compound interest (or rate of return) is a big part of future value. When interest gives birth to more interest, it is called *compound interest*. Since most people think of rates as a yearly percentage, many governments and U.S. banking regulators require financial institutions to disclose a comparable yearly interest rate on deposits. A compounded interest rate may be referred to as *annual percentage rate (APR)*, *effective interest rate*, or *effective annual rate*.

The basic formula for future value of a single amount is as follows:

$$FV_n = PV \times (1 + i)^n$$

Where:

FV_n is the future value at the end of period n.
PV is the initial principal (or deposit or investment), also called present value.
i is the annual rate of interest (or rate of return).

For example, if you invest $1,000 for one year at 8 percent interest, the future value would be $1,080, calculated as follows:

$$\$1,080 = \$1,000 \times (1 + .08)$$

If you invested $1,000 for three years at the same 8 percent interest, the future value would be $1,259.71, calculated as follows:

$$\$1,259.71 = \$1,000 \times (1 + .08)^3$$

In the second scenario, where the money is invested for three years, the power of compounding is evident. The total interest earned of $259.71 ($1,259.71 − $1,000) is the result of interest on top of interest. Note that the year 1 interest was only $80, but year 2 and year 3 interest ($86.40 and $93.31) are a bit more than $80, as the table below shows.

Year	Beginning-of-Year Value	Interest	End-of-Year Value
1	$1,000	$80.00	$1,080.00
2	$1,080.00	$86.40	$1,166.40
3	$1,166.40	$93.31	$1,259.71

Using a future value table, you can calculate the future value by using the future value interest factor (FVIF) found at the intersection of 8 percent and three years. That factor is 1.2597 (rounded).

$$FV_n = PV \times FVIF_{8\%,\, 3 \text{ years}}$$

$$FV = \$1{,}000 \times 1.2597 = \$1{,}259.70$$

FUTURE VALUE—ANNUITY

An annuity is a series of equal cash flows for a definite period of time. A fixed-rate home mortgage is an annuity. For example, if you borrow $100,000 for 30 years at 8 percent interest, the payment is about $774 per month for 360 months. As an insurance product, annuities are investment vehicles sold by insurance companies and other financial services companies that provide a monthly income of a set amount. There are many examples of annuities in the finance world.

Future value of an annuity (FVA) is the future value of a stream of payments (annuity), assuming the payments are invested at a given rate of interest. It is calculated as follows:

$$FVA = A \times (1 + i)^{n-1} / i$$

Where:

FVA is future value of an annuity.

A is the value of the individual payments in each compounding period.

i is the interest rate per period.

n is the number of periods.

Rather than use the above formula, it is probably easier to use the Microsoft Excel FV function or to use a time value of money table. If you use the table, you must find the future value interest factor for an annuity (FVIFA), which is found at the intersection of the number of periods and the rate. Here's the formula:

$$FVA = A \times FVIFA_{i,\,n}$$

Where:

FVA is future value of an annuity.

A is the value of the individual payments in each compounding period.

i is the interest rate per period.

n is the number of periods.

FVIFA is the future value interest factor for an annuity

For example, the future value of a five-year $1,000 annuity, assuming a 9 percent annual interest, is $5,984.70, found as follows:

$$FVA = A \times FVIFA_{9\%,\,5}$$

$$FVA = \$1,000 \times 5984.7 = \$5,984.70$$

Therefore, if you invest $1,000 per year for five years at an annual interest rate of 9 percent, the investment will accumulate to $5,984.70 by the end of year 5.

You can see how the future value of an annuity would have practical uses. If a company is attempting to put aside funds for purposes such as future capital investment, a sinking fund to pay off a loan or a bond, or a pension fund for employees, the future value of an annuity or some derivative of it would be used. For example, assume that in 10 years a company wants to retire a $10,000,000 bond issue. Assuming an interest rate of 7 percent, it could put aside about $145,000 per year, calculated as follows:

$$FVA \,/\, FVIFA_{7\%,\,10\ years} = A$$

$$\$2,000,000 \,/\, 13.8164 = \$144,755.51$$

PRESENT VALUE—SINGLE AMOUNT

The process of calculating the present value of a future amount is also called discounting. *Discounting* involves a mathematical extracting of interest (rate of return) from a future amount to reduce it to today's dollars. It is also called *reverse compounding*.

The formula for discounting a future amount is as follows:

$$PV = FV \times 1 / (1 + i)^n$$

Where:

PV is the present value of some future amount.

FV is the future value at the end of period n.

i is the annual rate of interest (or rate of return).

For example, the present value of $5,000 received at the end of year 5, assuming an annual interest rate of 8 percent, is $3,403, found as follows:

$$PV = FV \times 1 / (1 + i)^n$$
$$PV = \$5,000 \times 1 / (1 + .08)^5$$
$$\$3,403 = \$5,000 \times .6806$$

Once again, rather than using the formula, it is much easier to use the PV function of Microsoft Excel or a time value of money table. If you use a time value of money table, you must find the present value interest factor (PVIF) for a single amount and for the appropriate interest rate and number of periods. In the above example, the PVIF is .6806, which can be found at the intersection of 8 percent and 5 years in table A-3.

$$PV = FV \times PVIF_{8\%, 5 \text{ years}}$$
$$\$3,403 = \$5,000 \times .6806$$

There are many applications of present value. For example, if you have as your personal goal to accumulate $100,000 in five years and can invest your money at an annual rate of return of 7 percent, you can compute how much you must invest today to reach your goal. As the numbers show below, you would need to invest a lump sum of $71,300 now to achieve the $100,000 goal.

$$PV = FV \times PVIF_{7\%, 5 \text{ years}}$$
$$PV = \$100,000 \times 0.7130$$
$$PV = \$71,300$$

Present value is also used to value a series of uneven future cash flows, as is the case with many investments, such as commercial enterprises, equities, and real estate. The process of finding the present value of a series of uneven cash flows is called discounting, which is covered in a later section.

PRESENT VALUE—ANNUITY

A good example of a practical use of the present value of an annuity is a loan. It could be said that the value or the balance of a loan is the present value of its future payments. For example, if a loan arrangement calls for 20 annual payments of $1,000 with an annual interest rate of 8 percent, the loan balance (principal) would be $9,818.10.

$$PVA = A \times PVIFA_{8\%, 20 \text{ years}}$$
$$PVA = \$1,000 \times 9.8181$$
$$\$9,818.10 = \$1,000 \times 9.8181^{[1]}$$

When financial institutions sell loans, such as fixed-rate car loans, home equity loans, and mortgages to other institutions, the PVA formula is used to discount the future loan payments at a prevailing market rate. There are many applications of the present value of an annuity.

---

[1] Just as with the other examples of time value of money calculations, there is a formula for the present value of an annuity; however, it is much easier and less error prone to use the PV function of Microsoft Excel or to use a PVIFA table.

TIME VALUE AND A MIXED STREAM OF CASH FLOWS

The examples shown to this point in the chapter involve either a single amount or a stream of equal cash flows (annuity). There are times in the world of finance when the cash flow is a mixed stream—such as an income real estate investment (with rising rental income and depreciation and operating expenses that vary each period). How do you find the present value or future value of a stream of mixed cash flows? The answer lies in time value of money applications already presented in this chapter. To calculate the present or future value of a stream of unequal cash flows, you discount or compound cash flow values individually. For example, the following cash inflows occur on a prospective investment:

Period	Cash Flow
1	$1,000
2	$1,200
3	$1,500
4	$2,000

If you assume an interest rate of 9 percent, you would find the present value of these cash flows as follows:

Period	Cash Flow	PVIF $_{9\%, n}$	Present Value
1	$1,000	× 0.9174	= $917.40
2	$1,200	× 0.8417	= $1,010.04
3	$1,500	× 0.7722	= $1,158.30
4	$2,000	× 0.7084	= $1,416.80
		Total	$4,502.54

Each cash flow is multiplied by the appropriate PVIF for the period. The PVIF can be found by refering to the Time Value of Money tables found at *www.kaplanmbafundamentals.com*. For example, the cash flow for period 1 is multiplied by the PVIF for 9 percent and year 1, the period 2 cash flow is multiplied by the PVIF for 9 percent and year 2, and so on. Then the discounted cash flows are totaled to derive the present value of the stream of unequal cash flows. If this example was a proposed investment upon which a potential investor wanted a 9 percent periodic (e.g., annual) rate of return, then the investor should pay no more than $4,502.34 for the investment.

A similar procedure is used to find the future value of a stream of unequal cash flows. In that case, each periodic cash flow is multiplied by the appropriate FVIF. Using the same numbers, here's what a future value version would look like:

Period	Cash Flow	FVIF $_{9\%}$	Present Value
1	$1,000	× 1.4116	$1,411.60
2	$1,200	× 1.2950	$1,554.00
3	$1,500	× 1.1881	$1,782.15
4	$2,000	× 1.0900	$2,180.00
	$5,700	Total	$6,927.75

The total of $6,927.75 is the value of the unequal stream of cash flows at the end of year 4 (assuming the periods represent years). The future value includes $1,227.75 of interest that would accumulate period by period assuming a 9 percent periodic return.

Of course, the present value and future value calculations of unequal cash flows can be performed with a financial calculator or within Microsoft Excel using the preprogrammed functions. However, when those tools are not available, the time value of money tables and their interest factors are reasonable substitutes.

TEST YOURSELF

Note: In developing the solutions to these problems, you should use either a financial calculator, Microsoft Excel (with its finance functions), or the Time Value of Money tables found at *www.kaplanmbafundamentals.com*.

1. If you invest $10,000 today and assume that you can earn 9 percent per year, what will your investment grow to by the end of year 15?

2. Your investment advisor suggests that you invest $4,000 per year for each of the next 30 years for your retirement. Assuming a 7 percent annual rate of return, what will your retirement account be worth at the end of year 30? Alternatively, what would it be worth if you earned 9 percent per year?

3. You want to have $400,000 available to start a business in five years. How much must you invest today, at an annual rate of return of 8 percent, to accumulate that amount?

4. A bank wants to sell one of its loans to another bank. The loan calls for 10 annual payments of $6,000. If the prevailing interest rate on this type of loan is 9 percent per year, what is a reasonable value for this loan?

5. Consider the following cash flows:

Year	Cash Flow
1	$2,000
2	$3,000
3	$4,000
4	$5,000

If you assume that these cash flows represent projected returns from an investment and that the investor wants a 6 percent annual rate of return, what is the value of this investment today?

If you assume that these cash flows represent projected deposits into a savings account that will yield 5 percent per annum, what is the projected value of this account at the end of year 4?

KEY POINTS TO REMEMBER

- Discounting is the process of finding the present value of future cash flows and involves mathematically extracting the interest or earnings from cash flows.

- Compounding is interest giving birth to more interest.

- When finding the present value or future value, the key assumptions are cash flows and the timing of those cash flows, an interest rate, and the number of periods.

- An annuity is a series of equal cash flows per period for a specified number of periods.

- When finding the present value of an unequal stream of cash flows, each cash flow must be discounted into today's dollars and then summed.

- When finding the future value of an unequal stream of cash flows, you must find the future value of each cash flow and then total the future values.

- Time value of money (TVM) calculations can be performed using formulas, but an easier and less error prone approach is to use time value of money tables, a financial calculator with preprogrammed TVM functions, or the financial functions of Microsoft Excel.

Bond and Stock Valuation

INTRODUCTION

Investment valuation is a process that takes into account risk and expected cash flows. Any method of estimating the value of a financial instrument works on the assumption that the present value of an asset is the discounted value of the expected future cash flows. Different types of financial investments have different kinds of cash flows, and therefore it is important to understand the fundamentals of stocks and bonds when attempting to estimate their value.

It is also important to understand risk. Risk is incorporated into valuation models through the discount rate. In line with the risk/return trade-off is the simple valuation rule: the higher the risk, the higher the discount rate. The risk/return trade-off is the principle that states that potential return rises with an increase in risk. Therefore, if you take on more risk, you should expect more return. Alternatively, low levels of uncertainty (low risk) carry low potential returns. Accordingly, invested money can yield higher profits only if it is subject to the possibility of being lost. Keep that in mind as you review and work with the valuation models in this chapter.

WHAT'S AHEAD

In this chapter, you will learn:

- The fundamentals of bonds
- How to estimate the value of a bond based on its future cash flows
- How bond prices change and what influences bond price
- What is meant by the important bond yield called "yield to maturity"

- Preferred stock fundamentals and how to estimate the value of preferred stock
- Common stock fundamentals and the approaches to common stock valuation

IN THE REAL WORLD

Zero coupon bonds were introduced to the fixed-income market in 1982. They were a very unique concept in the marketplace. The first zero coupon bonds were created as investors detached coupons and sold the bonds. Trading the bonds without the coupons took away a portion of the bond's value, as the value of a bond is equal to the present value of the interest payments and the maturity value.

As the name implies, zero coupon bonds have no coupon, or periodic interest payments. Instead, the investor receives one payment—at maturity—that is equal to the principal invested plus the interest earned, compounded semiannually, at a stated yield.

Zero coupon bonds are sold at a substantial discount from the face amount. Here's an example: A zero coupon bond with a face amount of $20,000 will mature in 20 years. You may be able to buy that bond for $6,800. At the end of the 20 years, you receive $20,000. The difference between $20,000 and $6,800—which is $13,200—represents the interest.

There are many varieties of zero coupon bonds, but the safest ones are those issued by the U.S. Treasury. They are backed by the full faith and credit of the U.S. government.

KEY CONCEPTS

Stocks and bonds are two of the most common types of financial assets that individuals and institutions purchase as investments. The value of a share of stock of one bond is the function of anticipated future cash flows and required rates of return. As a general rule, bonds offer a stable and predictable stream of cash flows that can be discounted using present value techniques. The preferred stock valuation model is also relatively easy to work with, as preferred stock also promises a stable cash flow that goes on indefinitely, much like a perpetual annuity. The valuation of common stock is a bit more difficult. Dividend payments are more speculative than bond coupon interest and preferred stock dividends, and the growth of dividends is difficult to predict.

BONDS

A bond is a debt security, similar to a bank loan. When you purchase a bond, you are lending money to a government, municipality, corporation, federal agency, or corporation, known as the bond issuer. In return for the loan, the bond issuer promises to pay you a specified rate of interest during the life of the bond and to repay the face value of the bond (the principal) when it matures, or comes due.

Many entities issue bonds to raise funds to finance their operations, projects, and long-term assets. In the United States, the federal government is a big issuer of bonds. Then there are states and municipalities that issue bonds to provide funds for all types of programs and to help run school districts, fire and police departments, and to build and maintain the infrastructure.

Corporations, both for-profit and nonprofit, issue bonds. Some are extremely safe investments, such as the bonds of public utilities, while others are more risky, such as those issued by industrials and transportation.

Although anyone with enough money can buy a bond, institutional investors make up 90–95 percent of the trading of bonds. An institutional investor is an organization whose primary purpose is to invest its own assets or those it holds in trust for others, including pension funds, investment companies, insurance companies, insurances, and banks. Institutions, as a result of their massive financial resources, have a major impact on the bond market, and the value and yields of bonds.

Certainly, individuals also buy bonds for their own accounts, and they are offered many alternatives. Bond choices for investors range from the highest credit quality U.S. Treasury securities, which are backed by the full faith and credit of the U.S. government, to bonds that are below investment grade and considered speculative.

As is the case with any publicly traded financial asset, when a bond is issued, the issuer is responsible for providing details as to its financial soundness and creditworthiness. This information is contained in a document known as an offering document, prospectus, or official statement. Rating agencies assign ratings to many bonds when they are issued and monitor developments during the bond's lifetime. Financial services companies, securities firms, and banks also maintain research staffs that monitor the safety of bonds floated by the various corporations, governments, and other issuers.

Several financial services/research companies monitor bonds and provide ratings on individual bond issues. The four major rating agencies are the following:

- Duff and Phelps
- Fitch Investors Service

- Moody's Investors Service, Inc.
- Standard & Poor's

Grading by debt rating agencies provides classifications so that potential investors can determine the investment-worthiness of a bond.

Many personal financial planners recommend bonds as part of a diversified investment portfolio. Bonds typically have a predictable stream of payments and repayment of principal—features that are attractive to investors who want to preserve capital and receive a dependable interest income. But keep in mind that there are also risky bonds; the most risky are called junk bonds. Usually purchased for speculative purposes, *junk bonds* typically offer interest rates at least three to four percentage points higher than safer government bond issues.

Bond Fundamentals

There are three key fundamentals of bonds: interest rate, term, and principal (maturity value).

Bonds pay interest that is often fixed, but there are issues that also pay a variable (also called floating rate) or even interest that is payable at maturity—rather than periodic—which is most often the case.

Most bonds carry an interest rate that stays fixed until maturity and is a percentage of the face (principal) amount. Typically, investors receive interest payments semiannually. For example, a $1,000 bond with a 7 percent interest rate will pay investors $70 a year, in payments of $35 every six months. When the bond matures, investors are promised the full face amount of the bond—$1,000.

A bond's maturity refers to the specific future date on which the investor's principal will be repaid—usually an amount equal to $1,000. Bond maturities generally range from one day up to

30 years. In some rare cases, bonds have been issued for terms of up to 100 years.

Bonds are referred to by their maturities. Here are some useful maturity categories for bonds:

- Short-term notes/bonds: maturities of up to 5 years
- Intermediate notes/bonds: maturities of 5 to 12 years
- Long-term bonds: maturities of 12 or more years

While the maturity period is a good expectation as to how long the bond will be outstanding, certain bonds have features that can substantially change the expected life of the bond. For example, some bonds have redemption, or "call" provisions that allow the bond issuer to repay the investors' principal on a specified date before maturity. Bonds are "called" when prevailing interest rates have dropped significantly—an opportunity for the bond issuer to refinance the bond issue at a lower interest rate and therefore save significant expense. Bonds with a call provision usually have a higher annual return to compensate for the risk that the bonds might be called early.

As a general rule, bonds are considered a lower-risk investment because of their predictable cash flows. However, there are a number of risks associated with bonds and each bond investment should be analyzed carefully. Illustration 14.1 shows the risks inherent in bonds.

How to Value a Bond

The value of a bond is the present value of the expected cash flows from the bond, discounted at a required rate of return. Let's use a simple example of a bond that pays annual interest. Although most bonds pay semiannual interest, the annual interest example will clearly illustrate how the bond valuation model works.

Interest rate risk: The risk that interest rates will change and affect price of bond

Default risk (also called business risk): The risk that the bond issuer will fail to pay specified interest payments or principal at the promised time

Purchasing power risk (also called inflation risk): The risk that you will lose value because of a loss of purchasing power due to inflation

Reinvestment rate risk: The risk that interest rates will change and affect the rate that you earn on the reinvestment of your interest receipts

Liquidity risk: The risk that you will be unable to find a buyer for the bond if you want to sell before the maturity date

Interest rate risk (also called maturity risk): The risk that the value of the bond will be affected more by interest rate changes. This risk is higher in long-term bonds than it is in short-term bonds.

Exchange rate risk: The risk that exists in bonds that are denominated in a currency other than your own

Event risk: The risk that the issuing firm may experience an event that can affect the price of the bond

Call risk: The risk that a bond may be called by the issuer prior to maturity

Illustration 14.1. Bond Risks

Assume that a particular bond pays $100 interest per year, has a maturity value of $1,000, and will mature in 10 years. Additionally, assume that the investors' required rate of return on such an investment is 12 percent (based on a careful analysis of the risks involved and a review of the grades by the bond rating agencies (Moody's, Standard & Poors, etc.)).

Here are the cash flows (all inflows) associated with the bond investment:

Years	Cash Flow
1	$100
2	$100
3	$100
4	$100
5	$100
6	$100
7	$100
8	$100
9	$100
10	$1,100

In years 1 through 9, the cash flows are the interest payments, while in the last year (year 10) the $1,100 represents the last year of interest ($100) plus the maturity value ($1,000).

To estimate the value of this bond, you must discount the cash flows using the time value of money principles introduced in chapter 13. You can do it two ways:

1. You can discount each cash flow using the present value interest factors for a single amount.

2. You can find the present value of an annuity (10 years, $100) and the present value of a single amount (year 10 maturity value of $1,000) and sum them.

Here's the first approach. Working with the present value interest factors, you derive a bond value of about $887, as follows:

Years	Cash Flow	PVIF 12%	PV
1	$100	× 0.8929	$89.29
2	$100	× 0.7972	$79.72
3	$100	× 0.7118	$71.18
4	$100	× 0.6355	$63.55
5	$100	× 0.5674	$56.74
6	$100	× 0.5066	$50.66
7	$100	× 0.4523	$45.23
8	$100	× 0.4038	$40.38
9	$100	× 0.3606	$36.06
10	$1,100	× 0.322	$354.20
		Total	$887.01

Using the second approach, you value the annuity by multiplying the $100 interest payment by 5.6502, which is the present value interest factor for an annuity, assuming 10 years and 12 percent interest. That means the interest payments are presently worth $565.02. Then you must find the present value of the maturity payment using the PVIF 10 years, 12 percent ($1,000 × .322 = $322), and then you add the two present values ($565.02 + $322) to derive a bond value of $587.02 (off by one cent due to rounding).

BOND VALUE BEHAVIOR

Why is the bond value less than the maturity or face value of $1,000? The answer is this: when the investors' required return is greater than the bond's interest rate (also called its coupon rate), the bond value is discounted to compensate the investor. The reverse is also true: when the investors' required return is less than the bond's coupon rate, the bond will sell (be valued) at a premium—an amount greater than the face value. This last point is a great illustration of what is called *interest rate risk*—a risk inherent in all long-term bonds. As interest rates in the market rise, bond values fall, and when market rates fall, bond values rise. Interest rate risk is an inverse relationship between interest rate movements and bond value movements—a relationship all bondholders must understand.

Yield to Maturity

Whenever the required return by bond investors is different from the coupon rate, the yield to maturity becomes the key metric to follow. The *yield to maturity* (YTM) is the rate of return that investors earn if they buy the bond at a specific price and hold it to maturity. The YTM assumes that the bond issuer makes all promised interest payments and pays the maturity value to the investor on the promised maturity date.

Finding the yield to maturity of a bond is easy with a financial calculator or with Microsoft Excel. In Excel, there is a function called IRR (internal rate of return) which uses algorithms to find the rate that will discount the bond's cash flows (interest payments and maturity value) so that they exactly equal the bond's current market value. Without the aid of a financial calculator or MS Excel, the process of calculating the YTM is time-consuming. It is a process of trial and error. You must choose an interest rate, discount the cash flows, and see how close your present value comes to equaling the current market value of the bond. You conduct this process until you arrive at a net present value close to zero. The net present value is the present value of the cash flows (bond interest and maturity value) minus the market price of the bond.

Fortunately, it is rare that an investor would have to calculate the YTM of a bond, as the YTM of actively traded bonds can be found on any Internet service (e.g., Yahoo Bond Center) that allows you to look up bond prices, yields, and ratings.

PREFERRED STOCK

Preferred stock is called preferred because it gives its stockholders preferential treatment in a few ways. Although it usually carries no voting rights, preferred stock does have a superior priority over common stock in the payment of dividends and upon liquidation. Preferred stockholders will be paid out in assets before common stockholders and after debt holders in bankruptcy. Preferred stock may also have a convertibility feature—this means that the stock can be converted into common stock. Other possible features that can be attached to preferred stock ownership are shown in illustration 14.2.

A hybrid between a bond and a stock, preferred stock has the disadvantages of each of those types of securities without enjoying the advantages of either. Like a bond, preferred stock does not participate in earnings and dividend growth, and you rarely see any growth of preferred stock value (unless it is convertible into common stock) as you would see with the price of the common stock issued by a profitable company. On the other hand, preferred is not quite as safe as a bond. As a general rule, bonds have greater security than the preferred and have a maturity date at which the principal is to be repaid. Preferred stock is assumed to have an indefinite life.

Almost all preferred stock has a fixed dividend amount. The dividend is either specified as a percentage of the par value or as a fixed dollar amount per share. That idea of a constant cash flow helps make preferred stock a low risk investment.

How to Value Preferred Stock

The value of a share of preferred stock is derived from the following formula:

Value of Preferred Share = Annual Dividend /
Required Dividend Yield (Required Rate of Return)

Cumulative: Dividends accrue if they are not paid on time and must be paid before common stockholders receive a dividend.

Participating: Preferred stockholders are given a right to participate in earnings or value over and above the stated dividend rate.

Redeemable: Some preferred stock can have a fixed term and can be bought back by the company at a specified price, time, or interval. Redeemable shares may have a sinking fund, an investment held by a third party trustee into which the company pays over time to fund retiring them.

Voting: Refers to voting rights.

Put options: Company can repurchase the shares for a fixed price.

Convertible: The shares can be converted for common stock or into some other stock or debt instrument.

Illustration 14.2. Possible Preferred Stock Features

For example, if a preferred stock pays $10 per share and the investors, required rate of return is 10 percent, then the stock would be valued at $100 ($10 / .10).

The preferred stock valuation formula is the same as that of a perpetual annuity (perpetuity). A *perpetual annuity* is a stream of equal payments that last "forever," or at least indefinitely. The formula for the value of a perpetual annuity is as follows:

$$PV = A / r$$

Where:
   PV is the present value of the perpetuity.
   A is the periodic payment (the annuity).
   r is the required rate of return.

COMMON STOCK

The true owners of a corporation are the common stockholders who have what is referred to as a residual claim to the assets. That means they will receive what is left (the residual) in the event that the business is liquidated—assets sold and liabilities paid. However, as a common stockholder, there is no assurance of income, capital gain, or even return of investment. The only real assurances are that the common stockholders will not lose more than they invest (limited liability) and that they will have a voice, through their votes, in the management and direction of the entity. The common stockholders are the owners of the firm and have the right to vote on important matters to the firm, such as the election of the board of directors, major mergers, and acquisitions.

Common stockholders look for two types of income: dividends and capital gains; however, neither type of wealth is certain. To pay dividends, a corporation must have enough profit and cash. The board of directors will examine both the amount of retained earnings and the liquidity of the entity before declaring a dividend. The value of a share of common stock is a function of potential dividends and potential capital gains. But the key word is *potential*—common stock value is based on potential, if not speculative future cash flows.

How to Value Common Stock

As investors, we rarely have to estimate the value of a share of common stock because the market does that for us. The market, which is made up of rational, intelligent, and motivated buyers and sellers of all shapes and sizes—from individuals to security analysts to large institutions—takes into account all the available information about the company and assesses risk to determine whether a particular share of stock is a good buy. Certainly, the professionals estimate a company's value to determine if it is undervalued in the market, and they may use some of the basic approaches presented in this chapter.

CONSTANT-GROWTH RATE METHOD

The constant-growth formula, also known as the Gordon Growth Formula, assumes that a company grows at a constant rate forever. A constant-growth stock is a stock whose dividends are expected to grow at a constant rate in the foreseeable future. Certainly, many common stocks will not have constant growth of dividends, and so the constant-growth model is nothing more than a starting point of value estimation.

The formula is as follows:

$$P = D / (K_s - g)$$

Where:

P is the estimate price (value per share).

D is the next dividend.

K_s is rate of return.

g is growth rate.

PRICE/EARNINGS RATIO METHOD

Another method for estimating value of common stock is the price/earnings (P/E) model. The price/earnings model is especially useful when a company's stock is not traded publicly and no market price exists. Here are the steps:

1. Determine the P/E ratio for the industry.
2. Calculate the earnings per share (EPS) of the company.
3. Multiply the P/E of the industry by the EPS of the company.

For example, ABC Company is in an industry where the average price/earnings ratio is 12. ABC's latest earnings per share were $7. An estimated value for a share of its common stock is $84 ($7 × 12).

BOOK VALUE

Book value per share is not really a valuation technique, but it can be a consideration when trying to determine a market value because it reflects the residual amount per share if the assets were sold for their accounting value (what they are listed at on the balance). Most stocks sell at a price above book value, but there are times when a stock could be selling below its book value, especially if investors believe the assets are overvalued or that the assets are understated. Book value per share is calculated as follows:

Book Value per Share = (Total Shareholders' Equity – Preferred Stock) / Outstanding Common Shares

LIQUIDATION VALUE

The liquidation value per share is very similar to book value per share, except that the assets are valued at their estimated liquidation value (as opposed to historical cost). In the case of liquidation, the creditors would receive their money first, followed by the preferred stockholders. Liquidation value is calculated as follows:

Liquidation Value per Share = (Total Assets at Liquidation Values – Liabilities – Preferred Stock) / Outstanding Common Shares

TEST YOURSELF

1. A bond issued by Apex, Inc., pays $120 per year and will mature in 15 years at 9 percent. Assuming bondholders require a 12 percent required annual return, what is the estimated value of the bond?

2. If the required return on bonds similar to the one presented in question 1 drops to 8 percent, what would be the estimated value of the Apex, Inc., bond? What would the value be if the bond was a zero coupon bond?

3. A share of preferred stock pays an annual dividend that is 8 percent of its $60 par value. Assuming a 10 percent required return by preferred stockholders, estimate the value of a share of the preferred stock.

4. ABC, Inc., issued common stock that is projected to pay a dividend per share of $2 next year with growth estimated at 5 percent per year. If investors expect a 12 percent rate of return on the stock, what is its value?

5. Based on the following financial facts about a company, estimate the book value per share and liquidation value per share.

	Per Balance Sheet	Estimated Liquidation Value
Assets	$2,500,000	$2,650,000
Liabilities	$900,000	
Preferred Stock	$550,000	

Assume there are 300,000 shares of common stock outstanding.

Book value per share $_____

Liquidation value per share $ _____

KEY POINTS TO REMEMBER

- Bonds have more predictable cash flows (interest and maturity value) than stocks.

- The estimated value of a bond is the present value of its expected future cash flows, discounted at a rate equal to the investors' required rate of return.

- The yield to maturity is the expected annual return on a bond, assuming that it is held to maturity and the annual interest and gain on a discount or the loss on a premium is taken into account.

- Preferred stock also has predictable cash flows, but unlike bonds, those cash flows are over an indefinite period.

- The valuation formula for preferred stock is the same as the present value of a perpetual annuity, as the dividend from a preferred stock is assumed to continue into the indefinite future.

- Because of the complexity and the uncertainty of common stock investments, several approaches to value may be used as indicators of value, including the constant-growth (of dividends) model, the P/E multiplier, book value per share, and liquidation value per share.

Cost of Capital

INTRODUCTION

The cost of capital is the after-tax cost of the capital structure of an enterprise. It is not the cost of one component; rather, it is the cost of the blend of long-term financing—long-term loans, bonds, preferred stock, and equity—used by an organization.

In profit-seeking firms, the cost of capital is an important rate—a kind of hurdle—that must be surpassed on a consistent basis when investing in projects. The theory is that as long as the rates of return on investments (ROI) made by the firm equal the cost of capital, market value will be maintained. If the rate of return on investments surpasses the cost of capital hurdle, the market value of the firm will increase. Consistently earning rates of return above the cost of capital will help attract capital to the firm. Suppliers of capital, creditors, and stockholders are on the lookout for companies that can produce returns on investment greater than the cost of capital.

In this chapter, you will learn:
- A basic understanding of the cost of capital
- An understanding of the basic assumptions of the cost of capital calculation
- How to calculate the cost of capital for debt
- How to calculate the cost of preferred stock
- How to calculate the cost of common stock and retained earnings
- How to calculate the weighted average cost of capital (WACC) for a firm
- The uses of the cost of capital when making investment decisions

IN THE REAL WORLD

The cost of capital is used across the value chain in organizations and in many of the functional areas of business. In accounting, knowing the cost of capital for each capital component helps provide managers with the data needed to determine the firm's overall cost of capital—an important consideration when evaluating systemwide investments. In the operations area where investments in plant and equipment are necessary to increase productivity and returns on investment, the cost of capital helps managers assess the economic viability of proposed investments. Investment opportunities schedules (IOS) are prepared to rank investment possibilities from best to worst—all in light of the cost of capital. In finance, portfolio managers utilize cost of capital estimates to value investments; and in marketing, the return on investment of specific promotional campaigns is compared to the cost of capital needed to fund those campaigns in order to judge viability and performance.

KEY CONCEPTS

There are four basic sources of long-term funds for a business: long-term debt (loans and bonds), preferred stock, common stock, and retained earnings. Although not every entity will utilize all four types of capital, each source is a possibility and each source carries its own cost. The cost is calculated on an after-tax basis for the debt because interest expense is tax deductible—a feature that helps lower its effective cost.

Calculating the cost of capital is a step-by-step process. You first calculate the cost of individual components. What is the cost of the loans? What is the cost of bonds? What is the cost of preferred stock? What is the cost of common stock and retained earnings?

Then the proportions must be taken into account. If a company's capital structure is more heavily weighted toward debt, more weight must be factored in for debt versus equity. Eventually, the cost of capital is calculated on a company-wide, weighted average basis—a routine that is easy to learn and will be demonstrated in the last section of this chapter.

THE COST OF LONG-TERM DEBT

Debt capital is almost always a fixed cost source of funds. One important consideration in the United States is that the cost of debt—interest expenses—is tax deductible. This means that in effect, the use of debt is somewhat subsidized by the federal government as a result of tax law.

The cost of long-term debt is the after-tax cost of raising long-term funds through borrowing—be it through bank loans or by floating bonds. For example, if you assume that a long-term bank loan's interest rate is 8 percent and the enterprise is in the 30 percent tax bracket, the after-tax cost of the debt would be 5.6 percent, calculated as follows:

$$\text{After-Tax Cost of Debt} = \text{Interest Rate} \times (1 - \text{Tax Rate})$$
$$5.6\% = 8\% \times (1 - .30)$$

Calculating the after-tax cost of a bond is similar but a bit more complicated. The complicating factor is that most bonds have several interest rate or rate of return metrics to consider.

For starters, a bond has a coupon rate and an effective rate of interest. The coupon rate is how much interest is paid each year to the bondholder (the provider of the capital). But the coupon rate is not the true cost of debt. Then there is the effective rate, which is the coupon rate adjusted for the current bond value. For example, a bond's coupon rate might be 6 percent, but its effective rate might be 7 percent because the bond is selling at a discount. However, the effective rate is not the true cost of capital because it doesn't take into account enough cost factors.

The true cost of the bond is the yield to maturity. When investors buy bonds, they put much consideration into the yield to maturity (YTM). The YTM is the annual rate of return that investors will earn if all the scheduled interest payments are made and the face value is paid upon maturity. The yield to maturity takes into account interest and price appreciation due to a discount. It also takes into account the loss of value due to a premium.

For example, if you buy a bond at $900 that has a maturity value of $1,000, it is as if you will realize a $100 gain upon maturity. That gain along with the interest you receive on the bond must factor into the yield (cost), and it does through the YTM calculation.

On the other hand, a bond that sells for a premium at $1,200 will mature at only $1,000, and therefore a loss of sorts will be realized by the investor—a loss that will devour part of the yield provided by the interest payments.

The *internal rate of return* (IRR) is the discount rate that equates the cost of the bond (present value) with the cash flows (interest and maturity value). It is the compound annual rate of return that the investor earns on the bond, assuming the predicted cash flows (interest payments and maturity value).

The IRR can be calculated using a financial calculator or the IRR function in Microsoft Excel. To calculate it otherwise is a trial-and-error process that can be a bit time-consuming. Fortunately, the YTM on actively traded bonds is readily available through investment research publications and on the Internet.

Like the interest cost of bank loans, the yield to maturity of a bond must be adjusted for income taxes when estimating the cost of capital. For example, if a bond's yield to maturity is 10 percent and the corporation's income tax rate is 25 percent, then the estimated cost of the bond is 7.5 percent ($.1 \times (1 - .25)$).

THE COST OF PREFERRED STOCK

Preferred stock is a special type of ownership interest in a corporation. Preferred stockholders have the right to receive stated dividends before any earnings can be distributed to common stockholders, and in some ways, preferred stock is a lot like bonds. Preferred stock usually has a fairly stable market value (share price) and the dividends are fixed—much like the coupon interest payments on bonds.

Preferred stock dividends can be stated as an amount, such as $5.00 per share, or as a percentage of a par value, such as 8 percent of $60.00, which would be $4.80 per share. Since par value never changes, even the preferred stock dividend that is a function (or percentage) of par is fixed.

Unless otherwise specified, preferred stock has an indefinite holding period so that when you estimate the cost of preferred stock, you only consider the dividends. Therefore, if the dividend of the stock is $4 per share and the current price of the stock is $40, the cost of the preferred stock is 10 percent, found as follows:

$$D / P = \text{Cost of Preferred Stock}$$

Where:

D is the preferred dividend.

P is the current market price per share of the stock.

$4 / $40 = 10\%$

The dividend is not tax deductible, so there is no adjustment to the cost of preferred, as is the case with the cost of debt.

Another way to estimate the cost of preferred is to calculate the cost as a percentage of the net proceeds from the sale of preferred stock. For example, if a company is looking to issue preferred stock at $90 per share with a $9 dividend, they would also need to estimate the issuance cost per share (also called flotation costs) to calculate the net proceeds:

$$\text{Selling Price} - \text{Issuance Costs per Share} = \text{Net Proceeds per Share}$$

If we assume that the issuance costs are $3 per share, the cost of the preferred would be 10.3 percent, calculated as follows:

$$\text{Dividend per Share} / (\text{Selling Price per Share} - \text{Issuance Cost per Share})$$
$$\$9 / (\$90 - \$3) = \$9 / \$87 = 10.3\%$$

THE COST OF COMMON STOCK

The cost of common stock is the required return that investors in the market require. As was explained in chapter 14, the theory is that investors have some required return that is used to discount the expected future cash flows of the stock to derive a value. The challenge is to estimate that expected return. One way is to use a derivative of the constant-growth valuation model. The following formula can be used to estimate the cost of common stock:

$$\text{Cost} = D / P + g$$

Where:

> D is the dividend per share of the common stock.
> P is the current price (market value) per share.
> g is the estimated annual growth rate of the dividend.

For example, if a common stock pays an $8 dividend per share, is selling for $100 per share, and has an annual dividend growth rate of 5 percent, the cost of the common stock would be estimated at 13 percent, found as follows:

$$\$8 / \$100 + .05 = .08 = .05 = 13\%$$

There is another method that is used to calculate the cost of common stock. It is called the capital asset pricing model (CAPM). The CAPM is a model that describes the relationship between risk and expected return and that is used in estimating the value of risky securities—such as common stock.

Here is the basic formula for the CAPM:

$$\text{Expected Rate of Return of Common Stock} = R_f + (b \times (k_m - R_f))$$

Where:

> R_f is the risk-free rate of return.
> b is the beta of the stock—a measure of risk.
> k_m is the expected market return on common stock.

For example, if the risk-free rate is 3 percent, the *beta* (risk measure) of the stock is 2, and the expected market return over the period is 10 percent, the stock is expected to return 17 percent, calculated as follows:

$$3\% + (2 \times (10\% - 3\%)) = 17\%$$

The beta for a stock is calculated using regression analysis and is published for most actively traded stocks by a number of investment research services, such as Value Line. The beta is an indication of price volatility relative to the market as a whole. The whole market is usually the S&P 500, which is assigned a beta of 1. The S&P 500 is a stock price index comprised of the 500 largest companies in the United States.

Stocks that have a beta greater than 1 have greater price volatility than the overall market and are more risky. Stocks with a beta of 1 fluctuate in price at the same rate as the market. Stocks with a beta of less than 1 have less price volatility than the market and are less risky.

THE COST OF RETAINED EARNINGS

The cost of retained earnings is essentially the same as the cost of common stock. *Retained earnings* are profits that were not paid out as dividends, and as such should earn at least a rate of return equal to the expected rate of return on the common stock. Otherwise, the common stockholders would be better off if the earnings were paid to them as opposed to being reinvested in the corporation.

THE WEIGHTED AVERAGE COST OF CAPITAL

The *weighted average cost of capital* (WACC) is the expected cost of capital for a company. It is found by taking into consideration the cost of each type of capital utilized by the company and the amounts or proportions of specific types of capital used.

Here are the steps to calculate the WACC:

1. Calculate the after-tax cost of each type of capital used by the firm including long-term loans, bonds, preferred stock, common stock, and retained earnings.

2. Calculate the proportion (weights) that each type of capital component is of the total capital. This is done by dividing the amount of capital for a specific type by the total capital. It is best to keep the proportions as decimals (as opposed to percentages) so that you can easily multiply. Be sure that the sum of the proportions is equal to 1 (100 percent).

3. Multiply the proportions (in decimal form) of the capital by the specific costs of capital.

4. Sum the weighted cost of capital to derive the weighted average cost of capital.

Here's an example. Assume that a company has the following capital structure:

Sources of Capital	Capital
Long-term bank loan	$100,000
Bonds	500,000
Preferred stock	600,000
Common stock	1,000,000
Retained earnings	300,000

The bank loan carries an 8 percent interest rate, while the bonds have a yield to maturity of 9 percent. The preferred stock pays $9.00 per share and has a market price of $90.00. The common stock has a dividend of $1.50 per share, a selling price of $30.00, and an expected dividend growth rate of 5 percent per year. The company has an income tax rate of 30 percent. As the following table shows, the cost of capital is 9.548 percent:

Sources of Capital	Capital	Proportions	Cost	Weighted Cost
Long-term bank loan	$100,000	0.04	× 4.2% =	0.168%
Bonds	500,000	0.20	× 6.0% =	1.260%
Preferred stock	600,000	0.24	× 10.0% =	2.400%
Common stock	1,000,000	0.40	× 11.0% =	4.400%
Retained earnings	300,000	0.12	× 11.0% =	1.320%
	$2,500,000	1.00		9.548%

TEST YOURSELF

1. The company has a $1,040,000 loan from a bank with a 9 percent interest rate. The company is in the 40 percent income tax bracket. What is the cost of capital for the debt?

2. A corporation owes $2,080,000 on a bond. The bond has a coupon interest rate of 8 percent and a yield to maturity of 8.25 percent. With the corporate income tax rate of 30 percent, what is the after-tax cost of the debt?

3. A corporation has issued $2,080,000 of preferred stock with a dividend per share that is 10 percent of par value. The par value is $50, and the current share price of the preferred is $60. What is the cost of capital for the preferred stock?

4. A corporation has $4,160,000 of common stock that pays a $3 dividend per share on a current market price of $40 per share. Assuming a 7 percent annual growth rate in the dividends, estimate the cost of the common stock.

5. Using the information from problems 1 through 4 and assuming a retained earnings balance of $1,040,000, calculate the estimated cost of capital for the entire company.

KEY POINTS TO REMEMBER

- The cost of capital is an important factor considered by management when investing in long-term projects.

- The cost of a long-term loan is the after-tax cost of the interest.

- The cost of long-term bonds is the after-tax cost of the yield to maturity—the rate of return expected by the bondholders.

- The cost of preferred stock is the current dividend yield and is not adjusted for income taxes, as dividends are not tax deductible.

- The cost of common stock is the expected return that investors seek as they consider risk.

- The cost of retained earnings is approximately the same as the cost of common stock.

- The cost of common stock can be estimated using derivations of two models: the constant-growth valuation model for common stock and the capital asset pricing model (CAPM).

- The cost of capital for the enterprise is the weighted average cost of capital.

Capital Budgeting Cash Flows

INTRODUCTION

The capital assets of a company, the long-term projects of a nonprofit, and the new installation of a state-of-the art computer system at a university don't just happen. They are the result of a detailed planning process called *capital budgeting*—a technique used to determine whether a firm's long-term investments such as new machinery, buildings, new products, and research and development projects are worth pursuing. Keep in mind that there are not unlimited resources and that capital project proposals are often ranked in some manner that helps set priorities.

Capital rationing means that only a fixed amount of money is available each year for capital expenditures and that numerous proposals will in effect compete for the money. Will the projects be ranked on their rate of return? Will they be prioritized on how effectively they will contribute to the mission of the organization? Will they be ranked based on an urgency to satisfy government mandates or demands by important stakeholders? Each management team must decide how the ranking will occur.

Several formal techniques are used to evaluate potential capital asset investments, and the basics will be covered in chapter 17. However, before the techniques of capital budgeting analysis can be applied, the cash flows—more specifically the incremental cash flows associated with the proposal—must be projected.

WHAT'S AHEAD

In this chapter, you will learn:
- About the various reasons and motives for capital budgeting
- The process for capital budgeting
- How to calculate the initial investment/cash flows of a proposed capital investment
- Why incremental cash flows are the only relevant cash flows of a capital budgeting exercise
- How to calculate the incremental operating cash flows

- The reason why depreciation must be added back to incremental operating income to derive incremental operating cash flow
- How to calculate the terminal cash flow of a capital budgeting decision

---

IN THE REAL WORLD

Any type of organization, whether profit or nonprofit, must plan ahead for capital expenditures. Public colleges and universities are no exception. Through review and analysis of proposals, college administrators must prioritize projects such as building dorms, purchasing lab equipment, and installing new computers and then decide how to allocate capital—also called capital rationing—so that funds will be available for the capital expenditures.

For institutions of higher education, capital assets may be acquired through several methods of financing, including general obligation bonds, revenue bonds, capital leasing, and operating funds. General-obligation bonds can be repaid through a variety of tax sources, while revenue bonds are only payable from specified revenues. For example, the source of funds used to pay the interest and principal revenue bonds used to finance dormitories could be the room-and-board payments made by the students.

Growing colleges and universities are using tuition revenue bonds to pay for capital projects such as additional classrooms, new campus centers, and various other capital improvements that will help attract new students and grow admissions. A growing practice is to lease capital equipment. In many colleges and universities, a pool of laptops are acquired under a three- or four-year lease program and made available to faculty to use in their classes. In many cases, the lease represents a better alternative to owning the computers and ensures that the most current hardware and software are available to faculty. At the end of the lease, the institution returns all laptops and usually enters into a new multiyear lease, thereby always providing state-of-the art technology to faculty.

KEY CONCEPTS

The capital budget process has several steps, beginning with proposal generation. Once the acceptable proposals have been brought forth, the focus is on three types of incremental cash flows: initial, operating, and terminal. Careful projections of the relevant cash flows of a capital investment are needed to move on to analysis, which will help determine the economic viability of the proposal.

CAPITAL BUDGETING

Why do organizations take on long-term projects? Why are significant funds invested in plant and equipment? There are many reasons. Some capital expenditures—outlays of funds that will produce benefits over a period of time greater than one year—are mandated by government. Some capital expenditures expand the level of operations—usually through the purchase of fixed assets that give the organization greater capacity to produce. Very often, capital outlays are needed to replace obsolete or worn-out assets. In some organizations, there is a constant renewal process in place to rebuild, overhaul, and replace older assets so that efficiencies can be realized. During our most recent energy crisis of rising fuel costs, many companies have made investments in more energy-efficient operations that are producing costs savings. Capital expenditures might be made because of social responsibility (e.g., the "greening" of a business) or in the name of research and development.

There is a process to capital budgeting. Here are the steps:

1. Proposals are developed that describe the project and why it is necessary (mandated by government, replacement, R&D, etc.). Cash flows (costs, costs savings, and revenues) are projected.

2. A formal review is performed to determine if the projects are appropriate and in many cases, economically viable. Economic viability may be judged via techniques covered in chapter 17.

3. Management must decide which proposals take priority.

4. Expenditures are made for approved projects and they are implemented.

5. Results are monitored with actual costs and benefits compared to expectations. Corrective actions may be needed if significant variances from expectations exist.

6. A postaudit is often performed to gain valuable feedback.

The capital budgeting process exists to support the mission and goals of an organization. In companies, the process will support the goal of wealth maximization, while many nonprofit organizations also want to maximize the wealth they control. Decisions to expend capital funds to help produce more revenue streams or to lower energy consumption help maximize wealth and assure long-term survival. So like profit-seeking companies, nonprofits must be concerned about the efficient allocation of resources.

There may be many other reasons beyond wealth maximization for a nonprofit to follow a capital budgeting process. For example, a hospital may decide to spend huge sums of money on capital assets as a way to attach better doctors, provide better care, save more lives, and better meet community needs.

Since capital investments often require significant funds, the approval may be a multilevel process. Smaller commitments may possibly be authorized at the responsible manager level. For example, a plant manager might have a blanket authorization to approve capital investment proposals of up to $100,000, provided that organizational guidelines and policies are followed. Greater investments might have to go to a higher authority or even a capital budgeting committee composed of a cross-section of managers from different functional areas of the organization.

Implementation of the capital investment begins as soon as there is an approval. The same is pretty much true for the monitoring of the project. Variances—either good or bad—must be noted in a timely manner and if corrective action is needed, it too must be made in a timely manner. For example, a large plant and equipment investment could incur cost overruns from the start—during the construction and acquisition phases. Changes in purchasing, negotiations, and control procedures may make dramatic in-course adjustments to bring the project back in line with projections.

Much can be learned after a capital project has run its course. At the end of the life of a capital asset or project (that may include many capital assets), a postaudit should be performed. The postaudit process is yet another learning tool, an assessment of the actual performance. Just the existence of a postaudit function may cause managers to work harder to make reasonable assumptions when forecasting incremental cash flows. Information and feedback from the postaudit process can result in a fresh look at goals, strategies, techniques, and procedures connected with the capital budgeting process.

CAPITAL BUDGETING CASH FLOWS

The capital budgeting process usually involves some review and analysis of those cash flows relevant to the specific capital expenditure decision. *Relevant capital cash flow* is the cash flows that are caused (or triggered) by the capital expenditure decision. For example, if a manufacturer is deciding on making a $200,000,000 investment in new plant and equipment, initial investment will need to be made in the new physical assets and their installation. Additional working capital may also be necessary to support the new operation, and then there are the incremental revenues and expenses as a result of the decision. What additional revenues will be possible? What additional costs will be incurred? It is through the gathering and analysis of relevant cash flows of a capital project that economic viability can be judged and that scarce resources can be allocated.

Initial Investment

The initial investment is the relevant cash outflow for a proposed project at the very start of the project. Here is the basic format for calculating the initial investment:

> cost of assets acquired
> + installation costs
> − or + after-tax cash proceeds from sale of old assets or disposal of old assets
> + or − change in net working capital as a result of the capital project
> = initial investment

INSTALLATION COSTS

The installation costs are any costs that are necessary to place assets into operation. For example, machinery and computers usually require ancillary cost over and above their purchase prices to get them up and running.

Very often, a capital expenditure results in the replacement of existing assets. There may be a cash inflow that results from the sale of the old asset, or cash outflow if the old asset has no value and an expense must be incurred for its disposal (i.e., the cost of removal from the organization and proper disposal).

CASH FLOW ASSOCIATED WITH DISPOSAL

Many times a capital investment involves the replacement of an old asset with a new asset. The financial impact of the disposal—either by sale or costly removal and disposal—must be incorporated into the initial investment. Take the example of a building. If an old building must be razed to make way for a new building, there will be the cost of demolition, cleanup, and disposal of building materials. In other cases, replacement might mean that the old asset still has some value and can be sold as a salvage item or as a working asset—valuable to a new owner.

Keep in mind that the disposal of a capital asset can trigger tax consequences. This book does not cover U.S. tax laws and regulations because it is beyond the focus of the text; however, it is important to understand that whenever a capital asset is disposed of for a value not equal to the asset's book value, there is a tax consequence. For example, if the asset is sold for a value greater than book value, there will be a taxable gain. That tax should be deducted from the proceeds to show a true picture of incremental cash flow.

For example, assume that an old machine is replaced and that it can be sold for $300,000, while its book value (cost minus accumulated depreciation) is $250,000. To make this example simple, assume that the capital gain is taxed at 20 percent. The tax on the gain of $50,000 would be $10,000, and therefore the after-tax proceeds of the sale of the old machine would be $290,000, calculated as follows:

Proceeds from sale of old machine:	$300,000
Less tax on sale of old machine:	10,000
After-tax proceeds from sale of old machine:	$290,000

If a capital asset's value upon disposal is less than the book value, there will be a loss that results in a tax loss and therefore a tax savings. For example, if the old machine in the above example sold for only $190,000, the after-tax proceeds from the sale of the machine would be $202,000, calculated as follows:

Proceeds from sale of old machine:	$190,000
Plus the tax savings:	12,000*
After-tax proceeds from sale of old machine:	$202,000

*The tax savings can be found by multiplying the loss on the sale by the assumed 20 percent tax rate. The loss on the sale is found as follows:

Selling price:	$190,000
Less book value:	250,000
Loss:	$60,000

The loss of $60,000 is multiplied by the tax rate of 20 percent because the loss can lower taxable income and thereby save taxes at a rate of 20 cents for every dollar of loss.

To summarize, there are two key components to the incremental cash flow of the disposal of an old asset as a result of a new capital investment:

1. The proceeds from the sale of the old asset or the cost of disposing of the old asset
2. The income tax impact (either tax from the sale at a gain or tax savings from the disposal at a loss)

CHANGE IN NET WORKING CAPITAL

Net working capital is the difference between current assets and current liabilities. Net working capital needs are very often influenced by capital expenditures. If a capital expenditure is expected to help expand operations, activities, and revenue, then a reasonable assumption is that more cash will be needed and that accounts receivable and inventories will expand. However, the corresponding increase in spontaneous financing—such as accounts payables and other payables—may not be enough to cover the new needs.

The change in net working capital is the difference between the change in current assets and the change in current liabilities. For example, before a proposed capital project, current assets were $10,000,000 and current liabilities were $7,000,000. Projections showed that because of the capital project, the current asset needs would be $12,000,000, while post-capital expenditure of the current liabilities would be $8,000,000. The change in net working capital would be $1,000,000, calculated as follows:

Before the capital project: net working capital $3,000,000 = current assets $10,000,000 − current liabilities $7,000,000

After the capital project: net working capital $4,000,000 = current assets $12,000,000 − current liabilities $8,000,000

Therefore, the change in net working capital is found by comparing the $4,000,000 of net working capital needed upon implementation of the capital project versus the need for $3,000,000 of net working capital before the implementation. It is an incremental cash flow—which is the case in all cash flows considered in the capital budgeting process.

Operating Cash Flows

The operating cash flows of a proposed capital project are the incremental cash flows that are projected to occur if you adopt the project. *Incremental* means additional, so the exercise of projecting operating cash flows is a series of questions:

- What additional revenue can be expected over the life of the capital investment?
- What additional costs and expenses will occur as a result of the project?

The operating cash flows, like the initial investment, should be on an after-tax basis. Keep in mind that the calculation of operating cash flows must be just that—cash flows—not accounting income. The starting point can be a pro forma P&L (profit and loss statement) but the accounting profit or loss must be converted to cash flow. A standard format is as follows:

Incremental revenues
− Incremental expenses
= Incremental income before depreciation and taxes
− Incremental depreciation
= Incremental operating income before taxes
− Incremental income taxes
= Incremental operating income after taxes
+ Incremental depreciation
= Incremental operating cash flows

As you can see from the incremental operating cash flow calculation, incremental depreciation is initially deducted and then it is added back. One of the definitions of depreciation by the accountants is the systematic writing off or expensing of a physical asset over the useful life. The acquisition of an asset involves cash outflows but the depreciation does not. At first glance, the adding back of depreciation may seem confusing; however, it does make sense. Depreciation is a deduction for both accounting and income tax purposes—but it is a noncash item—so you need to subtract incremental depreciation to arrive at incremental taxable income but then add it back to the incremental operating income to derive incremental operating cash flows.

This type of "what if" analysis would need to be done for every year of the life of the proposed capital investment. For example, if you were looking to purchase new equipment that had a projected six-year life, the incremental operating cash flows for each year of the six years would need to be calculated. And then in the last year (i.e., year 6 in this example), the terminal (last) cash flow would also need to be calculated and incorporated into the analysis.

Terminal Cash Flow

The terminal cash flow is the cash flow resulting from the termination, disposal, and possibly, the liquidation of the capital investment. For example, if a capital asset has a projected life of six years, in year 6, you would need to estimate the amount of cash received as a result of selling the asset. It could also be that you believe the asset will cause a negative terminal cash flow. For example, if you believe the asset will be worthless at the end of its life, it may cost you something to dispose of it. Either way, you must project the after-tax cash flow that will result because of the termination of the asset. Keep in mind that whenever an asset is disposed of at a value different from its book value, a tax consequence will occur. If the asset is sold for more than the book value, an incremental cash outflow (taxes owed) will happen, and if the asset is sold for less than the book value, an incremental cash inflow (tax savings) will be projected because of the capital loss. Tax accounting and regulations are beyond the content focus of this book, but it is important to understand that the tax consequences of all incremental cash flows associated with capital investment must be considered in the review and analysis of the capital budgeting process.

TEST YOURSELF

1. Label each of the following types of cash flows related to a capital investment as either I (initial), O (operating), or T (terminal):
   A. _____ The cost of installing a new machine
   B. _____ The taxes owed on the sale of a capital asset at the end of its useful life
   C. _____ Incremental revenue generated by a new capital asset investment

D. _____ The freight charges on the delivery of a new computer system

E. _____ The proceeds from the sale of the old machine that
is being replaced by a new machine

F. _____ Annual incremental salary expense for the manager
of a proposed new plant

2. Calculate the initial cash outlay related to a proposed capital
asset investment based on the following:

- Purchase price of capital asset is $110,000.

- Installation and training costs are $15,000.

- Sale of old asset (asset being replaced) with a book value
of $80,000, for a price of $100,000. Assume a 30 percent
tax rate.

- As a result of the capital investment, an additional $10,000
of cash will be needed and inventory will increase by
$25,000, while accounts payable will increase by $12,000.

    Initial investment $ _____

3. A detailed analysis of the incremental operating cash flows
related to a capital investment with a three-year life has been
performed:

	Year 1	Year 2	Year 3
Revenues	$15,000	$20,000	$30,000
Cash expenses	$8,000	$9,000	$12,000
Depreciation	$3,000	$4,000	$6,000
Operating income before taxes	$4,000	$7,000	$12,000
Income taxes	$1,200	$2,100	$3,600
Operating income after taxes	$2,800	$4,900	$8,400
Add back depreciation	$3,000	$4,000	$6,000
Operating cash flow	$5,800	$8,900	$14,400

Assuming a 30 percent tax bracket, calculate the after-tax incremental operating cash flows for each of the three years.

Year 1 $_____

Year 2 $_____

Year 3 $_____

4. Assume the same cash flows as in problem 3, except that at the end of year 3, the asset will be sold for $100,000 and will have a book value at that time of $75,000. In addition, $10,000 of working capital will be freed up as a result of the termination of the capital project. What will be the total incremental cash flow as a result of year 3? Assume a 20 percent income tax rate.

Operating cash flows	$14,400
Sale of asset	$100,000
Less taxes on sale of asset	$5,000
Working capital	$10,000
Total incremental cash flow for year 3	$119,400

KEY POINTS TO REMEMBER

- The reasons for capital investment include commitments that will increase capacity to produce, efficiencies, cost savings, government mandates, accomplishment of social responsibility objectives, and research and development outlays.

- Capital budgeting is a process with steps such as proposal generation, economic viability review and analysis, prioritization of worthy projects in light of capital rationing, implementation, and monitoring, including postaudit.

- Only relevant capital cash flows are considered. They are the cash flows that are caused (or triggered) by the capital expenditure decision.

- Three major types of cash flows are generated by capital projects: initial, operating, and terminal.

- Initial investment cash flows consist of the cost of assets acquired, installation costs, after-tax cash flow from sale of old assets or disposal of old assets, and the anticipated change in net working capital as a result of the capital project.

- Operating cash flows include all of the following: incremental revenues, incremental expenses, incremental taxes, or tax savings. Incremental depreciation is eventually added back, as it is a noncash expense.

- Terminal cash flows from the termination, disposal, and possibly, the liquidation of the capital investment. It should be after-tax cash flows, so the tax impact of disposing of the asset(s) must be incorporated into the analysis.

Capital Budgeting Techniques

INTRODUCTION

In chapter 16 you learned about how to estimate the relevant cash flows of a proposed capital investment. The next step in the capital budgeting process is to evaluate those cash flows. There are several evaluation tools available—all designed to attempt to help us judge the economic viability of the project. Just about every manager on the verge of committing significant dollars to a capital investment wants to know if the decision will be a profitable one. Will the return on investment be enough to satisfy the providers of capital? Will the payback period be quick enough to satisfy top management? And the best question of all: Will the investment increase the wealth of the organization? This objective is important to both profit-seeking entities and nonprofits. In this chapter, we look at three basic evaluation tools—metrics that can help guide capital investment decisions: the payback period, net present value, and the internal rate of return.

WHAT'S AHEAD

In this chapter, you will learn:

- How to calculate and interpret the payback period for capital investments

- How to calculate net present value (NPV) and interpret the results of an NPV calculation

- How to calculate the internal rate of return (IRR) and interpret the results of an IRR calculation

IN THE REAL WORLD

Some studies have shown that higher IT capability directly correlates with superior revenue growth. Certainly, many IT managers would like to increase IT capabilities, but how should it be done? Should organizations outsource, particularly in the areas of application development and IT infrastructure? Or should organizations invest millions in projects that develop applications within the company and build expensive IT infrastructure?

Outsourcing is the practice of turning over responsibility of an organization's information systems applications and operations to an outside firm. This practice is widely believed to lead to cost savings and/or to free company resources for other activities. The real test is to determine if the present value of the benefits of outsourcing are greater than the present value of the costs of outsourcing.

Some studies have revealed that the outsourcing of IT can result in savings of 30–60 percent through lower-cost labor, lower technology investments, and process efficiencies. In addition, non-financial factors must be considered, such as access to skills and capabilities beyond those of the enterprise and speed of development (because of time zones, a 24/7 development cycle can be achieved).

However, there are risks associated with outsourcing. Privacy and security concerns must be weighed. So too must the possibility of diminishing technical returns, increased and hidden costs, loss of internal IT expertise, the negative impact on employees, and the possible impact of a failure of the outsource provider.

KEY CONCEPTS

Three capital budgeting techniques are covered in this chapter: the payback period, net present value (NPV), and internal rate of return (IRR) approaches. The payback period tells you how long it will take to recover the initial investment. NPV determines whether a project earns more or less than a desired rate of return (also called the discount rate or cost of capital) and is good for finding out whether a project is going to help create wealth within the enterprise. IRR goes one step further than NPV to determine a specific rate of return for a project. Both NPV and IRR give you numbers that you can use to compare competing projects and make the best choice for your business.

PAYBACK PERIOD

The payback period method is a commonly used approach for evaluating proposed capital investments. With cash flows projected, you can calculate the amount of time required to recover the initial investment. If all investments were annuities, the payback period calculation would be very easy. For example, if you invest $100,000 and believe you will receive $20,000 a year of cash flow, then the payback period would be five years ($100,000 / $20,000). However, rarely are the cash flows from capital investments in the form of an annuity. Usually, an investment pays back a mixed stream of cash flows, and therefore the cash flows must be accumulated to determine the payback period.

Below is an example of a capital investment with a mixed stream of cash flows.

Years	Cash Flows
0	($100,000)
1	$5,000
2	$6,000
3	$7,000
4	$8,000
5	$9,000

To calculate the payback period, you need to create a running total of cash flows—an accumulation of the annual cash flows of the project.

Years	Cash Flows	Accumulated Cash Flows
0	($100,000)	
1	$20,000	$20,000
2	$25,000	$45,000
3	$35,000	$80,000
4	$40,000	$120,000
5	$45,000	$165,000

According to this example, in year 4, the cash flows have accumulated to the point where they cover the initial investment. Assuming that the cash flows come in at an even pace during the year, the payback period for this example would be 3.5 years. The partial year (year 4) is calculated as follows:

The cash flow needed to accumulate the initial investment /
Total cash flow for that period = $20,000 / $40,000 = .5
.5 + 3 years = 3.5 years

You can see that by the end of year 3, $80,000 of cash flow is projected to have accumulated. Another $20,000 of cash flow is needed from year 4, with the cash flow for year 4 projected at $40,000. That means that halfway through the fourth year, the accumulated cash flows will have equaled $100,000.

Decision Criteria of the Payback Period

When the payback period is used to accept or reject a proposed capital investment, a *maximum acceptable payback period* must be set. There are no real guidelines as to the number of years to set as a maximum payback period. This benchmark is something that management must decide upon. It is based on experience and judgment. If management has a maximum payback period of five years and is presented with a proposed capital project of 3.5 years, then the proposed capital investment would be acceptable under the payback period decision criteria. If the payback period is greater than the maximum acceptable payback period, a proposed capital investment would be rejected.

The payback period is relatively easy to use and although other, more sophisticated methods of capital budgeting analysis are also relatively simple to use given software such as Microsoft Excel, the payback period is utilized today as supplemental information. People who don't understand discounted cash flows, net present value, and internal rate of return can understand the payback period.

Payback Period Drawbacks

Despite its popularity, the payback period method has some drawbacks. The method does not incorporate time value of money principles. It treats all cash flows the same—giving the same weight to cash flows received in year 1 as the ones received in year 6.

Another weakness of the payback period method is that the maximum payback period criteria is arbitrarily set by management. How does one select a benchmark? A payback of 3, 4, 5, or 10 years doesn't really connect with enterprise goals such as wealth maximization. That can only be done through methods that truly evaluate economic viability through the calculation of net present value.

NET PRESENT VALUE

Another method of evaluating the economic benefits of a proposed capital investment is the net present value approach. Net present value is the present value of the benefits of a capital investment minus the present value of the costs. It is an indication of the type of wealth that a proposed capital investment can contribute to the enterprise.

The rate that is used to calculate the present values is the minimum returned that must be earned on proposed capital investments. Management must decide what rate to use. Very often, the cost of capital for the enterprise is used because the theory is that if all capital investments earn rates of return greater than the cost of capital, capital providers—creditors, bondholders, preferred stockholders, and common stockholders—will be satisfied.

Decision Criteria of the Net Present Value (NPV)

When the NPV is used to make acceptance or rejection decisions about proposed capital investments, the following rules are followed:

- If the NPV is greater than or equal to $0, then the project can be accepted.
- If the NPV is less than $0, then the project can be accepted.

Consider the following example. Assuming a discount rate of 12 percent, the net present value of the proposed capital investment is $13,654. The present value of the cash inflows for years 1 through 5 is $113,654.23. If you subtract the initial investment of $100,000, you are left with $13,654.23—the net present value.

Years	Cash Flows
0	($100,000)
1	$20,000
2	$25,000
3	$35,000
4	$40,000
5	$45,000
Net present value	$13,654.23

In Microsoft Excel, there is an NPV function that makes the NPV calculation fast and easy. If you can't use MS Excel or a financial calculator, you can calculate the net present value using the time value of money tables. Below is an example of how the NPV would be calculated using the present value interest factors (PVIF).

Years	Cash Flow	PVIF 12%	PV
0	($100,000)		($100,000)
1	$20,000	0.8929	$17,858
2	$25,000	0.7972	$19,930
3	$35,000	0.7118	$24,913
4	$40,000	0.6355	$25,420
5	$45,000	0.5674	$25,533
		NPV	$13,654

Hopefully, you can see how a positive net present value helps to increase the value of the enterprise. If the NPV is positive, it means that its actual annual rate of return—also known as its internal rate of return—exceeds the cost of capital. When that happens, wealth is created. Some organizations favor the NPV approach over all other evaluation tools because it is the one method that reveals an indication of wealth creation while utilizing time value of money concepts. Some managers will rank projects based on the size of the NPV—especially when capital rationing is used. When a fixed amount of financing is available, wealth maximization can be achieved by selecting the combination of projects that will maximize NPV while staying within an established capital investment budget.

INTERNAL RATE OF RETURN

The internal rate of return (IRR) is another sophisticated method of evaluating the cash flows of a proposed capital investment. With cash flows projected, the IRR is calculated giving us the discount rate that equates the NPV of the investment opportunity with the initial investment. IRR is also one of the finance functions in Microsoft Excel. As the help file in Excel states: "IRR is based on NPV. You can think of it as a special case of NPV, where the rate of return that is calculated is the interest rate corresponding to a 0 (zero) net present value."

The IRR is very much like the annual percentage rate (APR) banks promise on savings vehicles like savings accounts, money market accounts, and certificates of deposit, as the IRR is an annual effective rate—a rate that takes into account the compounding of interest. Therefore, one advantage of the IRR method is that it results in a rate of return concept that is familiar to managers in that most investors think of wealth creation in terms of rates of return.

When calculating the IRR by hand, it is a time-consuming trial-and-error process. You discount cash flows using the present value interest factors for a given interest rate, and you do that until the NPV is equal to zero. Fortunately, the IRR function in Microsoft Excel makes the calculation significantly easier and faster to complete.

The Decision Criteria of IRR

The IRR can be used to accept or reject a capital investment by using these rules:

- If the IRR is greater than the cost of capital, accept the investment.
- If the IRR is less than the cost of capital, reject the investment.

The IRR can be used to rank the desirability of investments. A higher IRR is more desirable. However, there are some problems with IRR. It does not disclose, like the NPV method does, an estimate of the amount of wealth creation possible via a potential capital investment. In addition, the IRR method assumes that the reinvestment of periodic cash flows will be made at the IRR. That may not be possible. For example, if a proposed capital investment analysis results in an IRR of 15 percent, management will be attracted to that investment because the IRR will most likely exceed the cost of capital. However, is it realistic to believe that the cash flows in years 1, 2, 3, etc. will be reinvested at a rate of 15 percent? Probably not.

TEST YOURSELF

1. A capital investment has the following projected cash flows:

Years	Cash Flows
0	($75,000)
1	$3,000
2	$22,000
3	$20,000
4	$10,000
5	$45,000

What is the payback period? Payback period _____ years

2. Using the same cash flow numbers from problem 1, calculate the net present value. Assume a 12 percent required annual rate of return.

   NPV $_____

3. Use the projected cash flows below to estimate the IRR of this proposed capital investment. If you are using a financial calculator or the Microsoft Excel IRR function, you should be able to calculate the exact IRR. The firm's cost of capital is 12 percent.

Years	Cash Flows
0	($100,000)
1	$18,000
2	$26,000
3	$32,000
4	$37,000
5	$40,000

4. A company has budgeted $1,000,000 for capital investment during the upcoming year. There are seven proposals put forth. All seven proposals seem to be congruent with the mission, objectives, and goals of the organization. In analyzing these proposals, management is interested in wealth maximization and is assuming a 12 percent cost of capital. Which projects would you choose and why?

	Initial Investment	NPV	IRR
Project A	$550,000	$200,000	14%
Project B	$600,000	$125,000	13%
Project C	$200,000	$175,000	14%
Project D	$300,000	$180,000	12.50%
Project E	$250,000	$200,000	13%
Project F	$400,000	($100,000)	10%
Project G	$700,000	$300,000	14.50%

KEY POINTS TO REMEMBER

- The payback period is a metric that is often used in capital investment analysis because it is both easy to understand and to calculate.

- The payback period does give users an indication of risk, as longer payback periods have distant cash flows that are more uncertain than cash flows in earlier years.

- The payback method suffers from one important limitation: it doesn't consider the time value of money.

- The net present value (NPV) is the difference between the present value of benefits and the present value of costs.

- If the NPV is equal to or greater than $0, then the proposed capital investment is a candidate for acceptance. If the NPV is less than $0, the proposal is usually rejected.

- If the NPV is greater than $0, it means that the annual rate of return on the proposed capital investment is greater than the required rate of return.

- NPVs are used to rank potential capital investments, especially when the goal is wealth maximization and resources are scarce (capital rationing).

- Very often the required rate of return is the cost of capital for the enterprise.

- The internal rate of return (IRR) is the annual rate of return on the proposed capital investment.

- If the IRR is greater than the required return (cost of capital), the capital investment is a candidate for acceptance.

- If the IRR is less than the required rate of return (cost of capital), the proposed capital investment will not yield enough cash flow to satisfy capital costs.

- One drawback to the IRR calculation is that it assumes that periodic cash flows will be reinvested at the IRR—an assumption that is often unrealistic.

Acknowledgments

My father, Philip D. Griffin, often helped me many years ago with my accounting and finance homework when I was a young business student at Providence College. I couldn't have gotten through my accounting and finance courses without the tutorial help of my father. Dad had a successful career in finance. He was an accounting major who graduated from Bryant College and put his knowledge to work at Grinnell Corporation in Cranston, Rhode Island. He was later a finance executive for many years with ITT Grinnell in Providence, Rhode Island, and AT Cross in Lincoln, Rhode Island. When I teach and write about finance and accounting, I often draw on the lessons that I learned from my father. My dad still says: "You can't go wrong with a strong background in accounting." I have preached the same idea to hundreds of college students during my career as a professor of accounting and finance.

I want to thank Shannon Berning, Josh Martino, and Fred Urf er, my editors at Kaplan Publishing, for their assistance and ideas to help make this a good book. I also want to thank my family, my wife Nan and my children Brendan, Kate, Allison, and Trevor for their help and patience while I committed many hours to writing this book. I also would like to acknowledge the hundreds of students who have taken my accounting and finance courses for over two decades at the Charlton College of Business, University of Massachusetts—Dartmouth. I have always wanted to provide my students with clear and concise explanations of finance and accounting concepts; and when I don't quite get the points across with 100 percent clarity, my students let me know it. It is their need to understand that keeps me refining the content of my lectures and books.

Appendix A: Time Value of Money Tables

Table A-1: Future Value Interest Factors for the Future Value of a Single Amount

Period	1%	2%	3%	4%	5%	6%	7%	8%	9%	10%	11%
1	1.0100	1.0200	1.0300	1.0400	1.0500	1.0600	1.0700	1.0800	1.0900	1.1000	1.1100
2	1.0201	1.0404	1.0609	1.0816	1.1025	1.1236	1.1449	1.1664	1.1881	1.2100	1.2321
3	1.0303	1.0612	1.0927	1.1249	1.1576	1.1910	1.2250	1.2597	1.2950	1.3310	1.3676
4	1.0406	1.0824	1.1255	1.1699	1.2155	1.2625	1.3108	1.3605	1.4116	1.4641	1.5181
5	1.0510	1.1041	1.1593	1.2167	1.2763	1.3382	1.4026	1.4693	1.5386	1.6105	1.6851
6	1.0615	1.1262	1.1941	1.2653	1.3401	1.4185	1.5007	1.5869	1.6771	1.7716	1.8704
7	1.0721	1.1487	1.2299	1.3159	1.4071	1.5036	1.6058	1.7138	1.8280	1.9487	2.0762
8	1.0829	1.1717	1.2668	1.3686	1.4775	1.5938	1.7182	1.8509	1.9926	2.1436	2.3045
9	1.0937	1.1951	1.3048	1.4233	1.5513	1.6895	1.8385	1.9990	2.1719	2.3579	2.5580
10	1.1046	1.2190	1.3439	1.4802	1.6289	1.7908	1.9672	2.1589	2.3674	2.5937	2.8394
11	1.1157	1.2434	1.3842	1.5395	1.7103	1.8983	2.1049	2.3316	2.5804	2.8531	3.1518
12	1.1268	1.2682	1.4258	1.6010	1.7959	2.0122	2.2522	2.5182	2.8127	3.1384	3.4985
13	1.1381	1.2936	1.4685	1.6651	1.8856	2.1329	2.4098	2.7196	3.0658	3.4523	3.8833
14	1.1495	1.3195	1.5126	1.7317	1.9799	2.2609	2.5785	2.9372	3.3417	3.7975	4.3104
15	1.1610	1.3459	1.5580	1.8009	2.0789	2.3966	2.7590	3.1722	3.6425	4.1772	4.7846
16	1.1726	1.3728	1.6047	1.8730	2.1829	2.5404	2.9522	3.4259	3.9703	4.5950	5.3109

(continued)

17	1.1843	1.4002	1.6528	1.9479	2.2920	2.6928	3.1588	3.7030	4.3276	5.0545	5.8951
18	1.1961	1.4282	1.7024	2.0258	2.4066	2.8543	3.3799	3.9960	4.7171	5.5599	6.5436
19	1.2081	1.4568	1.7535	2.1068	2.5270	3.0256	3.6165	4.3157	5.1417	6.1159	7.2633
20	1.2202	1.4859	1.8061	2.1911	2.6533	3.2071	3.8697	4.6610	5.6044	6.7275	8.0623
21	1.2324	1.5157	1.8603	2.2788	2.7860	3.3996	4.1406	5.0338	6.1088	7.4002	8.9492
22	1.2447	1.5460	1.9161	2.3699	2.9253	3.6035	4.4304	5.4365	6.6586	8.1403	9.9336
23	1.2572	1.5769	1.9736	2.4647	3.0715	3.8197	4.7405	5.8715	7.2579	8.9543	11.0263
24	1.2697	1.6084	2.0328	2.5633	3.2251	4.0489	5.0724	6.3412	7.9111	9.8497	12.2392
25	1.2824	1.6406	2.0938	2.6658	3.3864	4.2919	5.4274	6.8485	8.6231	10.8347	13.5855
30	1.3478	1.8114	2.4273	3.2434	4.3219	5.7435	7.6123	10.0627	13.2677	17.4494	22.8923
35	1.4166	1.9999	2.8139	3.9461	5.5160	7.6861	10.6766	14.7853	20.4140	28.1024	38.5749
40	1.4889	2.2080	3.2620	4.8010	7.0400	10.2857	14.9745	21.7245	31.4094	45.2593	65.0009
45	1.5648	2.4379	3.7816	5.8412	8.9850	13.7646	21.0025	31.9204	48.3273	72.8905	109.5302
50	1.6446	2.6916	4.3839	7.1067	11.4674	18.4202	29.4570	46.9016	74.3575	117.3909	184.5648

(continued)

Period	12%	13%	14%	15%	16%	20%	25%	30%	35%
1	1.1200	1.1300	1.1400	1.1500	1.1600	1.2000	1.2500	1.3000	1.3500
2	1.2544	1.2769	1.2996	1.3225	1.3456	1.4400	1.5625	1.6900	1.8225
3	1.4049	1.4429	1.4815	1.5209	1.5609	1.7280	1.9531	2.1970	2.4604
4	1.5735	1.6305	1.6890	1.7490	1.8106	2.0736	2.4414	2.8561	3.3215
5	1.7623	1.8424	1.9254	2.0114	2.1003	2.4883	3.0518	3.7129	4.4840
6	1.9738	2.0820	2.1950	2.3131	2.4364	2.9860	3.8147	4.8268	6.0534
7	2.2107	2.3526	2.5023	2.6600	2.8262	3.5832	4.7684	6.2749	8.1722
8	2.4760	2.6584	2.8526	3.0590	3.2784	4.2998	5.9605	8.1573	11.0324
9	2.7731	3.0040	3.2519	3.5179	3.8030	5.1598	7.4506	10.6045	14.8937
10	3.1058	3.3946	3.7072	4.0456	4.4114	6.1917	9.3132	13.7858	20.1066
11	3.4785	3.8359	4.2262	4.6524	5.1173	7.4301	11.6415	17.9216	27.1439
12	3.8960	4.3345	4.8179	5.3503	5.9360	8.9161	14.5519	23.2981	36.6442
13	4.3635	4.8980	5.4924	6.1528	6.8858	10.6993	18.1899	30.2875	49.4697
14	4.8871	5.5348	6.2613	7.0757	7.9875	12.8392	22.7374	39.3738	66.7841
15	5.4736	6.2543	7.1379	8.1371	9.2655	15.4070	28.4217	51.1859	90.1585
16	6.1304	7.0673	8.1372	9.3576	10.7480	18.4884	35.5271	66.5417	121.7139

(continued)

17	6.8660	7.9861	9.2765	10.7613	12.4677	22.1861	44.4089	86.5042	164.3138
18	7.6900	9.0243	10.5752	12.3755	14.4625	26.6233	55.5112	112.4554	221.8236
19	8.6128	10.1974	12.0557	14.2318	16.7765	31.9480	69.3889	146.1920	299.4619
20	9.6463	11.5231	13.7435	16.3665	19.4608	38.3376	86.7362	190.0496	404.2736
21	10.8038	13.0211	15.6676	18.8215	22.5745	46.0051	108.4202	247.0645	545.7693
22	12.1003	14.7138	17.8610	21.6447	26.1864	55.2061	135.5253	321.1839	736.7886
23	13.5523	16.6266	20.3616	24.8915	30.3762	66.2474	169.4066	417.5391	994.6646
24	15.1786	18.7881	23.2122	28.6252	35.2364	79.4968	211.7582	542.8008	1342.7973
25	17.0001	21.2305	26.4619	32.9190	40.8742	95.3962	264.6978	705.6410	1812.7763
30	29.9599	39.1159	50.9502	66.2118	85.8499	237.3763	807.7936	2619.9956	8128.5495
35	52.7996	72.0685	98.1002	133.1755	180.3141	590.6682	2,465.1903	9,727.8604	36,448.6878
40	93.0510	132.7816	188.8835	267.8635	378.7212	1,469.7715	7,523.1638	36,118.8648	163,437.1347
45	163.9876	244.6414	363.6791	538.7693	795.4438	3,657.2620	22,958.8740	134,106.8167	732,857.5768
50	289.0022	450.7359	700.2330	1,083.6574	1,670.7038	9,100.4382	70,064.9232	497,929.2230	3,286,157.8795

Table A-2: Future Value Interest Factor for Ordinary Annuity

Period	1%	2%	3%	4%	5%	6%	7%	8%	9%	10%	11%
1	1.0000	1.0000	1.0000	1.0000	1.0000	1.0000	1.0000	1.0000	1.0000	1.0000	1.0000
2	2.0100	2.0200	2.0300	2.0400	2.0500	2.0600	2.0700	2.0800	2.0900	2.1000	2.1100
3	3.0301	3.0604	3.0909	3.1216	3.1525	3.1836	3.2149	3.2464	3.2781	3.3100	3.3421
4	4.0604	4.1216	4.1836	4.2465	4.3101	4.3746	4.4399	4.5061	4.5731	4.6410	4.7097
5	5.1010	5.2040	5.3091	5.4163	5.5256	5.6371	5.7507	5.8666	5.9847	6.1051	6.2278
6	6.1520	6.3081	6.4684	6.6330	6.8019	6.9753	7.1533	7.3359	7.5233	7.7156	7.9129
7	7.2135	7.4343	7.6625	7.8983	8.1420	8.3938	8.6540	8.9228	9.2004	9.4872	9.7833
8	8.2857	8.5830	8.8923	9.2142	9.5491	9.8975	10.2598	10.6366	11.0285	11.4359	11.8594
9	9.3685	9.7546	10.1591	10.5828	11.0266	11.4913	11.9780	12.4876	13.0210	13.5795	14.1640
10	10.4622	10.9497	11.4639	12.0061	12.5779	13.1808	13.8164	14.4866	15.1929	15.9374	16.7220
11	11.5668	12.1687	12.8078	13.4864	14.2068	14.9716	15.7836	16.6455	17.5603	18.5312	19.5614
12	12.6825	13.4121	14.1920	15.0258	15.9171	16.8699	17.8885	18.9771	20.1407	21.3843	22.7132
13	13.8093	14.6803	15.6178	16.6268	17.7130	18.8821	20.1406	21.4953	22.9534	24.5227	26.2116
14	14.9474	15.9739	17.0863	18.2919	19.5986	21.0151	22.5505	24.2149	26.0192	27.9750	30.0949

(continued)

15	16.0969	17.2934	18.5989	20.0236	21.5786	23.2760	25.1290	27.1521	29.3609	31.7725	34.4054
16	17.2579	18.6393	20.1569	21.8245	23.6575	25.6725	27.8881	30.3243	33.0034	35.9497	39.1899
17	18.4304	20.0121	21.7616	23.6975	25.8404	28.2129	30.8402	33.7502	36.9737	40.5447	44.5008
18	19.6147	21.4123	23.4144	25.6454	28.1324	30.9057	33.9990	37.4502	41.3013	45.5992	50.3959
19	20.8109	22.8406	25.1169	27.6712	30.5390	33.7600	37.3790	41.4463	46.0185	51.1591	56.9395
20	22.0190	24.2974	26.8704	29.7781	33.0660	36.7856	40.9955	45.7620	51.1601	57.2750	64.2028
21	23.2392	25.7833	28.6765	31.9692	35.7193	39.9927	44.8652	50.4229	56.7645	64.0025	72.2651
22	24.4716	27.2990	30.5368	34.2480	38.5052	43.3923	49.0057	55.4568	62.8733	71.4027	81.2143
23	25.7163	28.8450	32.4529	36.6179	41.4305	46.9958	53.4361	60.8933	69.5319	79.5430	91.1479
24	26.9735	30.4219	34.4265	39.0826	44.5020	50.8156	58.1767	66.7648	76.7898	88.4973	102.1742
25	28.2432	32.0303	36.4593	41.6459	47.7271	54.8645	63.2490	73.1059	84.7009	98.3471	114.4133
30	34.7849	40.5681	47.5754	56.0849	66.4388	79.0582	94.4608	113.2832	136.3075	164.4940	199.0209
35	41.6603	49.9945	60.4621	73.6522	90.3203	111.4348	138.2369	172.3168	215.7108	271.0244	341.5896
40	48.8864	60.4020	75.4013	95.0255	120.7998	154.7620	199.6351	259.0565	337.8824	442.5926	581.8261
45	56.4811	71.8927	92.7199	121.0294	159.7002	212.7435	285.7493	386.5056	525.8587	718.9048	986.6386
50	64.4632	84.5794	112.7969	152.6671	209.3480	290.3359	406.5289	573.7702	815.0836	1,163.9085	1,668.7712

(continued)

Period	12%	13%	14%	15%	16%	20%	25%	30%	35%
1	1.0000	1.0000	1.0000	1.0000	1.0000	1.0000	1.0000	1.0000	1.0000
2	2.1200	2.1300	2.1400	2.1500	2.1600	2.2000	2.2500	2.3000	2.3500
3	3.3744	3.4069	3.4396	3.4725	3.5056	3.6400	3.8125	3.9900	4.1725
4	4.7793	4.8498	4.9211	4.9934	5.0665	5.3680	5.7656	6.1870	6.6329
5	6.3528	6.4803	6.6101	6.7424	6.8771	7.4416	8.2070	9.0431	9.9544
6	8.1152	8.3227	8.5355	8.7537	8.9775	9.9299	11.2588	12.7560	14.4384
7	10.0890	10.4047	10.7305	11.0668	11.4139	12.9159	15.0735	17.5828	20.4919
8	12.2997	12.7573	13.2328	13.7268	14.2401	16.4991	19.8419	23.8577	28.6640
9	14.7757	15.4157	16.0853	16.7858	17.5185	20.7989	25.8023	32.0150	39.6964
10	17.5487	18.4197	19.3373	20.3037	21.3215	25.9587	33.2529	42.6195	54.5902
11	20.6546	21.8143	23.0445	24.3493	25.7329	32.1504	42.5661	56.4053	74.6967
12	24.1331	25.6502	27.2707	29.0017	30.8502	39.5805	54.2077	74.3270	101.8406
13	28.0291	29.9847	32.0887	34.3519	36.7862	48.4966	68.7596	97.6250	138.4848
14	32.3926	34.8827	37.5811	40.5047	43.6720	59.1959	86.9495	127.9125	187.9544
15	37.2797	40.4175	43.8424	47.5804	51.6595	72.0351	109.6868	167.2863	254.7385

(continued)

16	42.7533	46.6717	50.9804	55.7175	60.9250	87.4421	138.1085	218.4722	344.8970
17	48.8837	53.7391	59.1176	65.0751	71.6730	105.9306	173.6357	285.0139	466.6109
18	55.7497	61.7251	68.3941	75.8364	84.1407	128.1167	218.0446	371.5180	630.9247
19	63.4397	70.7494	78.9692	88.2118	98.6032	154.7400	273.5558	483.9734	852.7483
20	72.0524	80.9468	91.0249	102.4436	115.3797	186.6880	342.9447	630.1655	1152.2103
21	81.6987	92.4699	104.7684	118.8101	134.8405	225.0256	429.6809	820.2151	1556.4838
22	92.5026	105.4910	120.4350	137.6316	157.4150	271.0307	538.1011	1067.2796	2102.2532
23	104.6029	120.2048	138.2970	159.2764	183.6014	326.2369	673.6264	1388.4635	2839.0418
24	118.1552	136.8315	158.6586	184.1678	213.9776	392.4842	843.0329	1806.0026	3833.7064
25	133.3339	155.6196	181.8708	212.7930	249.2140	471.9811	1054.7912	2348.8033	5176.5037
30	241.3327	293.1992	356.7868	434.7451	530.3117	1181.8816	3227.1743	8729.9855	23221.5700
35	431.6635	546.6808	693.5727	881.1702	1120.7130	2948.3411	9856.7613	32422.8681	104136.2508
40	767.0914	1,013.7042	1,342.0251	1,779.0903	2,360.7572	7,343.8578	30,088.6554	120,392.8827	466,960.3848
45	1,358.2300	1,874.1646	2,590.5648	3,585.1285	4,965.2739	18,281.3099	91,831.4962	447,019.3890	2,093,875.9338
50	2,400.0182	3,459.5071	4,994.5213	7,217.7163	10,435.6488	45,497.1908	280,255.6929	1,659,760.7433	9,389,019.6556

Table A-3: Present Value Interest Factor for Single Amount

Period	1%	2%	3%	4%	5%	6%	7%	8%	9%	10%	11%
1	0.9901	0.9804	0.9709	0.9615	0.9524	0.9434	0.9346	0.9259	0.9174	0.9091	0.9009
2	0.9803	0.9612	0.9426	0.9246	0.9070	0.8900	0.8734	0.8573	0.8417	0.8264	0.8116
3	0.9706	0.9423	0.9151	0.8890	0.8638	0.8396	0.8163	0.7938	0.7722	0.7513	0.7312
4	0.9610	0.9238	0.8885	0.8548	0.8227	0.7921	0.7629	0.7350	0.7084	0.6830	0.6587
5	0.9515	0.9057	0.8626	0.8219	0.7835	0.7473	0.7130	0.6806	0.6499	0.6209	0.5935
6	0.9420	0.8880	0.8375	0.7903	0.7462	0.7050	0.6663	0.6302	0.5963	0.5645	0.5346
7	0.9327	0.8706	0.8131	0.7599	0.7107	0.6651	0.6227	0.5835	0.5470	0.5132	0.4817
8	0.9235	0.8535	0.7894	0.7307	0.6768	0.6274	0.5820	0.5403	0.5019	0.4665	0.4339
9	0.9143	0.8368	0.7664	0.7026	0.6446	0.5919	0.5439	0.5002	0.4604	0.4241	0.3909
10	0.9053	0.8203	0.7441	0.6756	0.6139	0.5584	0.5083	0.4632	0.4224	0.3855	0.3522
11	0.8963	0.8043	0.7224	0.6496	0.5847	0.5268	0.4751	0.4289	0.3875	0.3505	0.3173
12	0.8874	0.7885	0.7014	0.6246	0.5568	0.4970	0.4440	0.3971	0.3555	0.3186	0.2858
13	0.8787	0.7730	0.6810	0.6006	0.5303	0.4688	0.4150	0.3677	0.3262	0.2897	0.2575
14	0.8700	0.7579	0.6611	0.5775	0.5051	0.4423	0.3878	0.3405	0.2992	0.2633	0.2320
15	0.8613	0.7430	0.6419	0.5553	0.4810	0.4173	0.3624	0.3152	0.2745	0.2394	0.2090

(continued)

16	0.8528	0.7284	0.6232	0.5339	0.4581	0.3936	0.3387	0.2919	0.2519	0.2176	0.1883
17	0.8444	0.7142	0.6050	0.5134	0.4363	0.3714	0.3166	0.2703	0.2311	0.1978	0.1696
18	0.8360	0.7002	0.5874	0.4936	0.4155	0.3503	0.2959	0.2502	0.2120	0.1799	0.1528
19	0.8277	0.6864	0.5703	0.4746	0.3957	0.3305	0.2765	0.2317	0.1945	0.1635	0.1377
20	0.8195	0.6730	0.5537	0.4564	0.3769	0.3118	0.2584	0.2145	0.1784	0.1486	0.1240
21	0.8114	0.6598	0.5375	0.4388	0.3589	0.2942	0.2415	0.1987	0.1637	0.1351	0.1117
22	0.8034	0.6468	0.5219	0.4220	0.3418	0.2775	0.2257	0.1839	0.1502	0.1228	0.1007
23	0.7954	0.6342	0.5067	0.4057	0.3256	0.2618	0.2109	0.1703	0.1378	0.1117	0.0907
24	0.7876	0.6217	0.4919	0.3901	0.3101	0.2470	0.1971	0.1577	0.1264	0.1015	0.0817
25	0.7798	0.6095	0.4776	0.3751	0.2953	0.2330	0.1842	0.1460	0.1160	0.0923	0.0736
30	0.7419	0.5521	0.4120	0.3083	0.2314	0.1741	0.1314	0.0994	0.0754	0.0573	0.0437
35	0.7059	0.5000	0.3554	0.2534	0.1813	0.1301	0.0937	0.0676	0.0490	0.0356	0.0259
40	0.6717	0.4529	0.3066	0.2083	0.1420	0.0972	0.0668	0.0460	0.0318	0.0221	0.0154
45	0.6391	0.4102	0.2644	0.1712	0.1113	0.0727	0.0476	0.0313	0.0207	0.0137	0.0091
50	0.6080	0.3715	0.2281	0.1407	0.0872	0.0543	0.0339	0.0213	0.0134	0.0085	0.0054

(continued)

Period	12%	13%	14%	15%	16%	20%	25%	30%	35%
1	0.8929	0.8850	0.8772	0.8696	0.8621	0.8333	0.8000	0.7692	0.7407
2	0.7972	0.7831	0.7695	0.7561	0.7432	0.6944	0.6400	0.5917	0.5487
3	0.7118	0.6931	0.6750	0.6575	0.6407	0.5787	0.5120	0.4552	0.4064
4	0.6355	0.6133	0.5921	0.5718	0.5523	0.4823	0.4096	0.3501	0.3011
5	0.5674	0.5428	0.5194	0.4972	0.4761	0.4019	0.3277	0.2693	0.2230
6	0.5066	0.4803	0.4556	0.4323	0.4104	0.3349	0.2621	0.2072	0.1652
7	0.4523	0.4251	0.3996	0.3759	0.3538	0.2791	0.2097	0.1594	0.1224
8	0.4039	0.3762	0.3506	0.3269	0.3050	0.2326	0.1678	0.1226	0.0906
9	0.3606	0.3329	0.3075	0.2843	0.2630	0.1938	0.1342	0.0943	0.0671
10	0.3220	0.2946	0.2697	0.2472	0.2267	0.1615	0.1074	0.0725	0.0497
11	0.2875	0.2607	0.2366	0.2149	0.1954	0.1346	0.0859	0.0558	0.0368
12	0.2567	0.2307	0.2076	0.1869	0.1685	0.1122	0.0687	0.0429	0.0273
13	0.2292	0.2042	0.1821	0.1625	0.1452	0.0935	0.0550	0.0330	0.0202
14	0.2046	0.1807	0.1597	0.1413	0.1252	0.0779	0.0440	0.0254	0.0150
15	0.1827	0.1599	0.1401	0.1229	0.1079	0.0649	0.0352	0.0195	0.0111

(continued)

16	0.1631	0.1415	0.1229	0.1069	0.0930	0.0541	0.0281	0.0150	0.0082
17	0.1456	0.1252	0.1078	0.0929	0.0802	0.0451	0.0225	0.0116	0.0061
18	0.1300	0.1108	0.0946	0.0808	0.0691	0.0376	0.0180	0.0089	0.0045
19	0.1161	0.0981	0.0829	0.0703	0.0596	0.0313	0.0144	0.0068	0.0033
20	0.1037	0.0868	0.0728	0.0611	0.0514	0.0261	0.0115	0.0053	0.0025
21	0.0926	0.0768	0.0638	0.0531	0.0443	0.0217	0.0092	0.0040	0.0018
22	0.0826	0.0680	0.0560	0.0462	0.0382	0.0181	0.0074	0.0031	0.0014
23	0.0738	0.0601	0.0491	0.0402	0.0329	0.0151	0.0059	0.0024	0.0010
24	0.0659	0.0532	0.0431	0.0349	0.0284	0.0126	0.0047	0.0018	0.0007
25	0.0588	0.0471	0.0378	0.0304	0.0245	0.0105	0.0038	0.0014	0.0006
30	0.0334	0.0256	0.0196	0.0151	0.0116	0.0042	0.0012	0.0004	0.0001
35	0.0189	0.0139	0.0102	0.0075	0.0055	0.0017	0.0004	0.0001	0.0000
40	0.0107	0.0075	0.0053	0.0037	0.0026	0.0007	0.0001	0.000028	0.000006
45	0.0061	0.0041	0.0027	0.0019	0.0013	0.0003	0.00004	0.00001	0.000001
50	0.0035	0.0022	0.0014	0.0009	0.0006	0.0001	0.00001	0.000002	0.0000003

Table A-4: Present Value Ordinary Annuity

Period	1%	2%	3%	4%	5%	6%	7%	8%	9%	10%	11%
1	0.9901	0.9804	0.9709	0.9615	0.9524	0.9434	0.9346	0.9259	0.9174	0.9091	0.9009
2	1.9704	1.9416	1.9135	1.8861	1.8594	1.8334	1.8080	1.7833	1.7591	1.7355	1.7125
3	2.9410	2.8839	2.8286	2.7751	2.7232	2.6730	2.6243	2.5771	2.5313	2.4869	2.4437
4	3.9020	3.8077	3.7171	3.6299	3.5460	3.4651	3.3872	3.3121	3.2397	3.1699	3.1024
5	4.8534	4.7135	4.5797	4.4518	4.3295	4.2124	4.1002	3.9927	3.8897	3.7908	3.6959
6	5.7955	5.6014	5.4172	5.2421	5.0757	4.9173	4.7665	4.6229	4.4859	4.3553	4.2305
7	6.7282	6.4720	6.2303	6.0021	5.7864	5.5824	5.3893	5.2064	5.0330	4.8684	4.7122
8	7.6517	7.3255	7.0197	6.7327	6.4632	6.2098	5.9713	5.7466	5.5348	5.3349	5.1461
9	8.5660	8.1622	7.7861	7.4353	7.1078	6.8017	6.5152	6.2469	5.9952	5.7590	5.5370
10	9.4713	8.9826	8.5302	8.1109	7.7217	7.3601	7.0236	6.7101	6.4177	6.1446	5.8892
11	10.3676	9.7868	9.2526	8.7605	8.3064	7.8869	7.4987	7.1390	6.8052	6.4951	6.2065
12	11.2551	10.5753	9.9540	9.3851	8.8633	8.3838	7.9427	7.5361	7.1607	6.8137	6.4924
13	12.1337	11.3484	10.6350	9.9856	9.3936	8.8527	8.3577	7.9038	7.4869	7.1034	6.7499
14	13.0037	12.1062	11.2961	10.5631	9.8986	9.2950	8.7455	8.2442	7.7862	7.3667	6.9819
15	13.8651	12.8493	11.9379	11.1184	10.3797	9.7122	9.1079	8.5595	8.0607	7.6061	7.1909
16	14.7179	13.5777	12.5611	11.6523	10.8378	10.1059	9.4466	8.8514	8.3126	7.8237	7.3792

(continued)

17	7.5488	8.0216	8.5436	9.1216	9.7632	10.4773	11.2741	12.1657	13.1661	14.2919	15.5623
18	7.7016	8.2014	8.7556	9.3719	10.0591	10.8276	11.6896	12.6593	13.7535	14.9920	16.3983
19	7.8393	8.3649	8.9501	9.6036	10.3356	11.1581	12.0853	13.1339	14.3238	15.6785	17.2260
20	7.9633	8.5136	9.1285	9.8181	10.5940	11.4699	12.4622	13.5903	14.8775	16.3514	18.0456
21	8.0751	8.6487	9.2922	10.0168	10.8355	11.7641	12.8212	14.0292	15.4150	17.0112	18.8570
22	8.1757	8.7715	9.4424	10.2007	11.0612	12.0416	13.1630	14.4511	15.9369	17.6580	19.6604
23	8.2664	8.8832	9.5802	10.3711	11.2722	12.3034	13.4886	14.8568	16.4436	18.2922	20.4558
24	8.3481	8.9847	9.7066	10.5288	11.4693	12.5504	13.7986	15.2470	16.9355	18.9139	21.2434
25	8.4217	9.0770	9.8226	10.6748	11.6536	12.7834	14.0939	15.6221	17.4131	19.5235	22.0232
30	8.6938	9.4269	10.2737	11.2578	12.4090	13.7648	15.3725	17.2920	19.6004	22.3965	25.8077
35	8.8552	9.6442	10.5668	11.6546	12.9477	14.4982	16.3742	18.6646	21.4872	24.9986	29.4086
40	8.9511	9.7791	10.7574	11.9246	13.3317	15.0463	17.1591	19.7928	23.1148	27.3555	32.8347
45	9.0079	9.8628	10.8812	12.1084	13.6055	15.4558	17.7741	20.7200	24.5187	29.4902	36.0945
50	9.0417	9.9148	10.9617	12.2335	13.8007	15.7619	18.2559	21.4822	25.7298	31.4236	39.1961

(continued)

Period	12%	13%	14%	15%	16%	20%	25%	30%	35%
1	0.8929	0.8850	0.8772	0.8696	0.8621	0.8333	0.8000	0.7692	0.7407
2	1.6901	1.6681	1.6467	1.6257	1.6052	1.5278	1.4400	1.3609	1.2894
3	2.4018	2.3612	2.3216	2.2832	2.2459	2.1065	1.9520	1.8161	1.6959
4	3.0373	2.9745	2.9137	2.8550	2.7982	2.5887	2.3616	2.1662	1.9969
5	3.6048	3.5172	3.4331	3.3522	3.2743	2.9906	2.6893	2.4356	2.2200
6	4.1114	3.9975	3.8887	3.7845	3.6847	3.3255	2.9514	2.6427	2.3852
7	4.5638	4.4226	4.2883	4.1604	4.0386	3.6046	3.1611	2.8021	2.5075
8	4.9676	4.7988	4.6389	4.4873	4.3436	3.8372	3.3289	2.9247	2.5982
9	5.3282	5.1317	4.9464	4.7716	4.6065	4.0310	3.4631	3.0190	2.6653
10	5.6502	5.4262	5.2161	5.0188	4.8332	4.1925	3.5705	3.0915	2.7150
11	5.9377	5.6869	5.4527	5.2337	5.0286	4.3271	3.6564	3.1473	2.7519
12	6.1944	5.9176	5.6603	5.4206	5.1971	4.4392	3.7251	3.1903	2.7792
13	6.4235	6.1218	5.8424	5.5831	5.3423	4.5327	3.7801	3.2233	2.7994
14	6.6282	6.3025	6.0021	5.7245	5.4675	4.6106	3.8241	3.2487	2.8144
15	6.8109	6.4624	6.1422	5.8474	5.5755	4.6755	3.8593	3.2682	2.8255
16	6.9740	6.6039	6.2651	5.9542	5.6685	4.7296	3.8874	3.2832	2.8337
17	7.1196	6.7291	6.3729	6.0472	5.7487	4.7746	3.9099	3.2948	2.8398
18	7.2497	6.8399	6.4674	6.1280	5.8178	4.8122	3.9279	3.3037	2.8443

(continued)

19	7.3658	6.9380	6.5504	6.1982	5.8775	4.8435	3.9424	3.3105	2.8476
20	7.4694	7.0248	6.6231	6.2593	5.9288	4.8696	3.9539	3.3158	2.8501
21	7.5620	7.1016	6.6870	6.3125	5.9731	4.8913	3.9631	3.3198	2.8519
22	7.6446	7.1695	6.7429	6.3587	6.0113	4.9094	3.9705	3.3230	2.8533
23	7.7184	7.2297	6.7921	6.3988	6.0442	4.9245	3.9764	3.3254	2.8543
24	7.7843	7.2829	6.8351	6.4338	6.0726	4.9371	3.9811	3.3272	2.8550
25	7.8431	7.3300	6.8729	6.4641	6.0971	4.9476	3.9849	3.3286	2.8556
30	8.0552	7.4957	7.0027	6.5660	6.1772	4.9789	3.9950	3.3321	2.8568
35	8.1755	7.5856	7.0700	6.6166	6.2153	4.9915	3.9984	3.3330	2.8571
40	8.2438	7.6344	7.1050	6.6418	6.2335	4.9966	3.9995	3.3332	2.8571
45	8.2825	7.6609	7.1232	6.6543	6.2421	4.9986	3.9998	3.3333	2.8571
50	8.3045	7.6752	7.1327	6.6605	6.2463	4.9995	3.9999	3.3333	2.8571

Test Yourself Answers

CHAPTER 1

1. Three objectives of accounting:
    a. Helps users make investment and credit decisions
    b. Helps users determine risk
    c. Informs users about the economic resources of and claims against the enterprise

2. Accounting information is reliable if it is dependable and free from error or bias. Reliability should not be confused with absolute accuracy. Contrary to popular belief, reliable accounting information is often based on estimates and forecasts and therefore cannot always be precise. Relevant information is a bit different but equally as important in achieving usefulness.

3. Financial accounting is different from managerial accounting in the users it serves. Financial accounting primarily serves the needs of investors and creditors while managerial accounting serves the needs of internal constituents—managers and staffs—and helps support their decision making.

4. The four primary financial statements are balance sheet, income statement, statement of changes in equity, and statement of cash flows.

5. Despite audits, there are still limitations and risks associated with financial reporting. Since financial reports include mostly

numbers, they emphasize only those specifics about an enterprise that can be quantified. The cost principle and monetary unit assumption also present some important limitations, particularly when one considers inflation. The historical cost principle can lead to serious value distortions on balance sheets. Accounting is not a science but an art. Judgments and estimates are necessary and can be flawed. Financial statements may not be of uniform quality and reliability because of differences in the character and quality of judgments exercised by accountants and management. Then there is the risk that something significant has not been disclosed. Despite internal controls, fraudulent activity can sometimes render internal controls inadequate.

CHAPTER 2

1. A company purchases $1,500 of equipment paying cash. Update the accounting equation below based on this transaction.

Assets of $20,000 =	Liabilities of $12,000 +	Equity of $8,000
− $1,500 Cash + $1,500 Equipment	NO CHANGE	NO CHANGE
Assets of $20,000 =	Liabilities of $12,000 +	Equity of $8,000

2. A company provides $5,000 of services to a customer and is paid cash.

Assets of $30,000 =	Liabilities of $18,000 +	Equity of $12,000
+ $5,000 Cash	NO CHANGE	+ $5,000 Revenue
Assets of $35,000 =	Liabilities of $18,000 +	Equity of $17,000

3. A company purchases $25,000 of inventory on credit and a $100,000 parcel of land for cash.

Assets of $300,000 =	Liabilities of $180,000 +	Equity of $120,000
+ $25,000 Inventory – $100,000 Cash + $100,000 Land	+ $25,000 Accounts Payable	
Assets of $325,000 =	Liabilities of $205,000 +	Equity of $120,000

4. The steps of the accounting cycle are the following:

   A. Identify and gather transaction information

   B. Analyze and journalize the transactions

   C. Post to the ledgers

   D. Prepare the unadjusted trial balance

   E. Make adjusting entries

   F. Prepare the financial statements

   G. Close the books

5. An adverse opinion is given when the financial statements do not fairly present the financial position, results of operations, and the cash flows of the entity in conformity with GAAP.

CHAPTER 3

1. Current assets $345,000.

2. Balance sheet values:

Asset	Description	Balance sheet value
Cash	$10,000 in the bank with a deposit of $5,000 anticipated next week	$10,000 cash; the $5,000 might be an account receivable
Accounts receivable	$100,000 owed from customers with $20,000 estimated as uncollectible	$80,000 (net receivable)
Inventory	Cost of $200,000 with a market value of $150,000	$150,000 (lower-of-cost-or-market rule)
Property, plant, and equipment	Cost of $1,000,000 and accumulated deprecia-tion of $30,000	$970,000 (net book value)
Intangible assets	Cost of patents is $50,000 with $10,000 amortized	$40,000 (cost minus the amortized amount)

3. The liabilities are $230,000.

4. The equity is $380,000.

5. A. INT

   B. CA

   C. E

   D. LTL

   E. NC

   F. CL

   G. INT

   H. CL

   I. CL

CHAPTER 4

1. B, D, E

2. Gross profit $270,000

3. Single-Step Income Statement:

Revenues	
Net sales	$2,000,000
Gains	150,000
Total revenues	$2,150,000
Expenses	
Cost of goods sold	$1,100,000
Selling and administrative expenses	600,000
Interest expense	11,000
Losses	9,500
Income tax expense	160,000
Total expenses	$1,880,500
Net income	$269,500

4. Multiple-Step Income Statement:

Net sales	$2,000,000
Cost of goods sold	1,100,000
Gross profit	$900,000
Selling and administrative expenses	600,000
Operating profit	$300,000
Other revenues and gains	150,000
Other expenses and losses	20,500
Pretax income from continuing operations	$429,500
Income taxes	160,000
Net income	$269,500

5. ($2,500,000 − 600,000) / 750,000 = $2.53

6. Retained earnings, January 1, 2009: $500,000

    Less dividends: 200,000

    Plus net income: 350,000

    Retained earnings, December 31, 2009: $650,000

CHAPTER 5

1. A, E, F
2. C, D, G, H
3. $17,000
4. $123,000
5. $45,000

CHAPTER 6

1. Net realizable value: $490,000. Uncollectible accounts expense: $10,000.

    The net realizable value is found by subtracting the $10,000 uncollectible amount from the $500,000 owed by customers. Under the direct write-off method, the expense is taken when specific customers are recognized as uncollectible; therefore, the uncollectible expense is $10,000 as a result of the bankruptcy.

2. Net realizable value: $477,500. Uncollectible accounts expense: $22,500.

    The net realizable value is $477,500, which is the difference between the amount owed by customers ($500,000) and the estimated uncollectible amount of $22,500 ($500,000 × .03). The uncollectible accounts expense is $22,500—which is the estimated amount that is uncollectible. The $10,000 attributed to the customer who has entered bankruptcy would reduce the allowance for uncollectible accounts and would reduce the accounts receivable balance. It would have no impact on the uncollectible accounts expense because under accrual accounting rules, that is the function of an estimate of uncollectible accounts.

3. Here are the estimated uncollectible amounts from each age group:

Not yet due: $25,000 × .01 = $250

1−30 days past due: $36,500 × .04 = $1,460

31−60 days past due: $21,600 × .08 = $1,728

61−90 days past due: $6,400 × .1 = $640

Over 90 days past due: $38,900 × .3 = $11,670

Total uncollectible accounts: $15,748

Net realizable value: $112,652 ($128,400 − $15,748)

Uncollectible accounts expense: $15,748

4. FIFO: $1,705

LIFO: $1,495

Average cost: $1,600

FIFO: 35 units × $11 = $385 + 110 units × $12 = $1,702

LIFO: 100 units × $10 + 45 units × $11 = $1,495

Average cost: $11.03 × 145 = $1,600

5.

Face Value	Cost	Premium or Discount (Label P or D)	Carrying Amount
$100,000	$90,000	D	$90,000
$120,000	$150,000	P	$150,000
$110,000	$135,000	P	$135,000

CHAPTER 7

1. Initial cost is $21,350, found as follows:

Price:	$20,000 ($25,000 × (1 – .2)
Freight:	500
Electrician:	600
Inspection:	250
Cost:	$21,350

2. The initial cost is $3,250 ($3,000 + $250) with the depreciable cost equal to $3,050 ($3,250 – 200). The annual depreciation under the straight-line method is $610 ($3,050 / 5).

Years	Annual Depreciation	Accumulated Depreciation	Book Value at End of Year
1	$610	$610	$2,640
2	$610	$1,220	$2,030
3	$610	$1,830	$1,420
4	$610	$2,440	$810
5	$610	$3,050	$200

3. The rate for straight-line is 20 percent (1 / 5); therefore the double-declining-balance rate is 40 percent.

Years	Annual Depreciation	Accumulated Depreciation	Book Value at End of Year
1	$3,250 × .4 = $1,300	$1,300	$1,950
2	$1,950 × .4 = $780	$2,080	$1,170
3	$1,170 × .4 = $468	$2,548	$702
4	$702 – .4 = $280.80	$2,828.80	$421.20
5	$421.20 – 200 = $221.20	$3,050	$200

4. The depreciation rate is .20 per mile ($40,000 − 8,000 = $32,000 / 160,000 = .2).

Years	Annual Depreciation	Accumulated Depreciation	Book Value at End of Year
1	15,000 × .2 = $3,000	$3,000	$37,000
2	22,000 × .2 = $4,400	$7,400	$32,600
3	20,000 × .2 = $ 4,000	$11,400	$28,600
4	18,000 × .2 = $3,600	$15,000	$25,000
5	20,000 × .2 = $4,000	$19,000	$21,000

5. Copyright—net of amortization: $14,100

Assuming a 50-year life, the annual amortization would be $15,000 / 50 = $300 per year. Three years' worth of amortization would be $900.

CHAPTER 8

1. Warranty expense 201x = $84,000. Warranty payable as of the year-end 201X = $87,000.

2. Current portion of mortgage payable is $15,000. Under long-term liabilities, the mortgage payable balance would be reported as $485,000.

3. Discount amortized as a result of the interest payment is $6,000. Carrying value of the bond after interest is paid is $936,000.

4. Amount of premium amortized as a result of the interest payment is $7,000. Carrying value of the bond after interest is paid is $1,093,000.

CHAPTER 9

1.

Characteristic	Managerial Accounting or Financial Accounting?
The users are internal managers and staff	Managerial Accounting
The guidelines are spelled out in GAAP	Financial Accounting
The purpose is to provide information for credit and investment decisions	Financial Accounting
No independent review or opinion is required since the information is only examined by internal managers and staff	Managerial Accounting

2. Job 100 cost = $4,300 ($1,000 + 3,000 + (10 × $30)). The overhead rate is $30 = $1,500,000 of budgeted overhead / 50,000 machine hours.

Job 101 cost = $6,750 ($2,000 + $4,000 + (25 × $30))

3. Job 100 cost = $7,900 ($1,000 + 3,000 + ($3000 × 1.3)). The overhead rate is 130 percent of direct labor cost; therefore, a factor of 1.3 is used to estimate the overhead (i.e., $3,000 of direct labor cost × 1.3).

Job 101 cost = $11,200 ($2,000 + $4,000 + ($4,000 × 1.3))

4. Equivalent unit cost is $72.01, found as follows:

Direct materials of $56,000 / 1,300 units = $43.08

Conversion costs of $32,400 / (1,000 + 300 × .4) = $32,400 / 1,120 = $28.93

Direct material cost per unit $43.08 + conversion cost per unit $28.93 = $72.01 equivalent cost per unit

5. Finished goods: $72,010 (1,000 × $72.01)

    Work in process: $16,390 ($88,400 total cost minus $72,010 of finished goods)

CHAPTER 10

1. Total monthly cost = $167.99 ($39.99 + (2,100 − 500) × .08)

2.

Revenues	$100,000
Variable costs	47,500
Contribution margin	$52,500
Fixed costs	24,500
Operating Income	$28,000

The contribution margin ratio is 52.5% = $52,500/$100,000 = .525 = 52.5%.

3. $300,000 / (50 − 17) = 9,090.9 = 9,091 units

4. $300,000 + $50,000 / $33 = $350,000 / 33 = 10,606 units

5. $500,000 = $6x + 3 × $10x + 4 × $14x = $500,000 = $92 = $500,000 = 5,435; therefore, Product A = 5,435 units, Product B = 3 × 5,435 = 16,305, Product C = 4 × 5,435 = 21,740.

CHAPTER 11

1. Gross profit margin: 25%

    Net profit margin: 7%

    Return on assets: 14%

    Return on equity: 20%

2. A/R turnover: 7.63

    ACP: 47.82

    Inventory turnover: 43.33

    Total asset turnover: 2.08

3. Current ratio: 2.3 times

   Quick ratio: 1.8 times

4. Debt-to-total assets: 46.9%

   Times interest earned: 9

   Fixed charge coverage: 6

5.

Ratios	Industry Average	Company Ratio	Comment: "Good" or "needs improvement"
Gross profit margin	21.58%	30%	Good
Net profit margin	9.6%	5%	Needs improvement
Average collection period	37	32	Good
Inventory turnover	23.5	12	Needs improvement
Times interest earned	6	10	Good
Current ratio	1.38	2	Good

CHAPTER 12

1. Income Statement

	Actual	Budget	Variance	Favorable or Unfavorable
Sales in units	22,000	23,500	(1,500)	U
Sales	$484,000	$505,250	($21,250)	U
Cost of goods sold	264,000	282,000	(18,000)	U
Gross profit	$220,000	$223,250	($3,250)	U
Selling expenses	28,000	26,400	1,600	U
General and administrative expenses	19,700	21,000	(1,300)	F
Operating income	$172,300	$175,850	($3,550)	U
Interest expense	11,000	9,000	2,000	U
Income before income taxes	$161,300	$166,850	($5,550)	U
Income taxes	48,390	50,055	(1,665)	F
Net income	$112,910	$116,795	($3,885)	U

2. Income Statement

	Actual	Flexible Budget
Sales in units	22,000	22,000
Sales	$484,000	$473,000
Cost of goods sold	264,000	264,000
Gross profit	$220,000	$209,000
Selling expenses	28,000	28,000
General and administrative expenses	19,700	19,700
Operating income	$172,300	$161,300
Interest expense	11,000	0
Income before income taxes	$161,300	$161,300
Income taxes	48,390	48,390
Net income	$112,910	$112,910

3. Price variance = $4,750. Unfavorable, calculated as follows:

    ($3.25 – $3.00) × 19,000 = $4,750 Unfavorable

    Efficiency variance = $3,000. Favorable, calculated as follows:

    (19,000 – 20,000) × $3.00 = $3,000 Favorable

4. Price variance = $2,125. Favorable, calculated as follows:

    ($14.75 – $15) × 8,500 = $2,125 Favorable

    $14.75 = $125,375 / 8,500 hours

    Efficiency variance = $3,750. Unfavorable, calculated as follows:

    (8,500 – 8,250) × $15 = $3,750 Unfavorable

    8,250 = 5,500 units × 1.5 hours

    The efficiency variance is unfavorable because it took 8,500 hours when it should have (based on a standard of 1.5 hours per unit) taken 8,250 hours.

CHAPTER 13

1. This is a future value of a single amount problem. Here's how you find the answer using the time value of money table:

    $10,000 × 3.6425 = $36,425

    The FVIF for a single amount can be found at the intersection of 9 percent and 15 periods.

2. This a future value of an annuity problem. Here's how to solve the problem using the time value of money table:

    $4,000 × 94.4609 = $377,843.60

    The FVIFA of 94.4609 can be found at the intersection of 7 percent and 30 periods.

3. This a present value of a single amount problem. Here's how to solve it using the time value of money table (illustration 15.4):

$400,000 \times 0.6806 = \$272,240$

The PVIF for a single amount can be found at the intersection of 8 percent and 5 periods.

4. This is a present value of an annuity problem. Here's how to solve it using the time value of money table for the present value of an annuity:

$6,000 \times 6.4176 = \$38,505.60$

The PVFA of 6.4176 can be found at the intersection of 9 percent and 10 periods.

5. This problem involves the discounting of a series of even cash flows. The present value of the four cash flows is $11,875.40, as shown on the following case.

Year	Cash Flow	PVIF $_{6\%, n}$	Present Value
1	$2,000	0.9434	$1,886.80
2	$3,000	0.8899	$2,669.70
3	$4,000	0.8396	$3,358.40
4	$5,000	0.7921	$3,960.50
		Total	$11,875.40

To answer this part of the problem, you must find the future value of each cash flow and then total them—as shown below. The answer is $15,564.

Year	Cash Flow	FVIF $_{5\%}$	Future Value
1	$2,000	1.2155	$2,431
2	$3,000	1.1576	$3,473
3	$4,000	1.1025	$4,410
4	$5,000	1.05	$5,250
		Total	$15,564

CHAPTER 14

1. First calculate the present value of the interest payments: $120 × 8.0607 = $967.28.

    Then calculate the present value of the maturity value: $1,000 × .2745 = $274.50.

    Sum the two present values: ($967.28 + $274.50) = $1,241.78.

2. $120 × 8.5595 = $1,027.14

    $1,000 × .3152 = $315.20

    Sum the two present values: ($1,027.14 + $315.20) = $1,342.34.

    If the bond was a zero coupon bond, it would be valued at the present value of the maturity (face) value, which in this case is $315.20.

3. $4.80 / .1 = $48

4. $2 / (.12 − .05) = $28.57

5. Book value per share: ($2,500,000 − 900,000 − 550,000) / 300,000 = $3.50; liquidation value per share: ($2,650,000 − 900,000 − 550,000) / 300,000 = $4.00.

CHAPTER 15

1. 9% × (1 − .4) = 7.2%

2. 8.25% × (1 − .3) = 5.775%

3. The dividend is $5 (.1 × $50).

    $5 / $60 = 8.33%

4. $3 / $40 + .07 = .075 + .07 = 14.5%

5. See below.

Sources of Capital	Capital	Proportions	Cost	Weighted Cost
Long-term bank loan	$1,040,000	0.10 ×	7.20% =	0.720%
Bonds	2,080,000	0.20 ×	5.78% =	1.155%
Preferred stock	2,080,000	0.20 ×	8.33% =	1.666%
Common stock	4,160,000	0.40 ×	14.50% =	5.800%
Retained earnings	1,040,000	0.10 ×	14.50% =	1.450%
	$10,400,000	1.00		10.791%

CHAPTER 16

1. A. I

    B. T

    C. O

    D. I

    E. I

    F. O

2. Purchase price: $110,000

    Installation and training: 15,000

    Net proceeds from sale of old asset: 94,000*

    Increase in working capital: 23,000

    Initial investment: $242,000

    *The capital gain is $20,000 ($100,000 − 80,000 = $20,000). The gain is taxed at 30 percent, which results in a tax of $6,000. Therefore, the net proceeds are $94,000 ($100,000 − $6,000).

3. The following represent incremental cash flows:

Operating cash flows	$14,400
Sale of asset	$100,000
Less taxes on sale of asset	$5,000*
Working capital	$10,000
Total incremental cash flow for year 3	$119,400

*$100,000 − $75,000 = $25,000 gain × 20% = $5,000 tax.

CHAPTER 17

1. 4.44 years = 4 + 25,000 / 45,000

2. If you use a financial calculator or the Microsoft Excel NPV function, your answer will be ($8,658.17). Using the time value of money present value interest factors for 12 percent, your answer will be ($8,658.90), calculated as follows:

Years	Cash Flows	PVIF 12%	Present Value
0	($75,000)		($75,000)
1	$3,000	0.8929	$2,678.70
2	$22,000	0.7972	$17,538.40
3	$20,000	0.7118	$14,236.00
4	$10,000	0.6355	$6,355.00
5	$45,000	0.5674	$25,533.00
		NPV	($8,658.90)

The difference between the financial calculator/MS Excel−derived NPV and the NPV as a result of using the present value interest factors is because of rounding used in the tables.

3. The IRR of this investment is 14.03 percent, which you can find by using a financial calculator or Microsoft Excel. If you use the time value of money table for the present value of a single amount, you must try to find the discount rate that makes the NPV equal to zero (or as close to zero as possible). A good starting point is the discount rate of 12 percent (the cost of capital). Using the 12 percent discount rate, your NPV will be $5,786.50, which means that the IRR is some number higher than 12 percent. If you try 15 percent, the NPV will be negative, which means that the IRR is higher than 12 percent but lower than 15 percent. At 14 percent, the NPV is $80.30—which is as close to zero as you are going to get using the tables. Therefore, if you answered that the IRR is about 14 percent, you are correct.

4. With $1,000,000 to invest in capital investments and with the goal of wealth maximization, the optimal mix of projects would be G and E. That would involve a total up-front commitment of $950,000 with the greatest combined NPV ($500,000). The next closest would be the combination of G and D, which would commit the entire $1,000,000 budget but would only produce $480,000 of net present value. When wealth maximization is the goal and the budget is limited, prudent capital rationing would involve accepting the combination of investments that can contribute the greatest amount of wealth to the organization. Even though some projects might have a higher IRR, the greatest amount of wealth will be produced if the focus is on the NPV.

Glossary

Absorption costing: The method under which all manufacturing costs, both variable and fixed, are treated as product costs, with nonmanufacturing costs; e.g., selling and administrative expenses, being treated as period costs.

Accelerated depreciation: A method of calculating depreciation with larger amounts in the first year(s).

Account: The detailed record of a particular asset, liability, owners' equity, revenue, or expense.

Accountant's opinion: A signed statement regarding the financial status of an entity from an independent public accountant, after examination of that entity's records and accounts.

Accounting: The systematic recording, reporting, and analysis of financial transactions of a business.

Accounting concepts: The assumptions underlying the preparation of financial statements; i.e., the basic assumptions of a going concern: accruals, consistency, and prudence.

Accounting cycle: Series of steps in recording an accounting event from the time a transaction occurs to its reflection in the financial statements.

Accounting equation: Assets = Liabilities + Stockholders' Equity.

Accounts payable: Money owed to suppliers; trade accounts of the enterprise representing obligations to pay for goods and services received.

Accounts receivable: A current asset representing money due for services performed or merchandise sold on credit.

Accrual accounting: A practice of accounting but also an assumption that financial statement users make when reviewing the income statement. This rule says that the economic impacts of transactions are recorded in the period that they occur rather than in the period when cash is received.

Accrued liability: A liability that was incurred, but for which payment is not yet made, during a given accounting period. Some examples include wages owed and taxes payable.

Accumulated depreciation: The cumulative charges against the fixed assets of a company for wear and tear or obsolescence.

Activity-based cost accounting (ABC): A costing system that identifies the various activities performed in a firm and uses multiple cost drivers (nonvolume as well as the volume-based cost drivers) to assign overhead costs (or indirect costs) to products. ABC recognizes the causal relationship of cost drivers with activities.

Adverse opinion: Expressed if the basis of accounting is unacceptable and distorts the financial reporting of the corporation.

Aging of accounts: The classification of accounts by the time elapsed after the date of billing or the due date.

Allocation: The act of distributing by apportionment or distribution according to a plan; e.g., allocating costs is the assignment of costs to departments or products over various time periods, products, operations, or investments.

Allowance for doubtful accounts: An account established to record a contra-asset (subtraction from) to accounts receivable to allow for those customer accounts that will not be paid.

American Institute of Certified Public Accountants (AICPA): The national, professional organization for all Certified Public Accountants. Its mission is to provide members with the resources, information, and leadership that enable them to provide valuable services in the highest professional manner to benefit the public as well as employers and clients.

Amortization: 1. The gradual reduction of a debt by equal periodic payments to meet current interest and principal. 2. The process of spreading the cost of an intangible asset over the expected useful life of the asset.

Annual report: The requirement for all public companies to file an annual report to shareholders, with the Securities and Exchange Commission detailing the year's financial results.

Appraisal: A report made by a qualified person setting forth an opinion or estimate of value.

Appraised value: An opinion of an asset's fair market value, based on an appraiser's knowledge, experience, and analysis of the asset class.

Assets: What an enterprise owns. A probable future economic benefit obtained or controlled by a particular entity as a result of a past transaction or event.

Audit: The inspection of the accounting records and procedures of a business, government unit, or other entity by a trained accountant for the purpose of verifying the accuracy and completeness of the records. It could be conducted by a member of the organization (internal audit) or by an outsider (independent audit). A financial audit conducted by a CPA determines the overall validity of financial statements. A tax audit (IRS) determines whether the appropriate tax was paid. An internal audit generally determines whether the company's procedures are followed and whether embezzlement or other illegal activity occurred.

Auditing standards: Standards that provide guidance for the auditor and that help determine the audit steps and procedures that should be applied to fulfill the audit objective.

Auditor: An accountant, usually certified by a national professional association of accountants (AICPA, Institute of Internal Auditors), that conducts audits for businesses or other types of enterprises and organizations.

Available-for-sale securities: Equity securities with readily determinable values that are not classified as held-to-maturity or trading securities.

Balance sheet: One of the four required financial statements according to GAAP. It is also called the statement of financial position. The balance sheet provides information about the entity's financial position at a particular point in time, and it reveals the assets, liabilities, and equity of the enterprise.

Bank reconciliation: The verification of a bank statement balance and the depositor's checkbook balance.

Bankruptcy: A state of insolvency of an organization or individual; i.e., an inability to pay debts.

Beta: A statistical measurement correlating a stock's price change with the movement of the stock market. The beta is an indicator or statistical measure of the relative volatility of a stock, fund, or other security in comparison with the market as a whole. The beta for the market is 1.0. Stocks with betas above 1.0 are more responsive to the market but are also riskier investments. Stocks with a beta below 1.0 tend to move in the opposite direction of the market.

Book value: An accounting term which refers to a business's historical cost of assets minus liabilities. The book value of an asset is the cost of the asset minus accumulated depreciation.

Bookkeeping: The art, practice, or labor involved in the systematic recording of the transactions affecting a business.

Break-even analysis: An analysis method used to determine the number of services or products that need to be sold to reach a break-even point in a business.

Break-even point: The volume point at which revenues and costs are equal; a combination of sales and costs that will yield a no profit/no loss operation.

Budget: An itemized listing of the amount of all estimated revenue, along with a listing of the amount of all estimated costs and expenses that will be incurred in obtaining the revenue during a particular period, such as a month, quarter, or year.

Budget process: A systematic activity that develops a plan for the expenditure of resources, such as money or time, during a given period to achieve a desired result.

Business plan: A description of a business (normally over a one to five year period). A basic business plan includes information about the market, competitor analysis, the key people involved, financing needs, pro forma financial statements, budgets, project revenues from products and/or services, and the financial rewards if the business plan is implemented successfully.

Call provision: A provision of a bond or preferred stock issue, listed in its indenture (the formal agreement between the bond issuer and the holder), that allows the issuer to redeem the bond before the maturity date either at par or at a premium to par.

Capital asset: A long-term asset that is not purchased or sold in the normal course of business. Generally, it includes fixed assets; e.g., land, buildings, furniture, equipment, fixtures, and furniture.

Capital budget: The estimated amount planned to be expended for capital items in a given fiscal period.

Capital expenditure(s): The amount used during a particular period to acquire or improve long-term assets such as property, plant, or equipment.

Capital lease: A lease obligation that has to be capitalized on the balance sheet. It is noncancelable, has a duration of at least the life of the asset(s) being leased, and the lessor does not pay for the upkeep, maintenance, or servicing costs of the asset(s) during the lease period.

Capital rationing: The idea that resources are limited and the amount of funds for capital investment are limited and will need to be rationed (allocated) to only higher priority projects.

Capital stock: The ownership shares of a corporation authorized by its articles of incorporation, including preferred and common stock.

Capital structure: The permanent long-term financing of a company. Capital structure normally includes common and preferred stock, long-term debt, and retained earnings. It does not include accounts payable or short-term debt.

Cash and cash equivalents: All cash, marketplace securities, and other near-cash items.

Cash budget: Projects an entity's anticipated cash receipts and disbursements.

Cash cycle: The length of time, normally stated in number of days, between the purchase of raw materials and the collection of accounts receivable generated in the sale of the final product.

Cash management: The management of the cash balances of an entity in such a manner as to maximize the availability of cash not invested in fixed assets or inventories and to avoid the risk of insolvency.

Chart of accounts: A list of all the account names, usually organized by financial statement elements.

Commercial paper: Short-term debt investments issued by large corporations. Other corporations purchase commercial paper much like individuals purchase certificates of deposit from their banks, however the denominations of commercial paper are in the average millions of dollars and can be for a few days or up to 270 days under SEC rules. A major benefit of commercial paper is that it does not need to be registered with the Securities and Exchange Commission (SEC), making it a very cost-effective means of financing.

Compensating balance: The balance required to be kept on deposit at a bank by a borrower when taking out a loan.

Conservatism: The principle that guides the reporting of financial transactions and requires a prudent reaction to uncertainty to try to ensure that the risks inherent in a business situation are adequately considered.

Contingent liability: A possible obligation from past events that will be confirmed only by the occurrence or nonoccurrence of one or more uncertain future events not wholly within the control of the enterprise.

Contra account: 1. The reduction to the gross cost of an asset to arrive at the net cost; also known as a valuation allowance; e.g., accumulated depreciation is a contra account to the original cost of a fixed asset to arrive at the book value. 2. Reduction of a liability to arrive at its carrying value; e.g., bond discount, which is a reduction of bonds payable.

Contribution margin: The difference between sales and the variable costs of the product or service.

Control account: A summary account in the general ledger that is supported by detailed individual accounts in a subsidiary ledger.

Convergence: The process of making international accounting information more useful by bringing together the U.S standards with those of the rest of the world.

Convertible bond: A bond that can be converted to other securities under certain conditions.

Convertible preferred: Preferred stock that can be converted into common stock at the option of the holder of the preferred stock.

Cookie jar accounting: A type of unethical accounting whereby reserves are set aside in profitable years and then the reserves are used to cover losses to produce a type of income smoothing that understates income in good years and overstates it in bad years.

Copyright: The right to reproduce or sell a published work. Copyrights are granted for 50 years plus the life of the creator.

Cost accounting: A managerial accounting activity designed to help managers identify, measure, and control operating costs.

Cost center: A nonrevenue-producing element of an organization, where costs are separately figured and allocated and for which someone has formal organizational responsibility.

Cost control: The process and techniques of controlling the cost of a project, department, or activity within a predetermined amount.

Cost driver: Any activity or series of activities that takes place within an organization and causes costs to be incurred.

Cost-effective: Economical in terms of the goods or services received for the money spent.

Cost object: Anything for which cost data is desired; e.g., products, product lines, customers, jobs, and organizational subunits such as departments or divisions of a company.

Cost-plus pricing: Pricing that is based on the actual cost of production or service plus an agreed-upon markup.

Coupon bond: A bond that pays the holder a fixed interest payment (a coupon payment) every year until the bond reaches maturity.

Current assets: Assets of a company that are reasonably expected to be realized in cash, sold, or consumed during the normal operating cycle of the business (usually one year).

Deferral: Most commonly used as an abbreviation of deferred income (also called deferred revenue) or deferred expense (also called prepaid expense or prepayment).

Depletion: Expense for the physical reduction of natural resources owned by an entity.

Depreciation: The amount of expense charged against earnings by a company to write off the cost of a plant or machine over its useful life, giving consideration to wear and tear, obsolescence, and salvage value.

Direct cost: A cost that can be traced to a cost object in an economically feasible manner.

Economic entity: The accounting for an entity (i.e., a business) should be kept separate from the accounting for the owners of that entity. This assumption establishes the idea that economic resources and obligations shown on the balance sheet should not be confused with the resources and obligations of the owners of the entity.

Expense: A cost incurred in the process of delivering, producing, and rendering goods and services.

External audit: An audit conducted by an individual or firm that is independent of the company being audited. These independent auditors generally audit the books of a company once per year.

External auditor: An auditor, usually working for an audit firm (CPA firm), that is completely independent of the company it is auditing. External auditors report to the corporation's board of directors or the audit committee of the board of directors.

Face value: The value printed or written on the face of a bond.

Favorable variance: A variance created by using or spending less of a given resource than specified by the standard.

Financial accounting: The area of accounting concerned with reporting financial information to interested external parties.

Financial Accounting Standards Board (FASB): Created in 1973, it replaced the Accounting Principles Board and the Committee on Accounting Procedure of the American Institute of Certified Public Accountants. The FASB is a private body whose mission is to "establish and improve standards of financial accounting and reporting for the guidance and education of the public, including issuers, auditors, and users of financial information." The FASB publishes the generally accepted accounting principles (GAAP).

Financial audit: A historically oriented, independent evaluation performed for the purpose of attesting to the fairness, accuracy, and reliability of financial data.

Financial disclosure: A principle that requires financial statements and related notes to include any information that is significant enough to change the decisions of financial statement users.

Financial statement: A report that reveals various aspects of the financial condition of an entity. Financial statements include the balance sheet, income statement, and statement of cash flow.

Financial statement analysis: Analysis of a company's financial statement, usually by accountants or financial analysts. Includes several techniques, such as financial ratio comparisons over time periods.

Finished goods: Goods in inventory that have been completed and are available for sale.

Fixed asset: A long-term tangible asset that is not expected to be converted into cash in the current or upcoming fiscal year; e.g., buildings, real estate, production equipment, and furniture.

Fixed costs: Expenses that remain relatively constant and do not vary with revenue or activity volume. Examples of fixed costs consist of rent, property taxes, and interest expense.

Flexible budget: A budget based upon different levels of activity.

Franchise: The exclusive right to sell products or perform services in certain geographic areas. Franchises are usually granted (sold) by businesses to help expand their markets.

Freight: The charge for transporting something by common carrier.

Future value: The amount of money that an investment or an asset (the present value) will grow to by some future date.

Generally accepted accounting principles (GAAP): The standard framework of guidelines for financial accounting, including the standards, conventions, and rules accountants follow in recording and summarizing transactions and in the preparation of financial statements.

Generally accepted auditing standards (GAAS): The broad rules and guidelines set down by the Auditing Standards Board of the American Institute of Certified Public Accountants (AICPA) for carrying out an audit.

Going concern: The presumption that in the absence of any evidence to the contrary, an entity will operate indefinitely.

Goodwill: The excess of the purchase price to acquire a business over the value of the net assets acquired.

Governmental Accounting Standards Board (GASB): Oversees accounting standards for government entities. The mission of the GASB is to establish and improve standards of state and local governmental accounting and financial reporting. This is to result in useful information for users of financial reports and to guide and educate the public, including issuers, auditors, and users of those financial reports.

Gross margin: Also known as gross profit margin, it is the ratio of gross profit to sales revenue.

Historical cost: A principle that guides the valuation of assets and liabilities. This rule states that an asset or liability should be initially recorded (and reported) at its original (historical) cost.

Horizontal analysis: Comparison of one company's ratios to the ratios of other companies as well as to average industrial ratios and internal industrial deviation of these ratios.

Income statement: One of the four required financial statements according to generally accepted accounting principles (GAAP). It provides the net income (or net loss) earned by an enterprise over a stated period of time. It reveals the revenues earned and expenses incurred during a specific time period.

Indirect cost: A cost that cannot be traced to a given cost object in an economically feasible manner.

Information systems (IS) audit: An audit designed to ensure that internal controls are in place in the IS function so as to protect the operation and security of IS systems and to safeguard enterprise data.

Insolvency: When a business is unable to pay debts as they fall due.

Intangible asset: An asset that is not physical in nature. Examples are copyrights, patents, intellectual property, and goodwill.

Intellectual property: Creations of the mind, such as musical, literary, and artistic works; inventions; and symbols, names, images, and designs used in commerce, including copyrights, trademarks, patents, and related rights.

Interest rate: The rate of interest charged for the use of money, usually expressed as an annual rate.

Interfered tax allocation: The process of apportioning income taxes among accounting periods.

Internal audit: An independent audit function within an organization to examine and evaluate its activities as a service to the organization. The objective of internal auditing is to assist management in the effective discharge of their responsibilities.

Internal auditor: An auditor who works directly for an enterprise auditing its activities and testing internal controls.

Internal rate of return (IRR): The discount rate that makes the discounted cash flows equal to the initial investment. It is the rate that results in a zero net present value (NPV).

Internal Revenue Service (IRS): The agency of the U.S. government that enforces and interprets tax law and collects income taxes.

International Accounting Standards Board (IASB): Responsible for developing the International Financial Reporting Standards and promoting the use and application of these standards. The International Accounting Standards Board is an independent, privately funded accounting standard setter based in London, England.

Inventories: Raw materials and items available for sale or in the process of being made for sale (work in process).

Investigative audit: An audit that takes place as a result of a report of unusual or suspicious activity on the part of an individual or a department.

Investment center: The responsibility center within an organization that has control over revenue, cost, and investment funds.

Invoice: Detailed list of products sold or services rendered, with final prices charged for each item, tax, and a grand total of the amount owed.

Job costing: The allocation of all time, material, and expenses to an individual project or job.

Journal: A device (paper or computer file) used to record a transaction once the accountant or bookkeeper has examined a source document (such as an invoice, contract, loan agreement, calculation, etc.). Journalizing is the recording of the details of all of these source documents into multicolumn journals (also known as books of first entry).

Junk bond: A bond with a speculative credit rating of BB or lower. Such bonds offer investors higher yields than bonds of financially strong entities.

Ledger: A collection of accounts. The general ledger is the core of the organization's financial records. It constitutes the central "books" of a system, and every transaction flows through the general ledger—a permanent history of all financial transactions since day one of the life of the organization.

Leverage: The use of debt.

Liability: An obligation of an entity arising from past transactions or events, the settlement of which may result in the transfer or use of assets, provision of services, or other yielding of economic benefits in the future.

Liquidation value: The value of the assets at liquidation minus liabilities.

Lower-of-cost-or-market value: An accounting principle that states that an asset, such as inventory, should be reported on the balance sheet at the lower of two values: cost or current market value.

Management accounting: The process of identification, measurement, accumulation, analysis, preparation, interpretation, and communication of financial and other types of information. It is used by management to plan, evaluate, and control this information within an organization and to assure appropriate use of and accountability for its resources.

Markup: The amount added to the cost of goods in order to produce the desired profit.

Master budget: The entire budget of an entity—both the operational and financial budget.

Matching: A concept that states that expenses should be reported in the same period as the revenues to which they are related.

Monetary unit: A concept that assumes that currency is the appropriate unit of measure for assessing value and that the currency is not adjusted for inflation.

Net income: Revenues minus expenses.

Note payable: A payable evidenced by a signed promissory note.

Operational audit: A future-oriented, systematic, and independent evaluation of organizational activities.

Overhead: The indirect costs associated with providing and maintaining a manufacturing or working environment. Examples include renting the building, heating and lighting the work area, supervision costs, and maintenance of the facilities. Overhead includes indirect labor and indirect material.

Owners' equity: The owners' interest in the assets of the enterprise after deducting all its liabilities.

Par value: The value of a security that is set by the company issuing it. It is an arbitrary value and has no relation to market value.

Patent: The right to use, manufacture, or sell a product. A patent is granted by the U.S. Patent Office. Patents have a legal life of 20 years.

Periodicity: Also called the time period assumption, this rule states that it is meaningful to measure a firm's activities in terms of arbitrary time periods.

Present value: The discounted value of a payment or stream of payments to be received in the future, taking into consideration an interest rate.

Pro forma financial statement: A projected financial statement.

Profit center: A subunit of an organization that is responsible for producing profit, such as a division of a corporation that is to produce profits within the corporation.

Projection: An approximation of future events. A projection is made by extrapolating known information into the future, while considering events that could affect the outcome. Managers use projections to prepare budgets and pro forma financial statements.

Promissory note: A liability evidenced by a signed note (contract) that usually specifies the amount to be repaid (principal), the interest (rate), and the term (number of months or years the debt will be outstanding).

Purchasing power: The value of a particular monetary unit in terms of the amount of goods or services that can be purchased with it.

Qualified opinion: The auditor's opinion accompanying a financial statement that calls attention to limitations in the audit or exceptions the auditor has taken with the audit of the statements.

Reliability: The quality that makes information dependable and free from error or bias.

Responsibility accounting: The collection, summarization, and reporting of financial information about various subunits of an organization, tracking costs, revenues, or profits to the individual managers who are responsible for making the decisions.

Responsibility center: A subunit in an organization whose manager is held accountable for specified financial results of its activities.

Retained earnings: Profits of the entity that have not been paid out to the owners as of the balance sheet date but have been retained for use in the business. The retained earnings account is an equity account reported on the balance sheet.

Revenue: Sales of products, merchandise, and services, as well as earnings from interest, dividends, and rents.

Revenue bonds: A type of bond where principal and interest are secured by revenues such as charges or rents paid by users of the facility built with the proceeds of the bond issue. Projects financed by revenue bonds include highways, airports, dormitories, classrooms, and health-care facilities.

Revenue recognition: A rule that states that revenue should be recognized when the amount and timing are reasonably determined and when the earnings process is complete.

Securities and Exchange Commission (SEC): A U.S. government agency having primary responsibility for enforcing the federal securities laws and regulating the securities industry/stock market.

Sinking fund: A sum set apart periodically and allowed to accumulate in order to pay off a debt at some point in the future.

Spontaneous liabilities: Obligations that are realized automatically in the course of operating a company day to day, including accounts payable that are incurred when a company buys goods and services on credit, as well as salaries and wages payable that accrue each day that employees work.

Statement of cash flows: One of the four required financial statements according to GAAP. It shows the amount of cash collected and paid out by the enterprise over a specified period of time (same period as the income statement and statement of changes in equity) for operating activities, investing activities, and financial activities.

Statement of changes in equity: One of the four required financial statements according to GAAP. It summarizes the adjustments to equity over a specific period of time (same period as the income statement), including changes in capital and earnings retained.

Trademark: A symbol or name that allows a product or service to be identified; provides legal protection for 20 years plus an indefinite number of renewal periods.

Trading securities: Certain debt securities that are not classified as held to maturity and certain equity securities with readily determinable values. These investments are bought and held for the purpose of selling them in the near future.

Transaction: An exchange between a business (or some other type of organization, such as a nonprofit firm) and one or more external parties or a measurable internal event, such as certain adjustments for the use of assets in operations.

Trial balance: A worksheet in which the balances of all ledgers are compiled into debit and credit columns. Accountants prepare a trial balance periodically, at least at the end of every reporting period.

Unqualified opinion: An audit opinion not qualified for any material scope restrictions nor departures from generally accepted accounting principles (GAAP). The auditor may issue an unqualified opinion only when there are no identified material weaknesses and when there have been no restrictions on the scope of the auditor's work.

Variance: The deviation or difference between an estimated value and the actual value.

Variance analysis: Determining how a variance occurred.

Weighted average cost of capital: An average representing the expected return on all of a company's securities. Each source of capital, such as stocks, bonds, and other debt, is weighted in the calculation according to its proportion in the company's capital structure.

Work in progress: The inventory account consisting of partially completed goods awaiting completion and transfer to finished inventory.

Working capital: The excess of current assets over current liabilities.

Write off: To decrease the value of an item.

Yield: The annual return on an investment, expressed as a percentage.

Yield to maturity: The rate of return on a bond if the investor holds it to its maturity, incorporating the stated interest rate, accrual of discount, or amortization of a premium.

Zero coupon bonds: Bonds priced at a large discount from face value. The bonds pay no current interest during the life of the bond (hence the name zero coupon). The bonds mature at full face value (usually $1,000), so the difference between the original issue price and the face value represents interest income.

Index

Page numbers in *italics* refer to illustrations.

About the Author

Michael P. Griffin was born in Fall River, Massachusetts, in 1958. He was raised in Swansea, Massachusetts, and graduated from Joseph Case High School. He is a graduate of Providence College (BS, 1980) and Bryant University (MBA, 1982). Michael is currently the assistant dean of the Charlton College of Business and has been a faculty member of the school for over two decades, teaching accounting and finance courses. Michael is also the internship director for the college.

Prior to working for the university, Michael worked for a number of employers, including Fleet National Bank, E.F. Hutton and Company, and the Federal Home Loan Bank of Boston.

Michael is a Certified Management Accountant (CMA) and a Certified Financial Manager (CFM); both designations are awarded by the Institute of Management Accountants. In addition, he holds the Chartered Financial Consultant (ChFC®) designation from the American College.

Michael is the author of many business books and has developed several software packages both for commercial and academic use. He has been a consultant to a number of textbook publishers, including McGraw-Hill, Irwin, Addison Wesley, and Prentice Hall and has been a consultant for software content development for several software publishers. He has developed such software as the Personal Financial Organizer, the Ultimate Financial Calculator, the Ultimate Loan Calculator, and

OfficeReady Business Plans, all available through his company's website: *www.griffinfinancialconcepts.com*. He is the director of his own company, Griffin Financial Concepts, a developer of software and financial content for all types of media.

Michael is a member of Red Sox Nation and a fan of the Patriots, Celtics, and Bruins. He coaches youth sports in his hometown and is married with four children.